AND BABY
MAKES TWO

SHARYNE MERRITT
LINDA STEINER

AND BABY MAKES TWO

MOTHERHOOD WITHOUT MARRIAGE

Franklin Watts 1984 *New York / Toronto*

Library of Congress Cataloging in Publication Data

Merritt, Sharyne.
And baby makes two.

Includes index.
1. Unmarried mothers—United States.
2. Unmarried mothers—United States—Case studies.
3. Adoption—United States—Case studies.
I. Steiner, Linda. II. Title.
HQ759.45.M47 1984   306.8'56   84-11818
ISBN 0-531-09847-8

CONTENTS

AUTHOR'S NOTE

Although we've described the research and analysis in this book as a joint effort, we did have a division of labor. Sharyne Merritt conducted all of the interviews for the book and wrote chapters 1, 2, 3, 5, 8, and 10. Linda Steiner conducted all of the research for the Appendix and wrote chapters 4, 6, 7, and 9 as well as the Appendix.

We want to thank our editor, Liz Hock, for offering always helpful literary advice. We also want to thank attorneys Carol Donovan and Nancy Polikoff for reviewing the Appendix and offering their thoughtful comments. Any errors that may be present are, of course, not their responsibility.

And we want to thank all of the women who told their stories. Their candor and generosity of time and spirit made this book possible.

PREFACE

As two women in our thirties teaching at a university, we'd been musing about how women's values have changed in the years since we left college. In the 1970s we watched the move toward independence and remained single; now, in the 1980s, we are seeing an emphasis on nurturance and the desire to have children. While these values seemed to conflict, we sensed that the combination could produce a new option: adult single women raising children on their own.

Hints were all around us. An unmarried friend from graduate school appeared at a meeting pregnant; an adult student who was single towed her two-year-old daughter to class; a colleague told us that the topic of single-parent adoption had come up in her women's group.

But did these situations indicate the emergence of a social trend or simply some isolated instances of counter-cultural behavior in academia? Intrigued, Sharyne began some research, and placed an advertisement in *The Reader*, a free paper circulated in Chicago's "singles" neighborhoods, asking women who had had children while they were single and women who were single and thinking of having children to participate in a study.

Sharyne not only received several calls from women who had had children on their own, she was overwhelmed with calls from single women who were thinking about having a child and wanted information. Clearly, if we hadn't stumbled onto a social trend, we were onto something that might well become one.

Given the level of interest, Sharyne decided to embark upon a full-scale, nationwide study of single women who had become mothers between the ages of 28 and 42. We aren't interested in teenage pregnancy or even young adult pregnancy. We thought that the decision processes and experiences of younger women would be very different from those of adults who chose pregnancy or adoption "on their own." And we wanted to write a book for and about adult women.

We considered including men who had adopted while they were single, but because there are so few of them, we decided to limit our study to women. Perhaps our findings will be helpful to men.

Sharyne had posters printed to which were attached stamped, self-addressed postcards inviting single mothers to be interviewed. Friends were called upon to put the posters up in bookstores, day care centers, women's centers, YWCA's, and colleges in cities around the country. The response was strong, and Sharyne was able to set up interviews with single mothers in Los Angeles, San Francisco, Seattle, Portland, Denver, Phoenix, Chicago, Rochester, New York, Boston, Washington, and many smaller cities in between.

Sharyne talked to just over one hundred women who had children while they were single. Approximately a quarter of them got pregnant intentionally, another quarter "invited an accident," the third quarter became pregnant by accident, and the last quarter adopted. Some had not yet delivered, while others had children who were 30 years old. Most of the children, however, were under 7.

Because we were interested in women who became parents while on their own, we did not include women who had been cohabitating with their child's father at the time of the child's birth. Even though the woman remains legally single in such an arrangement, the practical implications of the father's presence make the situation quite similar to marriage. Sharyne did interview one woman who married her baby's father the day before she was due to deliver and divorced him a couple of weeks after the birth; she was not legally single, but the father's absence made her situation quite different from marriage.

The women interviewed worked in a variety of occupations; they were teachers, social workers, civil servants, doctors, nurses, psychologists, secretaries, machinists, telephone operators, business executives, a stockbroker, a flight attendant, a lawyer, an actress, and a shop owner. A few of them were graduate students and a few lived, at least for a while, on welfare. Almost all were white, socially mainstream and college educated. About one quarter would describe themselves as feminists—if the meaning of the term could range from favoring equal pay to thinking men are cheated by not being trained to be nurturing. Ten had been married and divorced before they had their children; five were lesbian or bisexual; and five were married at the time of the interview, only one to the father of the child.

Most of the women had been raised in warm, loving families. Their backgrounds ranged from army "brat" to old money elite to small town conservative. The majority came from middle-class homes in middle-sized or large cities. Few came from divorced homes, and few were only children. They were not "loners," nor were they "man haters," and they most certainly did not fit any stereotype of "unattractive and unlovable." On the contrary, almost all of them can be described as very warm, charming, and friendly.

Relatively few had married, though we suspect that women who subsequently married were less likely to fall into our research net. But since we wanted to know about all stages of single parenting, we consider this an advantage. Furthermore, we feel that readers who are considering single parenting ought to hear what it is like from women who have not married. It would appear to be safer to premise a decision on whether or not to have a child on remaining single than to base one's plans on something as unpredictable as finding a spouse.

We can't say with any certainty that the interviewees represent a cross section of adult women who become mothers while single. It *is* possible that people who volunteer to be interviewed are unusual in some respects. They may want to brag or to complain. They may be interested in furthering research, helping other women, or just having someone pay attention to them. On the other hand, we have no reason to believe that these women's situations are atypical, and we do think that their advice is useful.

While the sample selection was not scientific, we became more and more certain that we had tapped the key issues as patterns of experience and feelings emerged. Interviewing most of the women in person enabled Sharyne to observe emotional responses, probe for meanings, and in many cases see the mothers with their children. We have confidence in the sincerity and depth of the women's stories.

Our focus is on the women's experiences and feelings. We talked about their children, but we did not systematically interview the children themselves. Our reasons for this approach were threefold. First, most of the children were under seven—too young to be interviewed or to manifest effects that may emerge in adolescence. Second, the intelligence, articulateness, and frankness of the women inspired our trust in their observations and assessments of their children. Finally, we felt an understanding of the mothers' feelings and strategies would at least allow us to assess the environment in which the children were being raised.

Throughout the chapters that follow, our subjects speak for themselves. We have, however, changed the women's names and residences to preserve and protect their privacy.

CHAPTER

1

BECOMING
A MOTHER:
THE DECISION

"What about a family?"

It's a question many women without children ask themselves as they enter and move through their thirties. The idea may emerge suddenly, or it may have been there always. It may be a vague whisper—barely audible, ever present—or a thought that pops up now and again but repeatedly gets put on hold.

For a woman who is unattached, the first question generates a series of others: "Should I resign myself to never experiencing motherhood?" An unhappy prospect. "Should I marry someone I don't love just to have a child?" An unsound prospect. "Should I become a parent on my own?" An unusual prospect. Or is it? In 1978 over forty thousand babies were born to single women in their thirties, a 15 percent increase from ten years earlier. Going it alone, while not yet common, appears to be on the rise.

As the incidence of single women having children increases, the situation becomes clearly differentiated from what we typically think of as "the unwed mother problem." Even *The*

New York Times makes this distinction. In a recent editorial (November 1, 1981), the *Times* described the increase in births to unmarried women in the United States as "shocking." It goes on, however, to qualify the object of its outrage: "It is one thing for unmarried, adult, middle-class women to have babies. But when the mothers are poor teenagers, the consequences can be devastating." As the *Times* sees it, then, if you're mature and economically stable, it's OK to be unmarried and have a child. Or at least it is not truly "devastating."

Growing interest in the option of bearing children without marriage can be traced to several factors. The first is a matter of numbers. Women in their thirties, raised with the expectation of marrying a man older than themselves, are finding there just aren't enough eligible males! Landon Jones refers to this as a "marriage squeeze." "The first large cohort of baby-boom women born in 1946 and 1947 reached [their mid-thirties in 1981 and 1982]. Their prime market of potential marriage partners would be those men born during the last years of World War II. But those cohorts were considerably smaller than the baby-boom cohorts—up to 35 percent smaller. The scarcity of men gave older men an advantage in the marriage market, but the surplus of women disadvantaged baby-boom women."[1]

The more educated and more successful a woman is, the more severe the squeeze is; in addition to the tradition of "marrying up" in age, women also traditionally "marry up" in status. Consequently, the pool of men from which a woman chooses a mate is often limited to those who have achieved more than she has. And there is the added sting: A disproportionate number of the "good ones" are married. As Christine Doudna and Fern McBride note, "Educated, professional men marry earlier and stay married longer than other men, while their female peers marry later and have a higher probability of divorce . . ."[2]

[1] Landon Y. Jones, *Great Expectations: America and the Baby Boom Generation* (New York: Ballantine Books, 1980), 210.

[2] Christine Doudna with Fern McBride, "Where Are the Men for the Women at the Top?" in *Single Life: Unmarried Adults in Social Context*, ed. Peter J. Stein (New York: St. Martin's Press, 1981), 22. (Originally published in *Savvy*, February 1980).

The numerical discrepancy gets worse: the number of available successful women is increasing, while the pool of women from which a man tends to choose a mate includes those who have achieved less than he has. Achieving women find themselves in competition with less achieving women for a small number of older, achieving men. There simply are not enough successful fortyish males to go around.

Women in their thirties who are experiencing the marriage squeeze also are experiencing a biological squeeze—motherhood cannot be delayed indefinitely. As a woman's biological age increases, so too can the risks. Her fertility level may decrease. In a study involving artificial insemination, 74.1 percent of women between the ages of twenty-six and thirty got pregnant. The comparable figure for women between the ages of thirty-one and thirty-five was 61.5 percent, whereas the success rate was only 53.6 percent for those women older than thirty-five.[3]

Further, the likelihood of spontaneous abortion increases with age. "At age thirty-eight, the [spontaneous] abortion rate is approximately double what it is in the twenties, and in the forties, the rate may be triple."[4] There is the possibility of having a child with Down's syndrome, a form of mental retardation. For a twenty-year-old, the risk of having a child with Down's syndrome is 1 in 2,000; for a thirty-year-old, 1 in 895; for a thirty-five-year-old, 1 in 365; and for a forty-year-old, 1 in 109.[5]

A third factor arises out of the dynamic social changes of the sixties and seventies. Having children while single became a more viable and acceptable option. Also, women's career roles underwent what amounts to a sea change. In spite of continuing wage discrimination, more and more women wage earners are now financially self-sufficient and no longer need a spouse to provide for them and furnish "security." There also has been a significant change in attitude; growing feelings of independence

[3] Robert H. Glass and Ronald J. Ericcson, *Getting Pregnant in the 1980's* (Berkeley, CA: University of California Press, 1982), 69–70.

[4] Ibid., 70.

[5] Ibid., 72.

and competence have rendered more and more women emotionally self-sufficient, ridding them of the need for a spouse to make decisions for them. Not that spouses aren't desirable; they are just becoming less essential as providers, protectors, and mentors. And finally, there is the nuclear family. Given the high rate of divorce, marriage can hardly be considered a guarantee that a child will be raised by two parents. As women look around, they note the number of divorcees who are raising families successfully.

So the stage is set. A large group of single women is moving inexorably toward a biological "now or never" ultimatum with increased social supports for the idea of bearing and rearing a child on their own. As the components converge, having a child without marriage becomes an acceptable and less threatening option.

Of course, although this option may be acceptable, it is not necessarily the best possible one for *every* single woman. To become a parent under any circumstances is to undertake an enormous commitment. Ask anyone whose experience with children goes beyond watching "Little House on the Prairie," and you'll learn that raising a child consumes extraordinary amounts of time, love, patience, and money. Becoming a parent is accepting responsibility for another person. It's agreeing to meet this person's needs, even if that means overlooking your own. And you're in it for life.

Once you've become a parent, there's no turning back. If it's more work than you thought it would be, or if your child turns out to be not the sort of child you expected, or if you turn out not to be the sort of parent you expected, you can't do much about it. As Elizabeth Whelan says in *A Baby? Maybe,* "Children are not returnable. You can have an ex-wife, ex-husband, ex-job, but you cannot have an ex-child. The result of your decision, in other words, is not only unpredictable, it is irrevocable. That is why it's the most fateful decision of your life."[6]

[6]Elizabeth Whelan, *A Baby? Maybe.* (Indianapolis: Bobbs-Merrill, 1975, 1980) 16.

And for a single woman the decision to become a mother—whether by intentionally conceiving, adopting, or "accidentally" getting pregnant—is quite complex. It involves a series of personal, strategic, and ethical issues that may be dealt with consciously, subconsciously, or not at all. The resolution or nonresolution of these issues strongly influences the experience of motherhood.

MAKING THE DECISION

Almost every time we mentioned our research to someone who had never considered the possibility of a single woman having a child, we were met with the same question: "Why would someone who's single want to become a mother?" Immersed as we were in the topic, the question struck us as a bit silly at first. Our response was pat. "For the same reasons a married woman would want to become a mother." But we soon realized we were not giving the question the serious consideration it demanded.

Why indeed? We cannot separate the single women from the married women on this point because this particular decision is a *highly* personal, emotional one that does not lend itself readily to rational analysis. As author Hazel Scott says, "There's a time when you have to explain to your children why [they were] born, and it's a marvelous thing if you know the reasons by then."[7]

While wanting a child may not be purely rational, it's also not irrational (no doubt many parents of teenagers would dispute this point). It's nonrational—a matter of sentiment. Some people say wanting a child is innate, "an internal bubbling, an arousal, a tug for a baby that is an instinctual desire to reproduce."[8] Others contend that it is something women learn from the society: they get dolls when they're children and pressure from parents and peers when they're adults. Whatever the origins,

[7] Hazel Scott, quoted in *A Woman's Notebook II*, ed. Amy Shapiro (Philadelphia: Running Press, 1981) unpaged.

[8] Lois Leiderman Davitz, "Baby Hunger," *McCall's*, November 1981, 14.

it is a desire that's widely experienced at a level that permits little explanation beyond "I wanted a family" or "I've always wanted children."

But wanting a child isn't enough. Babies don't, after all, grow on trees. There are purposeful steps to becoming a mother, whether by pregnancy or adoption.

The decision actually has two parts. First, there is the option of becoming a parent while single. Second, there is the choice of how to do it. These two parts may not be clearly separated. For many women who become pregnant intentionally or who adopt, the questions of effect (on mother *and* child) of raising a child alone and of the strategy for becoming a mother are worked out simultaneously. In fact, resolving the question of birth versus adoption and/or the question of paternity is often the key to finalizing the decision to become a mother while single. And women who become pregnant unintentionally—by "allowing" pregnancy or making a "passive" choice—often have subconsciously dealt with both questions prior to conception but may not be able to say which influenced which.

Nevertheless, for analytical purposes it seems to us important to treat the question of why a woman would become a parent while she is single as separate from the question of how she goes about accomplishing it.

ENHANCING A FULL LIFE

Middle class and methodical—that's how Margaret Richards would describe herself. You could see it in her tidy tasteful living room. You could hear it when she explained her decision to become a single parent.

Growing up in Sacramento, Margaret learned all the traditional values and moral teachings of her middle-class parents. She would go to college, become a teacher (because it was a "nice" profession and good to fall back on if you were widowed), and then, of course, she would marry and have children—two would be nice.

In 1958, when she was eighteen, Margaret left her sheltered

home for UCLA. The sorority house she lived in was also sheltered. Universities in the late fifties and early sixties weren't yet hotbeds of dissent and radicalism. But the people she met were mainly from Los Angeles—certainly more interesting and less conservative than the ones she had left behind in Sacramento.

Much to her parents' dismay Margaret chose to stay in Los Angeles after her graduation. She thought she could meet more men there. But the men she went out with were not what she had hoped for. They expected more than the boys at the university and offered less. Nor did the job she secured teaching in the inner city fit her expectations. "I loved the kids," she told us, "and I even learned to handle the problems of their not being able to come to school because they didn't have shoes or because they had been beaten up, but I couldn't handle the fear. And it got worse. First there were episodes of teenage gangs throwing eggs at my car as I drove out of the school yard. Then one of the other teachers was raped, and I started thinking 'this isn't for me.'

"So I left teaching with no regret, and I found a great fund-raising job. One year later I was offered a similar job in New York. This time a couple of thousand miles away from Sacramento.

"By then I was too busy to even think of marriage and children. I was meeting famous people, had my own expense account, my own bank account, my own apartment. I loved my work, and my career was my highest priority. Twice I ended relationships with men because they threatened my career. One really super man wanted me to marry him and move to Atlanta, but I knew I couldn't find a job there to even compare with the one I had, so I gave him a flat no. A few years later I had an offer from a foundation in Dallas; it meant packing up and leaving in two weeks. I barely had time to say good-bye to the man I had been dating seriously. But again I had no regrets. I was climbing up the career ladder, and my personal life didn't matter."

As Margaret approached her mid-thirties, however, panic set in. It was getting late to have a baby. (Back in Sacramento she had always planned on a family.) She had reached a biological "now or never" point. But the years had been kind. They had given her the security and independence that encouraged her to consider parenting on her own.

Many women, having met their goals of marrying and bearing children, reach a point where they are ready to switch their attention to careers. Margaret had met her career goals and was now ready to switch her attention to home and family. "I had it made professionally," she said. "I had made a name for myself in my field and had the bank account to prove it. I could afford to slide for a while if I wanted to. I was really looking forward to taking a break from the struggle onward and upward. I'd paid my dues . . . and I wanted a baby . . . so very much."

But why have a child alone? Why not find a suitable partner, marry, and have a traditional nuclear family? Margaret had a lot of reasons for not waiting. Her biological time clock was ticking away. If she waited, she might not be able to conceive, or her child might have birth defects, common to older mothers. But that wasn't all. She just didn't feel the need for having a man around.

"As I moved through my thirties, marriage seemed less and less important. Oh, I dated a lot, but the relationships didn't seem to go anywhere. The most exciting and successful men either didn't want to make commitments, or they had already made them. So the bottom line was the same—no future with any of them. In fact, I knew so many interesting and extraordinary women that I could be perfectly happy with their company.

"I'd look at my married women friends and think that I wasn't certain what they saw in their husbands, but I was beside myself with envy over their children. In fact, I remember saying to a friend, 'There are a lot of mixed pros and cons about marriage, and I probably wouldn't have any great regrets if I never married, but I would have very strong regrets if I didn't have any children.' I knew having a child would mean that I would have to settle down more, but I was ready for it. I had done those things; I had made those trips; I had spent that money. I remember sitting in a café in Paris thinking, Well, if you have a child, you won't be able to come to Europe any more. You won't be able to have these fascinating conversations. And I thought, That's OK. I've done it. I know what it is. I'm not going to sit at home and long for it. And I was tired of longing for a child. Getting rid of that pain was more than a trade-off for not having more trips to Paris. I never heard a woman start a sentence with 'My son' or 'My daughter' without feeling a little knife in my gut. So I didn't have a great deal of anxiety about trade-offs. I made peace with the idea that they existed.''

Methodical and cautious, Margaret had not only computed a costs/benefits analysis, she had also been assessing her ability to be a single parent. And in this sense she also felt ''ready.''

She started going to conferences on single parenting to get a taste of the life-style. She was not discouraged. ''None of the women I met there or heard about had problems that applied to me. Mostly they lacked the resources that I had. I had stable employment; I was a homeowner; basically, I was a good manager. I was concerned about day care because that's what everyone always discussed, but I felt that I could find somebody to sit.''

She gave serious thought to what she had observed in her friends' homes. She had enough involvement with families to have some feeling for the day-in/day-out business of coping with children. But again she was not discouraged. ''I knew it would be an upheaval, but I was confident in my ability to deal with problems as they came up. I certainly felt I was much more mature than the average new parent. I guess I had a sense of strength about my parenting competencies.''

But although Margaret felt comfortable and positive about becoming a parent, she was not certain she was prepared to deal with the social repercussions of an unmarried pregnancy. She was firm in her desire to have her own child rather than adopt but was fearful that giving birth to a child as a single woman might jeopardize her career, alienate her family, and ultimately be unfair to the baby.

''I worried about my career and my parents and what my child would think when he grew up. My parents are really middle class and conservative. After all, I was brought up in Sacramento, and you know darn well people in Sacramento don't have babies unless they're married! I had a lot of conflicts—I yearned for a child . . . I could care for a child and love it so much . . . but it would be illegitimate!

"I would wake up in the middle of the night with my heart pounding. . . . All the taboos about unmarried mothers were haunting me. I had visions of some of the older, distinguished managers in my office throwing up their hands and gasping with horror at my big stomach. Could I really carry it off? And then there were my parents; I never discussed anything with them— certainly not this—and if they couldn't handle the situation, I would feel so guilty. My father could possibly manage, but my mother would surely fall apart. How could I do that to her? And to my baby—would he grow up hating me because he didn't have a father?"

Margaret spent a lot of sleepless nights and troubled days trying to arrive at a decision, but in fact she was beginning to make one. She discussed single parenting in a general way with acquaintances whose opinions she valued. She watched mothers with their young children, noting how they looked, how they acted toward each other, whether they seemed happy. Then she began to take her temperature every morning and chart her ovulation carefully—just in case. She still used birth control, but she was getting very close to welcoming a pregnancy.

On her fortieth birthday, Margaret realized that she could no longer postpone making the decision. She had a long talk with herself and concluded that her fears, while not unwarranted, were also not insurmountable.

"I thought back on a rather scandalous sexual episode I had had at a previous job and decided, I lived through that; I can stand this." Besides, she was certain that once the pregnancy was over and the baby was at home, people at work would adjust or forget all about it in a short time.

Margaret also convinced herself to put aside her fears about her parents: "I didn't want to hurt them, but I couldn't be defined by them either. I finally told myself, They will either come around or they won't." Secretly, though, she hoped they would be won over by a grandchild—even if its origins were unconventional.

And the question of fairness to the baby?

"I decided my baby would be fatherless—or never exist at all on the face of the earth. That's the only choice the child had. I felt I could handle the social issues if they turned out to be serious—they would be something we would both have to live with. Of course, it's better to have a father, but no child is born into an ideal situation. And look at the number of children with divorced parents. At least my child would be spared angry scenes and quarrels—and wouldn't live in poverty. He'd have many breaks that other children didn't have."

The only remaining issue was getting pregnant. Somewhat hesitantly, Margaret spoke with an intermittent lover (who lived out of town and visited her every several months) about her desire to have a child. He agreed to be the biological father, although, she still contends, "I've never understood his motivation, really I haven't."

Margaret is now the mother of a four-year-old boy. None of her fears about her colleagues, her parents, or her son have come to pass. She describes her sacrifices as irrelevant compared to her almost overwhelming joys. Yet she stops short of recommending single parenting to other women. "I'm hesitant to give advice to other women about anything. I wouldn't try to convince another woman that she should do the same thing, though I know beyond a doubt that my son is the most wonderful, most important, most satisfying part of my life."

It would be hard to find someone more different from Margaret than Julie Holmes. Margaret had been devoted to moving up the career ladder; Julie had been devoted to moving around. Even their surroundings were polar opposites: compared to Margaret's coordinated, uncluttered home, Julie's Manhattan apartment was a study in chaos. Books, photographs, and plants covered not only the walls but the floors, the countertops, and the overstuffed Salvation Army furniture.

Margaret's concern about having a child was based on her

fear of being unconventional. Julie only worried about appearing too conventional. Margaret was a product of Sacramento in the serene fifties; Julie was a product of protests in the turbulent sixties. Yet both opted for single motherhood in order to enhance their already satisfying life-styles.

When we met Julie, she was thirty-one years old and five months pregnant. She was teaching at an alternative day-care center, and "alternative" was the key to her life. "After college I worked and studied and traveled, always maintaining that there was never a time when I had anyone else supporting me. I'd always get a part-time job, or do some freelance work in photography, or sell some of my paintings. I didn't want to settle down. I was Julie the Gypsy. The model that my friends had followed—finish college, work a few years, get married, get a mortgage, have some children, settle down—never seemed right to me. That model seemed like it would thwart my creativeness, my need for independence. Somewhere in the back of my mind I knew I wanted children, but I never seriously thought about it because you had to be married and have a mortgage in order to have children, and that wasn't for me."

At twenty-eight Julie returned from her travels and took her current teaching position. It was the perfect job for her: unstructured, creative, free-flowing. She taught "Julie's Drama," using puppets, "Julie's Art," finger-painting murals on the walls, and "Julie's Science," planting vegetables in a plot near the playground. Julie found she could be expressive without moving from place to place. Although she still didn't have a mortgage and a husband, Julie had at least parked her gypsy wagon and was getting a sense of roots.

Shortly after she turned thirty-one, Julie found herself reconsidering her thoughts on motherhood. "It was real strange. I started thinking about getting pregnant after one of the women I worked with got pregnant by accident and miscarried. We talked about it a lot. She told me her feelings about losing the baby, and I started realizing how important family really was to me. I thought about how close I was to my father and mother and how happy my childhood had been and how much I wanted my own little family.''

So Julie started thinking about having a child. But like Margaret, she had to resolve a conflict. For her the conflict was not over the impropriety of becoming a mother while single but over the propriety of becoming a mother at all. Julie wasn't afraid of being deviant; she was afraid of being normal. And she had to overcome this fear in order to become pregnant.

Julie had spent her twenties fighting being traditional, doing what some women are supposed to do. She had made a point of being nontraditional, not getting trapped in the role of ''suburban mother of two.'' Her image of motherhood sounded as if it came directly from Marilyn French's novel, *The Women's Room*. Motherhood was a tedious, thankless, endless drudgery of serving a husband and children and never fulfilling yourself. As far as Julie was concerned, ''Mothers lived through their children and then resented the children for stopping them from doing what they really wanted to do.'' Julie didn't want to be like that.

She did, however, want to fulfill herself, to live up to her potential—not through working up the organization, as Margaret did, but through travel, art, and proof of self-sufficiency. Now, just as Margaret was ready to shift priorities, so was Julie. ''I've done all the stuff I want to do. I don't mean that life is over; I just feel ready now. I don't feel the child is stopping me from doing anything. Maybe I just needed to prove my identity or to realize that a mortgage isn't a prerequisite for pregnancy. I'm ready to move on now and share my life.''

Unlike Margaret, Julie wasn't worried about how other people would respond. In fact she was certain that her decision would be met with approval by the people who counted most. And perhaps it was in part because she expected approval that she discussed her plans with her father (her mother had died when she was five) and her closest friends. This was not a bid for reinforcement but a wish to involve the people she loved in her decision. After all, they would be the ones to whom she and her child would turn for emotional sustenance.

Julie, an only child, had always received unconditional approval from her father. "He's always supportive of everything I do. It's 'Whatever makes you happy, baby.' " Therefore she had little doubt about her father's response to her idea of single parenting.

"I told my dad I was thinking about having a baby on my own, and he was worried at first. Not worried as much that I wouldn't be able to handle it financially, as emotionally. You know—the responsibility. I think he was thinking how lonely his life had been since my mother died. He kept saying, 'Do you understand it's not all roses; it's stomachaches and fevers and doctors' appointments and orthodontists?' And I told him I could handle it. And he agreed. He just wanted me to know what I was getting myself in for and then he said, 'If that's what you want, it's what I want.' "

Her most "free-spirited" friend was the only one to respond negatively. "She worried about my selling out, giving up the artist's dream, giving up my freedom." From her other friends Julie received what she calls "total loving support." Friends who were parents themselves were certain she would be a great mother, and friends who did not have children were looking forward to being "aunts" and "uncles."

Julie had little concern about how the people at her school would react, not because as an "alternative" school it provided a liberal environment but because she was respected for being exactly who she was. "I was sure everyone would accept it. Basically, I think if you feel good about what you're doing and you feel it's right, people are willing to accept it—even if they wouldn't do it themselves."

Julie had successfully gained the support of her father and friends. As she puts it, "There would be people to share life with me and the child." She had no concern about her job security or the things she would be giving up. She admits that she didn't know if her decision would hurt the child, but she doubted that either social stigma or the adequacy of one parent were important concerns. Julie thought that single parenting would be so common by the time the child entered school that it wouldn't be noticed. But if the child were uncomfortable and wanted to tell a story, Julie would back it up. Of the adequacy of one parent Julie says, "Mothers raise children anyway. Even in two-parent families, fathers are often not part of the family in the sense of really sharing parenthood. Children may have their material needs met by their fathers, but they get their physical needs and emotional needs met by their mothers. Besides, my child will probably get love from more adults than most children raised by divorced parents."

Julie's boyfriend did not care for her plan. He was forty-six and had three grown children. He said he didn't want to be responsible for another family. Julie didn't want anyone to assume responsibility. She only wanted a baby, not a marriage. He insisted he didn't want to be a father, though he knew that Julie wanted to become a mother and that she was using no form of birth control. Still he continued their intimate relationship, and Julie conceived.

Shortly after she received a positive report on her pregnancy test, Julie went through a period of self-questioning. "I thought, Now that I'm pregnant, did I make the right decision? Do I want an abortion? I thought about all the responsibility and I got real scared: How am I going to do this myself? Can I support myself and a child? It's a long haul. I had a million questions. I spent five days talking to myself. At the end I was real solid, very committed to the idea. And I was really happy. It felt like I'd made a life change. I felt a new direction, a new meaning in my life."

We spoke with Julie again when her daughter Susan was six months old. Now that she was actually involved in it, what was her assessment of single parenting? "I wouldn't trade it for anything in the world. I have never been this happy. I'm working hard. Between teaching and taking care of Susan I don't have any time to myself any more. I have to schedule an appointment with myself just to shave my legs. But it's the best thing I've ever done. I'm not saying that everyone should do it, and I'm not saying it's easy. I don't like getting up earlier in the morning. And I don't like having to drag this child out in the cold to the sitter. I haven't come upstairs with nothing in my arms since she was born; if it isn't her, it's diapers or laundry or her stroller. But I've never been happier. I just can't explain it. I'm not standing on a cloud singing about it, because I don't have the time, but there has not been one day that I have thought of caring for Susan as drudgery. Not even when she's been sick, not even when I've been sick. She's the best thing that ever happened to me.''

The stories of Margaret and Julie are significant because they both represent the motivational push of "enhancing a full life." Although Margaret and Julie came to very different stylistic resolutions of the issues, they based their decisions on the same criteria.

First of all, both women were ready to change their paths to fulfillment. They had proven themselves as individuals and were ready to shift their priorities. Margaret had worked diligently at her career and was ready for an emotional commitment. Julie had met her needs for individuality and was ready to "settle down."

This sense of being "ready" is expressed by over half of the women we spoke to. Here's how a woman who adopted described her decision: "It was really a coalescence of a lot of things that made it seem the right time. I was living here in Philadelphia. I've lived in various parts of the country, and I've always enjoyed the different places I've lived, the different lifestyles, the different types of people. But I never felt like they were places I could settle into on a long-term basis. But I really felt I could do that in Philadelphia. Another very significant factor was I got a promotion. It wasn't just the promotion, though the financial benefits helped; it was that it gave me a sense of stability. So that was a part of it—the sense that I had some stability and permanence in terms of a job and a place that I would be willing to stay. I was psychologically ready. I had really done the things I wanted to do, and a child would not only not hamper me from doing anything but would also really enrich my life. It was all of those factors. I was ready—not just financially but emotionally, and certainly in terms of career.''

The other part of being "ready" to enhance life is feeling that you have what you want, that you won't be sacrificing. Margaret had taken the trips to Europe, had the feathers in her cap. Julie had moved around, proved her independence. Neither thinks that life has stopped; they are just aware of having accomplished important goals. As another single mother put it, "I think you need to be able to say, 'I have done everything for myself that I wanted to do. I've traveled all that I wanted to travel; there's not really any place I want to see right now. I've been to Europe; I've been to South America. I've bought a home. I've invested. I've sat on the beach five days a week. I've screwed around. I've got my career all sorted out.' I can honestly look my daughter in the face and say, 'I've made no sacrifices for you.' Because I think that's a hard burden for a child to bear—thinking, My mother sacrificed everything for me."

In addition to being ready to move on to being mothers, Julie and Margaret and women like them are also ready to move on without being married. They aren't hostile toward men; they simply don't feel they need husbands. They don't regard having a partner as a requisite to feeling complete. Margaret notes that she wouldn't have any great regrets if she didn't marry; Julie sees marriage as an incursion on her independence. Here's how three other women see it.

Barbara: "It occurred to me after several years of looking around at the available crop that I was very content to be single. It's not a makeshift sort of thing as it is for many of my friends. I'm not marking time. As far as I can see, I'm not fooling myself. I enjoy my life without answering to another person."

Veronica: "I started realizing that I hadn't met Prince Charming, and there wasn't any reason to wait any longer. I liked living alone, and I wasn't sure I was ready to have some guy checking up on me, or having me fix his meals or do his laundry, or having to stumble over him in the bathroom in the morning. If in the future I meet somebody who has his ego in the right place and likes my kids and likes himself, maybe I'll consider getting married. But it's just not essential for me to have a husband."

Laura: "When I got pregnant, I told people that at this point I could visualize myself more as a mother than as a wife—at least as a wife of any of the men I knew. For me marriage is not out of the question; it's just that most of the men that I've become involved with have completely different ideas of where I should be than I do. I believe marriage should basically be a partnership and a real kind of giving and taking on both sides. If I found a man who thought that too, I might get married. But as it is, I'd rather be single."

Being satisfied with being single not only means a willingness to forgo a certain amount of companionship, it also means a readiness to manage child rearing without the help of an ever-present mate. Again, there are different interpretations of this issue. For Margaret, this form of preparedness is based on her financial security and her confidence in her abilities to cope with problems she knows will arise. For Julie, preparedness to go it alone is based on her establishing a "support system" of friends and relatives who will be a part of the baby's life.

Other women see themselves as not only capable of raising a child without a mate but *preferring* to raise a child without a mate. When we asked Carol Mead, a single woman in her seventh month of pregnancy, whether she expected any benefits from single parenting, she replied, "Definitely." According to Carol, "You can do what you want. There won't be anyone telling me I'm doing it wrong. I don't want the kinds of conflicts that can occur between the mother and the father over rearing the child. It fits in well with my independence. It sounds silly to say that I won't have to answer to anyone, but that's the way I feel. My mother tells me my first words were 'Me do it, Mom.' And all my life has been 'I want to do it myself'—even having a child."

The mother of a two-year-old girl echoes this view. "The way I see it, women want children and what's happened in our culture is there's been a moral law that says you have to get married in order to have children. The way it looks to me is that that's a real lie and a rip-off. What I've noticed is that when Tom and Tina got married, they did fine. And then Tina had a baby and all of a sudden Tom feels left out. Well, where's Tina?

She's nursing and diapering and in love and having this relationship, and Tom's on the outside. So it looks to me like there's a real lie in there somewhere—wanting to have a baby and saying you want to be married, when in fact they're two separate things. And it's the rare couple that has it all together, that has the baby as a couple, instead of it really being hers.''

Yet another advantage to mateless mothering was seen by a woman with a one-year-old. ''I think you can focus more of your energy on the relationship with the child. I've thought about what it would be like if I were married. God, if I had to spread my time between taking care of Linda and taking care of a husband, I don't know if I could do it. For me it's real satisfying to be a single parent and focus my energies on my needs and her needs and building up a relationship. I don't feel in any way that I've lost part of my identity. If anything, I've added to it. If there were a man here, I wouldn't be as much myself. That's my personality. I have a tendency in my relationships with men to adapt to the image they have of what a woman should be like. I sort of bend to them, become what they want me to be instead of what I am. For me it wouldn't be an advantage to have a man around; it would be a real disadvantage.''

Ready to be parents, ready to be single, these women are also ready to face the social consequences of being single parents. After much internal debate, Margaret concluded that she could face the possible negative responses of her colleagues and her parents and that her son would have advantages to compensate for lacking a father. Julie doubted that there would be any negative social consequences for either herself or her child. Both women noted that, given current divorce rates, their children would be unlikely to be seen as social outcasts; living in a single-parent home, after all, is no longer unusual.

Like Margaret and Julie, most of the other women who had children in order to enhance an already full life cited personal abilities to cope and general changes in attitudes toward non-nuclear families as reasons not to fear social stigma. Those who were not able to escape concern about negative response to an unmarried pregnancy chose to adopt. This is not to say that all single women who adopt do so because of concern about illegitimacy. It does reveal, however, that this is an available option that circumvents both social and moral questions. (Adoption is discussed in Chapter 3.)

A second group of women were ready to be parents in that they had fulfilled themselves and did not desire a day-to-day adult companion, but they were not ready to forgo the help of a mate. For these women single parenting was premised on the on-going, though not full-time, involvement of the child's biological father.

COUNTING ON A CO-PARENT

At least a dozen of the women we interviewed bore children with the expectation that the biological father would be involved in the child's life on a steady basis, although this expectation was seldom shared by the men involved. A potentially dangerous situation, it leaves the woman open to great disappointment. Such was the case for Ann Parker.

Ann was tall, painfully thin, and painfully ill at ease. We arrived at her apartment promptly for our scheduled meeting, but her puzzled expression indicated she wasn't expecting us. When we introduced ourselves, she was obviously embarrassed at having forgotten the appointment and not particularly eager to invite us in. Having driven fifty miles to her home, we were reluctant to reschedule and tried to encourage her to talk with us. Finally, Ann opened the door a little wider and said nervously, "This is a terrible day to talk to anybody, but if you don't mind, I guess I don't."

We told her that we didn't mind, that interviewing some women on bad days was actually advantageous for it guarantees our not getting only rosy pictures of a single parent's life. We went into the living room, where she introduced us to her four-year-old daughter Patricia. But something was wrong. Patricia was lying on the couch covered with a blanket, awake and alert but absolutely still. Ann explained that Patricia had had an asthma attack an hour earlier and was just back from the hospital where she received an Adrenalin shot.

This was hardly the sort of bad day we'd anticipated, so we apologized for even suggesting that there was some research advantage to interviewing her and offered to return another time. She then explained that it wasn't a bad day because Patricia was sick—she was quite used to periodic trips to the emergency room—it was a bad day because she had talked to Patricia's father and was terribly sad. Talking about it, she suggested, might make her feel better.

"Michael, Patricia's father, and I were together for five years. We never lived together, but we saw each other almost every day.

"I wanted to get married, but he didn't. And then I got pregnant. My first thought was to have an abortion, but it was a real soul-searching kind of thing. I had just finished my master's degree and had a good job, so I had some independence and security, and I was moving toward thirty—and possibly, though I haven't figured this out yet, I sensed that Michael was drifting away. So there might have been something there about wanting to hold onto some part of him. I'm not sure of that.

"I don't know. It's gotten confused with the years. I knew I wanted her, but before the first six weeks were up, when I had to decide if I was going to have an abortion, I asked Michael what he thought. He said, 'Well, the only thing I can say is that I can't tell you no. If you really want a baby, go ahead and have it, and I'll do what I can.' And we'd had a good relationship before then, so I guess I pinned a lot of hope on his being part of our life. My dream of a father was someone who would share even if we didn't live together. Later I found out he had been seeing a twenty-one-year-old girl, so there were probably a lot of vibes mixed up that I wasn't even aware of. I was feeling rejected. So maybe it was a now-or-never thing—like if I'm going to have my child with him, I better have it now because he's going to be gone. I don't know."

Although Ann hoped Michael would be involved, she was

prepared to raise the child on her own. "I knew I could make it even if he didn't come through. I had a lot of wonderful friends, two of whom offered to have me live with them. I had a good medical plan and a maternity leave. I was worried about what my boss would say, but I knew he wouldn't fire me."

And yet, she admits, she had always held onto a fantasy. "I guess I thought we'd be a family eventually. My fantasy was that at least we could be co-parents—not live together but share parenting. And she would love her daddy and get to visit him, and he would send her things, and maybe we could live nearby."

As Ann approached the end of her first trimester, Michael changed his mind and insisted that she have an abortion. He told her if she didn't, he would never see her again and would never see the child. It brought an end to Ann's fantasy.

"It was awful. Whenever I think about it, I just start crying. How could a father never want to see his child? And what would I tell her? It was almost impossible to believe. But I knew I wanted to have the baby, and I think when you're pregnant there's some self-preservation thing that keeps you going. I think it took me until Patricia was one and a half to decide that it was OK— that I was going to be the mom, and I wasn't going to try to push him into being any kind of dad at all. It was awful then, and it's still awful for me."

What's Ann's overall evaluation of single parenting?

"I know Patricia was something I really wanted, but it's just a lot more work than you can ever imagine. I feel like she needs more than I have to give. And I miss not having anyone else love her as much as I do. That's been there all along."

Would she recommend single parenting?

"I used to think if you want to have a child and you're not married, it's better to go through the hardship of single parenting than to look back when you're fifty and say, 'Oh, my gosh, I wish I had done that.' But that's not what I think now. I would never try to dissuade anyone from doing it, but I would say that if you have the least bit of ambivalence, don't do it."

Sandra Franklin presents a very different example of a single mother who was counting on a co-parent. She got what she wanted, but it proved to be no more satisfactory than Ann's situation.

Sandra is an advertising consultant. When she conceived her daughter, now three years old, she was thirty-two and the divorced mother of a ten-year-old boy, Howard. At that time she was living with Ron, her lover and business partner.

Sandra started considering having a second child when she was thirty-one. Her profession gave her both a flexible schedule and a high income. She had always wanted a second child and felt that time was moving on. If she were going to do it, it should be soon. She also realized that having a child was more important than keeping Ron. "I talked to Ron about it, and I told him I wanted to have another baby, and if he didn't want one, he should leave so I could begin a relationship with another man who did."

Ron wanted to think about it, and they decided to wait six months. At the end of the six months Ron told Sandra that he really didn't want to be a father. If she wanted, he would "get her pregnant," but he would move out. He would stay in the area and visit her, her son, to whom he was attached, and the new child, but he wouldn't be a "live-in daddy."

Sandra agreed. She loved Ron enough to want to have his child. Besides, she had no overwhelming desire to go through the lengthy task of entering another relationship. Given her experience as a single parent, she knew that she was capable of raising children on her own. That Ron would stay in touch was a bonus for her, her son, and the child to be. Her ex-husband had, in fact, maintained no contact with her son and Ron would at least guarantee some continuity in their lives. Her only condition was that he be present at the birth. Ron agreed.

Shortly after Sandra conceived, Ron left their home and moved in with a woman very unlike Sandra. In contrast to Sandra, who has a high-powered, achieving, rapid-fire style, Ron's new partner was nonverbal, passive, and pleasing. "In one way I took it as an insult. But in another way it seemed OK. At least she wasn't any competition."

Ron lived up to his bargain—and more. Not only does he

visit once a week, he voluntarily gives Sandra child support—five hundred dollars a month, which is far more than most courts would award. But his visits, while very welcome, give Sandra the taste of pleasure that ultimately becomes pain. "He comes over every Wednesday night and sees the kids for a couple of hours, and then he stays and we talk until two or three in the morning. I'm his source of intellectual stimulation. His lover is nice but bland, so he's comfortable with her but needs me for some wit and challenge. That would be OK, but it's made it awfully hard for me to cut my attachment to him. It's like getting a weekly fix, so I can't get over loving him, and I can't have him. I can't tell him to leave my life so I can get through the separation and pain, because both kids would miss him. And I can't tell him to leave as soon as the kids go to sleep and not stay and talk, because I value those hours as much as he does. It's really a no-win situation."

Does Sandra regret having contracted for a co-parent? "Given it all to do over again, I probably would have done it the exact same way, but I don't think I'd recommend this type of arrangement to another woman."

Many of the women who enter single parenting with the help of a co-parent resemble Ann. They are in love with their baby's father. They "allow" a pregnancy by not using birth control. They hope to remain involved with the man on an intimate level and to share responsibility for the child. They are frequently disappointed.

What these women appear to be seeking is a modified form of single parenting. They are prepared to remain single in terms of their legal status and probably in terms of their housing arrangements, but they anticipate an on-going relationship with a man to satisfy their and their baby's emotional needs.

Such expectations, if not shared by the father, are unlikely to become reality. Then, in sharp contrast to a path paved with emotional security and shared responsibility, the mother may find herself on a path that is both lonely and burdensome.

The sense of being alone and burdened expressed by women like Ann is foreign to women like Margaret and Julie. It may be that women who embark on single parenting with the assumption of a relationship with the man are not as emotionally self-sufficient as the women we have classified as "enhancing their lives." For them, being alone with and solely responsible for a child may seem frustrating, if not overwhelming.

But even if these women are just as self-sufficient, hoping for love and help and getting neither is bound to lead to unhappiness. If the man does not want to be part of the family, not only has the woman been rejected by her lover, but this wonderful extension of her—and him—also has been rejected. The depression that results can last for years.

On the other hand, counting on help and not receiving it can lead to exhaustion. If you expect endless work and you get it, you manage. If you expect relief and you don't get it, you become tired—and resentful.

A few of the women we interviewed remain involved with the man, not as a lover but in a parental role. Sometimes the woman wants to revive a romantic relationship with the biological father and work out a long-term commitment. In other situations the woman becomes hostile over his not participating enough in child rearing. Either way, until the emotions settle and a satisfactory arrangement is achieved, the situation can be both frustrating and painful.

WHEN LIFE IS CHANGING

The third motivational push occurs when a crisis or change precipitates seeking fulfillment in motherhood. Considering motherhood at such times is not odd; it conforms to the social norm that females find happiness in having babies. As Jessie Bernard says in *The Future of Motherhood*, "The bearing of children has been almost intrinsic to femaleness, evidence and proof and validation of competence as a female." [9] She goes on to describe how little girls are "processed" to become mothers: "If one asks a little boy what he is going to be when he grows up, he will

[9]Jessie Bernard, *The Future of Motherhood* (New York: Penguin, 1974) 19.

reply in a wide variety of ways: fireman, aviator, astronaut. Not so the little girl. She will reply that she is going to be a mother.'' [10]

FILLING A VOID

The above-mentioned change may be brought about by dissatisfaction with career, a lack of purpose, or a need for focus. Consider Cheryl Valin's story.

You know Cheryl (or someone very much like her). Perhaps you met her in high school. She was bright but not brilliant, pretty but not a prom queen. She never did anything notable and certainly never did anything outrageous. She was raised in a traditional suburban home. Her father, a lawyer, took the train to work every day; her mother, a homemaker, stayed home and raised the children. Cheryl aspired to a life just like the one in which she was raised. If you had asked her at yearbook signing time what her goal was, she would have replied, ''to go to college, meet a boy [preferably one in pre-med or pre-law], get married, and have babies.'' Cheryl was a classic case of standard socialization.

She finally achieved part of her goal—motherhood—but it didn't happen the way she had planned it. When she became pregnant, Cheryl was thirty-four years old—and single. To explain why her life had not gone according to plan, she said she would have to go ''way, way back in my life.''

''I always thought I'd have babies. I was married when I was twenty-three, and I thought I'd get pregnant right away, but while we were on our honeymoon, I suddenly found out that my husband didn't want to have any children. I guess we had never really discussed it before we got married. I might have thought that we discussed it, like when we talked about how cute babies were, but it never occurred to me to talk about what we were going to do. It just seemed obvious. Well, he said he didn't want any children because it was a terrible world to bring children into. I was just crushed. I was shocked and I felt so betrayed.''

The marriage lasted five years. Childlessness wasn't the only

[10] Ibid., 26.

issue leading to their separation, but it played a significant part. Cheryl always felt "something was missing." After the divorce she spent several years "recovering." She considered going back to college to get a teaching certificate, but the thought of taking education courses for two years was dismal. She worked as a teacher's aide for a while, then as a clerk in a florist shop. She began studying art at a local junior college. Life was no longer full of pain, as it had been at the end of her marriage, but it wasn't full of anything else either. It was, she says, pretty empty.

When she was thirty-three, Cheryl took an art class with a woman who had lived in Phoenix. Moving to the Southwest became Cheryl's goal. "I was starting to save some money. It was fall, and I was thinking I would probably move out to Phoenix the following summer. That was when I met Robert, my son's father. I was really getting tired of being where I was, and I was getting ready to pull up my roots and move. It was a big move after living there so many years. So anyway, when I met Robert, I told him I was planning on moving to Phoenix, but he started getting very serious."

Robert couldn't get too serious, however, because he was married. Nevertheless, Cheryl says she "started thinking about having babies again, not wanting to think about it, but thinking about it all the time." Then Cheryl got pregnant. "I'm not entirely sure that I didn't get pregnant on purpose." She decided she would have the baby but follow through with her plans to move.

Apparently Cheryl sought a focus for her life, and the baby supplied it. "At the time I got pregnant, I had stopped what I was doing. I had decided that I was going to move and I was waiting. I was just waiting to try something else. I think it was time for me to have a baby, but I wasn't brave enough to tell myself that I was going to get pregnant. I just told myself that I was going to let my life change."

For other women the need for focus is prompted by the ending of a relationship or a divorce. Sara Destry's is a case in point. "It was a few months after I broke up with the man I had been seeing. That was the first relationship I thought might really work—you know, go all the way to marriage. Anyway, it was over, and I met this guy and we had this mad, passionate fling, and for the first time in my thirty-three years I did not use birth control. I did want to have a baby, but I didn't want to have it with this person as such. But you know, to paraphrase an old song, 'if you can't be with the person you love, then love the person you're with.' " Of her son, now five, she says, "He came at a time when I needed him. Needed him, meaning I was lonesome. He could fill an emptiness—not as a lover but as someone to love."

And how does having a child in the midst of change work out? Our research would indicate that for those who desire a change because life isn't going well, having a baby may *not* be the best answer.

For example, Cheryl, who moved while she was pregnant, with neither friends nor a job, describes her first year of single motherhood as "horrendously lonely."

Although Cheryl feels she has now "set roots down" in Phoenix, she says of single parenting, "It's still isolating. Maybe a little less bad than it was. I don't have any friends who are not single mothers. We stay together and kind of hold ourselves up."

Compounding Cheryl's despair is her reliance on Aid for Dependent Children (AFDC) for support. Her bachelor's degree in English literature did not train her for a profession, and she claims that secretarial jobs don't pay enough. After paying for transportation, lunches, and after-school care for her son, she would end up earning less than she does on welfare. But even if she tries to convince herself that raising a child is a worthwhile thing to do, living with the poverty and disrespect that come with being on welfare—especially if you don't see it as escapable—invariably leads to a sense of failure and dependency.

Would she recommend becoming a single parent to other women? "I wouldn't. I would tell them, 'You're never going to belong to yourself again. Ever. You're never going to be able to do what you want. For eighteen years you'll never be free of the responsibility. You're stuck.' "

Sara too has found single parenting more difficult than she had expected. She describes her sacrifices as her "plight." "My social life has been completely interrupted. I can't go on a date, I can't go on trips, I can't even go out to dinner with friends."

Would Sara recommend single parenting? "I said yes when I first had him, but I'm not sure I would say yes now. I wouldn't say yes; I wouldn't say no. I was used to an enormous amount of freedom, and it's been cut down to zero. I absolutely adore my son, and I can't imagine what it would be like to not have him, but it's very, very hard."

CHANGE FOR THE BETTER

For another group of women, however, entering motherhood at a time of personal change is a positive experience.

For Lucy Kramer the change arose out of a human development workshop she took a year before she got pregnant with her daughter. In the years prior to the workshop she had "accidentally" gotten pregnant four times and intentionally had abortions four times.

One of the personal issues she sought to resolve in the workshop was why she kept getting pregnant. She concluded that "maybe what I want is a baby." That may not seem a particularly profound insight, but the workshop also gave her the skills she felt she would need to be a mother.

"The training has improved my ability to do a lot of things, one of which is to be with children. Children used to drain me. I always loved them, but I couldn't stay much more than an hour with one. You know how active they are. Well, I'd watch them and I'd get tired. And since the training that doesn't happen any more. I think that was the big difference that made my having a baby possible."

For Stephanie Burns the change involved going back to college. Stephanie had been working as a paralegal and going to school part-time. When she was thirty-two, she decided it was time to push her career ahead. She quit her job and became a full-time student, with the knowledge that she could live off her savings for the two years it would take her to complete her bachelor's degree. During her first year back at school she began looking into adoption. "I think I've always been a maternal-type person, and I was getting a nesting instinct and getting ready to be able to afford a child. It was all starting to fit into place, and since school gave me more time at home than a job did, it would be a good time to establish a relationship with a child. I knew that in two years I'd have less time and more money, so it was the right point to get started."

For Martha Stevens change meant moving across the country. But unlike Cheryl, Martha wasn't escaping an empty life and walking into the unknown. She had been promoted to a job that would require her to move every three or four years. This mobility would limit her role as an "aunt" to her friends' children.

"I always liked kids, but I never thought I'd have any of my own. I'd never been married and I'd never really had that sort of expectation of myself—being a wife and mother. But I love kids. So I got real involved with my friends' kids. It was the perfect resolution. I never believed that you had to be a biological parent in order to have a relationship with children, so this way I was a pseudo-parent—every kid's favorite aunt, every mother's favorite baby-sitter. But then it wasn't such a perfect resolution, because I moved to Chicago, and the children I was involved with were all in California. I knew I could make friends with women in Chicago who had kids and be a pseudo-parent to a new crew, but when I moved again, I'd lose those relationships, too. So I realized that if I was going to have a consistent relationship with a child in my life, I was going to have to have my own child."

And how do these women pushed by "positive change" fare? None mentions how hard it is. None mentions sacrifices. What they do mention are the financial disadvantages of the one-paycheck family.

Lucy says that the chief problem with single parenting is economics. But she insists that's no reason to get married. "If what you really want is to have a baby, then have a baby and the economics will work out; they just always do. And the emotional cost of being married in order to cover yourself financially is just too high.''

Stephanie also points to finances. ''I think the only times I've felt resentment were when I wanted to do things with the kids but I couldn't afford to. But that's not resenting the kids; that's merely resenting circumstances.''

And Martha echoes, ''The major problems are material. I think for single women who are thinking about having kids, the financial aspect is one of the most important ones to consider, because you really don't have anything else to fall back on except yourself. That is one of the advantages of a two-parent household: you have twice as much opportunity to get money.''

Being pushed by the desire to enhance one's life or by positive change does not provide absolute assurance that a woman will be delighted with motherhood. Nor does being pushed by the hope for a co-parent or by negative change guarantee the onset of depression. Yet patterns exist. It may be that one's initial steps set the tone for the future. Whatever the reasons, motivation, while not the only factor, is certainly an important part of the overall experience.

Obviously, there are good reasons to have a child and bad reasons to have a child—not good and bad in terms of idealistic standards but in terms of whether women are likely to see single parenting as mostly joyful or mostly difficult, and whether women are likely to encourage or discourage other single women from becoming mothers.

CHAPTER
2

BECOMING A MOTHER: GETTING PREGNANT

She wants to start a family on her own. The question is how?

For those fantasizing about the prospect of single parenting, all sorts of possibilities come to mind. "I'd hang around Harvard and seduce a graduate student so I could be certain the child would be smart." "I'd adopt a child no one else wanted." "I'd find a donor, maybe a gay guy." "I'm dating this man and I could just . . ." "I'd ask my ex-husband." "I'd ask my old friend." "I'd find a doctor who did artificial insemination." "I'd go to Italy or Poland or some other Catholic country and adopt."

Selecting a strategy for becoming a mother while single involves a series of choices. The first is whether to adopt or to conceive. Then come the specifics. If adoption, an infant or an older child? A healthy child or a needy one? An American-born child or a foreign-born child? If conception, "accidentally" or intentionally? If intentionally, by artificial insemination or by intercourse? If by intercourse, with the man's knowledge or without?

Because the strategies of conception and adoption are very different, we will discuss them in separate chapters. In this chapter we look at the questions surrounding getting pregnant; in the next chapter we examine paths to adoption.

All in all, it's easier to get pregnant than to adopt—though this doesn't mean that conception as a strategy to single motherhood is without complexities.

First, there's the issue of intent. Some women want to get pregnant and purposefully set out to do so. Theirs is an "active choice." Others want to get pregnant, but rather than acknowledging their plan—to themselves or the man—they simply fail to use birth control; theirs is a "passive choice." Finally, there are women who don't wish to be pregnant, but having conceived, they choose not to abort and not to place the child up for adoption. For them it is an "after choice."

The second issue is the biological father. If a woman actively decides to get pregnant, who should be the father? A lover? A friend? An unknown donor? Should she ask him or just "do it"? (Of course, if the pregnancy is a result of passive choice or after choice, the issue of who the biological father should be isn't dealt with—at least not consciously—prior to conception. As we will discuss later, this can lead to other concerns.)

ACTIVE CHOICE

Women who choose conception seldom give serious thought to adoption. Only three of the women we interviewed who bore children had considered adoption first. Yet the reasons these three women gave for not adopting may shed some light on the subconscious concerns of some of the women who didn't overtly consider that alternative.

Throughout her twenties and thirties Margaret Richards had said to herself, "If I don't marry, certainly I'll adopt." Yet when she reached the point of deciding to become a single parent, she found herself thinking that adoption was second best. She really wanted to have her "own" child.

"We had an adoption in our family which didn't turn out well," Margaret said. "My brother and sister-in-law adopted a boy who's a real mess. They gave him every possible advantage and he should have turned out beautifully, but instead he's a constant disappointment. I don't know, maybe they spoiled him because he wasn't really theirs—you know, went overboard— or maybe it was just his makeup. But whatever the reasons, he's always upsetting them. He was a disciplinary problem in high school and then refused to go to college—it's just not what they had hoped for. That kind of scared me off.

"I kept thinking, I'd rather have my own child. It sounds snobbish, but I thought I could have a quality child. The idea of a dull child or a child full of problems—well, to be honest, it just wasn't appealing. I come from a very bright, talented family; there are musicians and inventors and teachers and successful businessmen. And I thought, Why waste this great genetic material? So it was a snobbish thing. I thought I could get a better-quality child if I had it myself."

A second woman, Dorothy Wold, had other reasons for preferring birth. "I didn't rule adoption out," Dorothy began, "but it was never very high on my list of priorities. My preference was to have my own child if I could . . . for several reasons that are hard to explain.

"First, I don't deal well with the thought of giving up a child for adoption. I'm a social worker, and I realize intellectually that there are circumstances in which it makes a lot of sense, but to me it's a level of rejection that's just too severe. And I felt somehow that I wouldn't be the best person in the world to explain to a child why his parents had given him up. So that was part of it.

"And part of it had to do with how important my own family is to me. We're very close, and having a heritage, family background, blood ties, seems essential to me.

"The other thing was the fact that I work with emotionally disturbed kids. I knew the chances of a single parent adopting a newborn healthy infant was zip, and I couldn't work with emotionally disturbed kids all day and come home to my own problem child at night. If my own child developed problems, that would be different. But somehow I felt that an adopted child might end up feeling like a patient or a client, or 'a case,' or whatever, as opposed to *my* child. I'm not sure that that would actually have happened, but that was my fear.''

The third woman who considered adoption prior to conception actually tried to adopt for two years before giving up and getting pregnant.

As Marsha Baker recalled, ''I filed with an agency and had to go in for a bunch of interviews. It was *not* pleasant. It was like being in in-depth therapy except worse, because you not only had to dredge up all sorts of garbage from your past, you knew every word was being evaluated. I felt like I was under a microscope. I know they want to make certain that you're fit for parenting, but I'd walk out of the sessions dazed. And then when they finally figured I was OK, they referred me to these books of pathetically needy children. I don't question the need of these children—mongoloid children, terribly handicapped children—but I just didn't think I could raise one. I would have considered a multiracial infant or an older healthy child, but there were none available.''

At the same time, Marsha was trying to arrange an independent adoption. As a nurse in a large urban hospital, she was well placed to hear of available infants—and she nearly got one. ''One of the doctors I work for had heard about this little Puerto Rican boy, and I rushed over and talked to his mother. She was a child herself—only fifteen—and she seemed rather blasé about the whole thing. Anyway, we made arrangements for me to take him, and I saw a lawyer and got all the paperwork done, and then the mother changed her mind at the last minute. She had found a couple that offered her ten thousand dollars for the baby. I would have taken custody the next day, when she called and said she'd gotten a better offer. I couldn't compete in that market. I couldn't pull it off financially, and I couldn't justify it morally. And if I had bought a baby, I would have always feared that somebody would be able to take him away from me.''

Margaret, Dorothy, and Marsha are unusual. The other women who actively chose pregnancy responded to our query with comments such as: ''I never even thought about it''; or ''I was certain no one would let me adopt, so I didn't even try''; or most commonly, ''I wanted to have my own child.''

But a woman can't have "her own" child on her own. The biological reality is that she needs a man's help. Which man, then?

People who heard about our research for this book almost invariably assumed that a woman who intentionally gets pregnant selects the father on the basis of his genes. After all, if she's not married and can have anyone father her child, why not go for the most handsome and the most intelligent man around? But is that necessarily possible?

Think about it. How many women have a corral of handsome genius studs just waiting to go to bed with them? And how many women could go to bed with a man they may not know or care for just to get pregnant? Some, but probably not most. So a man's availability, a woman's attraction to him, and the acceptability of his potential involvement in her and her child's lives may loom as the key issues in her decision.

Candidates may be current lovers, former lovers, or friends. Yet the fact remains that the choice may be based more on convenience than on genes.

And if a man is available, attractive, and acceptable, should she ask him to father a child, or should she silently obtain his "help"?

Most of the active-choice women did ask the man. They saw it as a simple matter of honesty or a wish to avoid "using" someone. They felt that trickery ultimately would anger and alienate the man, and they did not want to deny a man's "equal" right to make a choice about procreation. Others remained silent, assuming that if the man had wanted to have sex and would not be asked for financial or emotional support, he was not being used. Still others chose to avoid the issue of the father altogether by having artificial insemination. That way the donor volunteered, was paid, and would be unknown.

LETTING HIM KNOW

Micki Herlinger's story is fairly typical. Like so many single women, Micki had a man in her life who had been her lover on and off for years, one of those forever affairs in which marriage is not really a question.

"Bruce and I have known each other for six years. We've sort of ebbed and flowed in and out of each other's lives. There's been a lot of love, a lot of emotion between us. We've lived together, we've traveled together, we've meant a lot of things to each other. But one thing we could not be was married to each other. Bruce is very charming and delightful. He has a million good qualities, but he has as many bad qualities. He is neurotic and irresponsible and can't find a job to suit him. I'm very stable, very settled. If we're together too much, we both get irritable and angry. So we can't have a long-term relationship. He's not as responsible as I am or as interested in settling down. He would never consider marriage, and I would never consider marrying him."

For Micki, marrying Bruce was not sensible, but when she decided she wanted to have a child, she turned to Bruce.

As Micki saw it, "If I had this wonderful man in my life that I wanted to marry and have a family with, that would have been great. But since there wasn't such a person around and since I didn't want to wait for him in order to have a child, Bruce was the best choice. You see, we really do care for each other, but I knew he wouldn't be involved and that's what I wanted."

Micki and Bruce talked about it. "I told him that I wanted to have a baby, and he was real pleased. He thought I'd be a good mother, and while he could never see himself as a day-to-day father, there was no one else he'd rather make a baby with."

So Micki put away her diaphragm and arranged to see Bruce around the middle of her cycle. Some months he cooperated, and some months he didn't. "As I said," she laughed, "he's not very responsible." But four months later Micki was pregnant.

Lucy Kramer asked a lover and received an enthusiastic response. "This was a man I was seeing, sleeping with, and I considered just not using birth control but thought that would be unfair to him. So one night he was here, and I was real scared, and I said, 'Oh, Jeff, I've got something to tell you and I don't know how to tell you!' I was real nervous, and I finally just said, 'OK, listen, I want to get pregnant and I want to know if you will help.' He said, 'What do you mean by help?' and I said, 'Well, make sure that I get pregnant.' I said, 'As far as anything else is concerned, any more involvement on your part is negotiable, and you can choose if you want to or not, and that's not what I'm asking.' And he said yes.

"He was actually excited about it. He'd call me and say, 'Are you taking your temperature?' and 'When should we do it?' He was really cute. When I told him I'd be ovulating, he'd come over and rub his hands together and say, 'Let's go to it.' And the second month we tried I got pregnant!''

Carolyn Norton got pregnant by a married man with whom she was very much in love. "He had known that I wanted to have a baby, and he offered. Basically, he said, 'Are you ready for this?' and I said, 'It's what I want.' I got pregnant the first time we tried.''

But although she had been certain, when their relationship ended in her third month of pregnancy, Carolyn began questioning her decision. Her concern did not come from the loss of his potential participation. He was married and she had known all along that they couldn't raise the child together. So it wasn't that she'd be alone—that was a given. Rather, she was so angry with him—and perhaps hurt by him—that she wondered about having his child.

"I started thinking, Oh, my God, I don't want to have his kid. I don't want part of him in my life. I was really working myself over. So I took a long, long walk in the woods, and I asked myself, Shall I get an abortion or shall I have the baby? And the answer just came so clear and so strong and it was, You would be a fool to have an abortion. This is what you've wanted for so long. It doesn't matter what you feel about him. It's a baby.''

Martha Stevens was in a different position when she decided to have a child, because she wasn't involved with any man. She considered chance sexual encounters but not very seriously. "I toyed with the idea of just picking guys up, but I didn't really want to do that. How could I go to bed with someone I didn't know? Besides I'm not the sort of person who hangs out in bars and picks up men. I wouldn't even know how to go about doing that. And even if I could, I'd be too uptight to go to bed unless I got *really* drunk. The whole concept is alien to me. Besides, I didn't like the idea of tricking someone into it. It didn't seem right.

"But I had this buddy at work who I really liked, and I thought he'd be good to father my baby. He was married and had several kids and felt bad for me because I didn't have a family. And I knew he had affairs. Also, since he was married, I didn't think I would have to worry about his wanting anything to do with his kid.

"So I started having an affair with him. Before we started the affair, I told him that I wanted to get pregnant and asked if he would mind. He said he thought it was a good idea—that it would be good for me to have a kid. I said, 'You won't have to give me any money or anything. I just want to have the baby, and it's my baby.' He didn't say anything, so we just left it at that.

"I didn't see him very often—he would come over every week or ten days, so I was a little worried about whether I'd get pregnant. Then after about three months, when I still hadn't conceived, I told him I was serious about having a kid, and I wanted to see him more often, and he started to come by every other day or so. Three months later I got pregnant."

NOT LETTING HIM KNOW

Of course, not every woman asked. Some, like Christina Lash and Gail Jordan, simply failed to use birth control with their current lovers.

For Christina it was a matter of "arranging." "I really wanted to have a baby since I was thirty-two. I had my IUD taken out and made a sort of halfhearted attempt at rhythm. At that time I had been dating Robert for two years, and he knew I wanted to get pregnant, though he was really against it. Of course, he also knew I was only using rhythm, and he never offered to do birth control, so I guess he was willing to take the chance.

"Anyway, when I was thirty-three, my doctor told me that

if I wanted to get pregnant, I'd better do it soon because I had little fibroid cysts that might get bigger. So I started juggling the dates around on my charts. As far as Robert is concerned, it was an accident, but the truth is I arranged it, and I was thrilled to death when I got pregnant.''

For Gail it was even easier. ''I was dating a man who was perfect. I kept on thinking, If I ever got pregnant, I would love to have his child. He looks right, he talks right, he has the right personality.

''One night he came over and we were sitting around talking, and I was looking at him and thinking about how special he was. He has lovely blue eyes and a wonderful, gentle face and thick dark hair, and he was lean and soft-spoken. . . . And a little while later we went to bed. I hadn't put my diaphragm in yet, and I knew it was the middle of my cycle and I could get pregnant. I had been thinking for a long time about how much I wanted a child and that I didn't need to wait for a husband. So I got pregnant. I had the opportunity and I took it.''

Women who are not involved in an ongoing relationship have to create opportunities. That is what Marsha Baker did after she decided that adoption was not a possibility. A nurse, Marsha described her baby's father, Bennett, as a good ''donor.'' ''He's very smart and good-looking and healthy. Genetically, he was perfect.''

He was also available as a lover. ''Bennett and I have known each other for years. We might see each other every week, or we might not get together for months. And sometimes when we're together, we just have dinner, and sometimes we spend the night.''

All she had to do was time their visits. ''I started taking my temperature and checking my cervical mucus to chart my ovulating, and when my temperature dropped and my mucus got sticky, I'd pop over to Bennett's looking sexier than usual.''

It took Marsha eight months to get pregnant. Amazingly, Bennett never noticed the twenty-eight-day intervals between visits. ''If he had realized that I was trying to get pregnant, he would never have touched me. He has a child by an ex-wife, and he doesn't see the kid. He thinks fatherhood is out of the question for him. If he were ever to know that this was deliberate, he'd kill me.''

Did Marsha have any concerns about deceiving Bennett? ''No. This is my baby, so I'm not using him. I'm not trying to get money. I'm not trying to get emotions. It doesn't matter who did it because it's not going to be any skin off his nose. It's no different than if I were artificially inseminated, as far as I'm concerned, except this way I'll be able to tell the baby who her father is.''

ARTIFICIAL INSEMINATION

While some active-choice women let the man know their intentions and others do not, still others avoid the issue of a man's participation by having artificial insemination. There are no moral or emotional issues involved; the sperm donor is a volunteer and remains anonymous. And while not every gynecologist and fertility clinic will artificially inseminate single women, it is done in every major city in the United States. One study estimates that in recent years some 1500 single woman have been successfully artificially inseminated each year.[1]

Although we talked to a few women who obtained sperm from a donor they knew and then inseminated themselves, Dorothy Wold, who went through a doctor, struck us as more typical. When Dorothy decided to get pregnant, she was not emotionally involved with a man. She talked with four male friends about the possibility of fathering a child. She asked two what they thought of the idea and asked the other two whether they would father a child for her. She told each one that there would be two conditions: they would not be involved with her and the child, and they must at some point acknowledge paternity.

''Their reactions were interesting. For each one the initial response was 'Oh, sure, I'd do that.' Then the more we talked about it, the more they'd say, 'But I might find myself wanting

[1] Anne Taylor Fleming, ''New Frontiers in Conception,'' *New York Times Magazine*, July 20, 1980, 14.

to come around to see how you're doing.' And some were concerned about telling a future wife and children, 'By the way, there's this kid . . .' Each time I talked about it, it seemed like the emotional and logistic complications were so great that it didn't make great sense. It didn't feel right. I think had I been involved in a special relationship that was significant to me, that would have been different. But since the specific man was not that important, I ended up feeling better about not knowing who the donor was at all and going with artificial insemination.''

Armed with arguments about how her single status should not be an issue in artificial insemination, she made an appointment with her gynecologist. Much to her surprise, he didn't care about her marital status. "His only concern was that I would 'miss all the fun.' He even offered to find a donor so I wouldn't have to use frozen sperm.''

They scheduled a first try on her next ovulation. Dorothy describes the actual process of getting pregnant by artificial insemination as "one of the least sexual feelings I'd ever had.

"It was all very clinical—about the same as having an internal. I was on my back with my feet in stirrups. He put the sperm into a cervical cap and slid the cap into position. Like putting in a diaphragm. The cap looks like a Ping-Pong ball cut in half. They just slide it in and you don't feel it any more than you do a tampon. I stayed there on the table for thirty minutes. It was not the most exciting thirty minutes of my life. When I got home I masturbated, thinking that an orgasm would help pull the sperm up—though I don't know if that's fact or fiction.

"I left the cap in place for about the next eight hours and then removed it by pulling the string. Two days later I went in for a second try. I saw my doctor's associate that time, and he injected some sperm into my cervix with a dull-tipped syringe and then put the cervical cap in. He had me lie on my back in a knee-chest position for half an hour—another rather uninteresting, not to mention uncomfortable, half hour. I don't know which time I got pregnant, but one of those two did it.''

Of the choice of artificial insemination over knowing who the father was, Dorothy says, "I think it was best. I don't know anything about the donor other than his medical history, the color of his hair and eyes, and his education. Actually, I'm not supposed to know his education. It was crossed out on the form, but you can still read it. It said four years postgraduate education, so I assume he had gone to medical school and was an intern or a resident.

"I think I'm better off not knowing who he was. If I knew him, I might want to call him—to use him as some kind of father as opposed to a donor. It would have a different feel about it. I might want him to know what's going on with my son. There would be some emotional ties. It would be much more complicated. As it is, I have this feeling of clinical distance. It was really neat, and I was glad somebody was willing to do it, but there's no attachment, and when I talk to my son or other people, I use the word 'donor,' because that's the way I feel. He was a donor, not a father."

PASSIVE CHOICE

For another group of women pregnancy was less deliberate.

We asked each of the birth mothers we interviewed whether they became pregnant intentionally. The women who made an active choice responded yes. The women who got pregnant accidentally and made an after choice to not abort responded no. The women we categorize as passive-choice responded, "Good question" or "More or less" or "Perhaps subconsciously."

Some passive-choice women actually acknowledge intent but report that they pursued their goal in a haphazard manner. It could be said that they "invited an accident."

Irene Sullivan's story supports this. When asked if she had gotten pregnant on purpose, she responded, "Sort of accidentally on purpose. It's complicated. I had been in a relationship with a man for a couple of years, and it didn't work out. He definitely didn't want to have a kid; I definitely did. I was about thirty-five when we split up. Then for the next year or so there was just nobody around that might become a serious relationship. It was a combination of this relationship ending, the fact that I was in my middle thirties, and being ready. It was in the air. Friends talked about getting pregnant. It was a good time careerwise for me to have a baby. Well, I didn't use birth control and I got pregnant. It was a man I'd known only briefly—more an affair than a relationship. When I realized I was pregnant, I was elated. The thought of abortion crossed my mind for about three minutes. So it was clear that it was a choice. It wasn't a super-organized plan—but it was a choice.''

For other women, not only was the process of becoming pregnant unplanned, the intention to become a mother was also confused. Eleanor Gates, who had been firmly opposed to having children throughout her twenties, at thirty started wondering about whether she could get pregnant.

''I had my Dalkon Shield removed when there was all that FDA stuff about their being dangerous. I got a diaphragm but didn't use it that seriously. And I got pregnant. And without giving it a great deal of thought I had an abortion. It was the right decision at the time. I wasn't enough in control of my life to have a child. I just wasn't ready to take care of another person. Yet even though the abortion wasn't traumatic, and I was comfortable with the decision, I knew that if I ever got pregnant again, unless it was rape or something, I would continue with the pregnancy. I think everyone should have the choice to have an abortion or not, but for me I had decided that once was enough.

''After that I became almost obsessed with the idea of getting pregnant. Not that I really wanted to, but I couldn't get it off my mind. I started another relationship, and I would approach the time I would be getting my period and I'd think, Oh, God, what if I'm pregnant, what if I'm pregnant. And I'd get my period and I'd think, Oh, good, or Oh, shit. I was *very* ambivalent. And then two years later I did get pregnant. This time I felt stronger, more in charge of my life. I was in a good position personally and financially. I think subconsciously this is what I wanted, but it was easier to deal with it more or less from the back door instead of asking a man. I just wish I could have been more up front with myself and others.''

For still other women the desire to have a child was wrapped up in the desire to have a husband. But when they recognized that marriage was not an option after they allowed themselves to get pregnant, they chose not to abort.

Cheryl met Robert when she was thirty-two. She had always wanted to have a family, but her first marriage ended without children. Although Robert was married when she met him, there was the chance of his leaving his wife, a thread to which Cheryl held fast.

"I didn't know that Robert was married until we had seen each other a couple of times. He was separated from his wife, and I thought, Well, that isn't *really* married. So I thought I'd continue dating him and see what happened. He was a very sweet, sincere person, and I knew he wouldn't purposely hurt me.

"He was separated off again and on again, and he told me after we'd been seeing each other about two months that he had two children. That made it different. I told him we shouldn't see each other anymore unless he firmly decided to get a divorce. We tried that for a while, but we missed each other and started seeing each other again. It was off again, on again. I have a real hard time realizing that something isn't good and leaving a situation. It always takes me a long time. Anyway, one time when they were separated, he decided to get a divorce. The marriage was bad. It sounded like it had always been bad. I started thinking about our getting married and having a baby. So I was thinking about having a baby, and then I got pregnant."

Was Cheryl using birth control?

"Well, I was and I wasn't. I used a diaphragm but not all the time. The night I got pregnant I was pretty sure it wasn't the right time of the month for me to get pregnant so I didn't use my diaphragm.

"Meanwhile he decided he couldn't leave his kids. So we broke up, but by the time he decided he wouldn't get the divorce, I was already pregnant.

"I wasn't really surprised when I skipped my period. I avoided thinking about it for awhile. By that time I knew that he couldn't leave his wife and we couldn't get married, but I really didn't let myself think about being pregnant. I didn't consider having a child, and I didn't consider having an abortion. I just avoided it.

"After a few weeks I went to Planned Parenthood for the test, and they gave me this sheet that asked what I would do if I were pregnant and I checked off 'keep the baby.' And as soon as I did that, my mind was made up. I felt very strongly about it. I decided, Yes, I'll keep the baby. And I was surprised at how sure I was that it was the right thing to do. I knew that I'd be doing it alone, and that felt OK. Looking back on it now, I realize how much I wanted to have a child. He's everything I ever hoped for."

Bonny Thompson also told us she had hoped for marriage. Bonny had been dating her baby's father for four years prior to conceiving her daughter. "We'd talked about marriage on and off, never very seriously—I wanted to; but he kept finding reasons to wait. I got pregnant three times by him before I got pregnant with my daughter, and I had three abortions. People had said, 'Why did you let yourself get pregnant if you didn't have to?' And I think it was because I really wanted a child. But each time I got pregnant, I couldn't face it yet, so I'd have an abortion. It was an easy out. I don't have any religious ties, so it was very simple. But the last time was different. I think I felt ready, and I think I finally realized that we'd never get married."

It's worth noting that Bonny is one of two women who had had several abortions prior to having a child. Both women acknowledge that previous conceptions and abortions attested to their desire to have a child *and* their feeling that they weren't ready. Several other women whom we interviewed had had one abortion. For them the issue seemed to be less one of confused motives than of an actual accident and the acceptance of abortion as after-the-fact birth control.

AFTER CHOICE

Not all of the women identified conscious or unconscious motivations to become pregnant. About a third are certain it was an accident. They made their choice—after they conceived—to keep the baby.

Four of the women who got pregnant accidentally had been told by their gynecologists that they were unable to conceive. Each was upset at the thought she would never be able to bear a child, each stopped using birth control, each got pregnant, and each rejected out of hand the idea of abortion.

A woman named Sherry described her decision. "I can't tell you how sick I was when the doctor told me that I could never have children. 'Devastated' is probably the only word that comes close to describing how I felt. As long as I can remember, I had wanted children, and now I was told I never would. It was like being punched in the stomach.

"Well, since I couldn't get pregnant, I didn't have to use birth control. But the doctor, it turns out, was wrong. A few months after the diagnosis I was pregnant.

"I didn't see being a single parent as ideal, but I felt like the chance might not come again. As far as I was concerned, the baby was a miracle and I wasn't going to give it up. Abortion was not an option."

Abortion was not an option for Rochelle North, but her choice was based on religious beliefs. "I never considered abortion because I see it as the taking of a life, although I did consider adopting the baby out.

"From the time he was born until he was a year old, I agonized over whether I should have given him up for his own sake. I had so much guilt. Guilt because I was single and working, and leaving him with a sitter who was incompetent. I agonized and agonized. I had nightmares and cried and felt guilty until he was a year old. Then suddenly I realized it didn't really matter. It was too late. It was too late for him to be separated from me, and of course it had always been too late for me to be separated from him. So it was irrelevant. The decision had made itself."

For others abortion *was* an option, and an option seriously considered. Norma Egan's description was surely more detailed than other women's stories but not unusual.

"John and I had known each other since I was twelve. Our

relationship was more a friendship than a romance. I traveled a lot, and when I came to LA, I would stay with him, and we would have fun together. It wasn't a big sexual relationship. We probably slept together only three or four times. Sometimes I used my diaphragm and sometimes I didn't. But that wasn't atypical for me. In the past I had often not used the diaphragm because of not wanting to interrupt the spontaneity of what was taking place. It was irresponsible but not atypical of me. I didn't want to get pregnant—not even in my most private unconscious thoughts. But I did.

"I had planned on having an abortion. I scheduled it once and canceled it, and then I scheduled it again. I had had an abortion six years before, and that wasn't a particularly negative experience; but for some reason this time the idea of having an abortion was very disgusting to me. I couldn't just take care of business like I had the first time. Instead I found myself thinking, Why am I having an abortion? Maybe I should have the baby. I'm twenty-eight and I really want to be a mom, so why wait?

"One of the reasons I thought I should go ahead and have the child is that I felt there was a good chance I would never marry. Most marriages I've seen are pretty traditional, and I don't want to be part of all those mate expectations and stereotype things. So I was thinking about that.

"I didn't feel like it was now or never—I was twenty-eight and I had a good six years left—but it was convenient that I was pregnant. I was ready. I'd done a lot of neat things and been a lot of fun places. I had gotten my master's degree, and I had been out working at a job which I like doing, so it was a good time to have a child.

"The other issue was the father. John is thirty-eight and has never been married and never had any cildren, and he *loves* children. And I thought who would I rather co-parent my kid with than John? He doesn't have to be a husband to me, but he'd be an outstanding father."

This wasn't all that went into Norma's decision to not abort. She also did research. "I read articles and books on single parenting, I called single-parent organizations, I interviewed single parents, I talked with a therapist. There were all these issues to consider: your economics, your profession, your desire to have a child, your support systems. I got very analytical and weighed all these objective criteria. I didn't want to be irresponsible. I didn't want to screw the kid and set him up for a terrible life. So I weighed all these things and felt like most of them were in my favor. I had savings, I was well set in my career, and I had a slew of single friends who would like to have kids and who I could count on for help.

"I talked with John. I told him I was considering having the child, and his bottom line was 'Norma, I'll support you in any way, shape, or form I possibly can.'

"So once I had mapped out the objective stuff and realized it could work, I decided to just let my emotions roll. And my emotions were telling me that I wanted the kid real badly.

"I remember my abortion was scheduled for Monday, and it was the weekend and I had to decide. So I went and got the money that I needed for the abortion, and at the same time I went to the bookstore and got books on pregnancy, so whatever way it would go, I'd be prepared. I was all by myself and I had done all my research, and now I had to decide. And I finally decided. I just decided I was going to do it. I'll tell you, though, John was a very important factor. If he hadn't said he'd help out, if he had said, 'Forget it, have the abortion, I don't want to have anything to do with it,' I don't know what I would have done. I don't know whether I still would have gone through with it. He was a big deciding factor. I knew I was going to get my own emotional support from my friends and family, but knowing he would help pay for things was an important backup. Anyway, it seemed like it could work, so I just decided."

Whether pregnancy resulted from an active choice, a passive choice, or an after choice, few of the women reconsidered abortion or gave thought to putting their child up for adoption. They love their kids and cannot imagine life without them. Yet few had a second child. This is due in part to the physical and emotional strains of pregnancy (which we examine in Chapter 4) and in part to the father question (which we discuss in Chapter 9).

CHAPTER
3

BECOMING
A MOTHER:
ADOPTION

There is both good news and bad news about adoption. The good news is that it *is* possible for single people to adopt. The bad news is that it is very difficult to adopt American-born infants. In fact, fewer and fewer American-born infants are available for adoption by any prospective parents—married or single. Widespread access to birth control and abortion in the last several years has dramatically decreased the number of unintentional pregnancies and unwanted births. Furthermore, there is the increased likelihood that women—both older and younger—who do become pregnant unintentionally and opt against abortion will decide to raise their children themselves. Consequently, demand for infants to adopt exceeds the available supply, and the few who *are* adopted almost invariably go to married couples.

Single women who apply to adoption agencies are told in no uncertain terms that they cannot adopt healthy infants or toddlers. The agencies' rationale: two parents are better than one, so two-parent families should have first choice. It goes without saying that the first to be chosen are young healthy children. The children left for placement with a single parent are usually older or handicapped children.

There may be some advantages for a "difficult" child in a single-parent home. Single adoptive parents tend to be older than married adoptive parents and to live in urban rather than suburban environments. Children placed with them therefore tend to get the benefits of a more experienced and confident adult as well as the benefits a city provides: greater services, activities, and tolerance of differences. And for some children, having one person with whom to establish an especially close relationship and one person to provide an unambivalent source of authority may boost emotional growth and sense of security.

Yet most single people who want children, like most married people who want children, are not motivated by such a humanitarian goal as helping a child with problems. They are simply people who want to experience parenting and enjoy the emotional rewards of a family. And even if a single person wants a handicapped child, she may not get one. As one social worker explained, "You have to be an unusual person to parent an emotionally or physically handicapped child. Whether you are a single parent or a part of a couple, you have to have an extraordinary level of patience and an extraordinary desire to give of yourself. Not everyone has what it takes. Agencies don't just 'dump' hard-to-place children on single people, assuming that some home is better than none. The last thing kids like that need is to be placed somewhere they don't belong and then be bounced from home to home. We only give children to applicants who have the emotional, financial, and physical resources to provide adequately for the extraordinary demands and needs of a handicapped child."

Not all children who are adopted go through agencies, however. A somewhat more likely, though still not *very* likely, avenue for adopting an American infant is independent adoption.

In independent adoptions a pregnant woman who wishes to put her infant up for adoption asks a doctor or a nurse or a lawyer, rather than an adoption agency, to find a home for her child. Prospective adoptive parents either informally tell obstetricians and nurses to "keep their eyes open" for an adoptable infant or they formally register with an adoption lawyer.

Infants put up for adoption through hospital staff are somewhat more likely to be placed with single adoptive parents than are infants put up through lawyers. A pregnant girl who has not sought the help of a lawyer or an agency may accept the judgment of the people at the hospital. She may be young or frightened or anxious to have it over with and get on with her life—or all three. This doesn't mean she is not thoughtful or not concerned. She is simply accepting the option offered. And if the people at the hospital recommend that she give her baby to a single woman, she may well do so.

The doctor or nurse route is fairly haphazard and informal. It may take months or years for them to hear of an infant—and perhaps they never will. When an infant *is* found, the birth mother may accept the home recommended by the hospital staff member or may seek another on her own. After she decides, the process in most states is a relatively simple matter of having a social worker approve the new home (a pro forma matter if the birth mother has already given her OK) and of signing legal papers.

When one uses a lawyer, the prospective adoptive parent pays a retainer to the lawyer and completes a personal data file. The lawyer then provides the pregnant client with descriptions of a series of adoptive parents from which to choose. There is no waiting list; each birth mother can choose from all existing applicants. The decision is typically made before the birth, and the lawyer arranges for the newborn to go directly to its adoptive home on release from the hospital. As with a doctor or nurse placement, a pro forma home study is completed by a social worker.

A pregnant girl following the more formal lawyer process may also be young and frightened and anxious to move on. If, however, she is given the choice of putting her child in a home with one parent or a home with two parents, she is likely to choose the latter. After all, she probably feels unable to raise the child herself because she is unmarried. Why then would she choose to have the child raised by another unmarried woman—even one who is older and more financially secure?

The adoptive parent usually pays the birth mother's hospital bill and adoption fees. If one adopts through a doctor or nurse, total costs average about five thousand dollars; if one uses a lawyer, costs can run up to ten thousand dollars.

There are several differences between the independent process and an agency adoption. Agencies theoretically perform a more thorough screening of applicants than do doctors, nurses, or lawyers. In some states agencies do not place infants immediately in adoptive homes but give the newborn to a foster mother for two to six weeks while the birth mother finalizes her decision to relinquish the child. Second, agencies do not pay the birth mother's hospital expenses. And finally, agencies are less likely than doctors and lawyers to arrange open adoptions, whereby birth mothers and adoptive parents know who each other are and can, if they wish, meet each other and maintain contact throughout the child's life.

In addition to agency and private adoption there is a third route—foreign adoption. As with U.S. adoptions, it can be done through an agency or through a personal contact. Agencies in Korea, India, and Latin America will place children in single-parent homes, although their preference is often two-parent families.

Financial costs of international adoptions vary. If they include money under the table and extensive travel or legal fees, they can reach the ten-thousand- to fifteen-thousand-dollar range. Adoptions through reputable offices, however, usually can be completed for five thousand to seven thousand dollars. Yet the process of foreign adoption is not necessarily easy; it may take years of writing and waiting with no guarantee of success.

And there are other routes. Personal contacts through mainstream channels offered by medical people or bureaucrats and marginal channels offered by individuals (such as prostitutes) may lead to a pregnant girl who, from shame or poverty, wants to give up her child.

Whatever the route, adoption is a popular option for many single women who desire to be mothers.

THE EXPERIENCE

ADOPTING A FOREIGN INFANT

Jeanne Nichol's experience of adopting her "little charmer" is fairly typical of the process of adopting outside the United States.

As with so many women, the catalyst for Jeanne's decision to become a parent was a birthday. Every woman has a different idea of the age at which she can no longer put off the decision to become a mother. For some it's forty; for others it's thirty-five. For Jeanne it was thirty. "I always wanted a family. I grew up believing you went to college, got married, and had children. But that was not happening. When I turned thirty, I knew I had to do something about this family business, and I started looking into adoption."

Jeanne never seriously considered bearing a child herself. As she saw it, "There were two big counts against pregnancy: one, the suburban school district I work for; and two, my family. No way would the principal or the superintendent or the teachers or parents have tolerated an unwed pregnancy. I mean, it would have been seen as a major moral outrage. I don't know if they could have fired me, but they might have tried, or at least they would have let me know that I was an outcast and a slut."

She expected a similar response from her family, and her fears were confirmed the one time she mentioned the possibility of pregnancy to her mother. "When I was in the depths of my depression from having no luck at adopting, I talked to my mother on the phone about the option of my giving birth to a child. She said it would *devastate* my father. And I thought, Wow, that would really cut me off. I could handle other people thinking I'm different, but hurting my father was one thing I wasn't willing to do."

Jeanne began her quest with three months of research. She spoke with social workers, attended meetings of adoptive parents, and read everything she could find on adoption. During those months Jeanne personally resolved the two key issues that precede adoption. First, she explored her feelings about raising a child that was not born to her. "For some women there's a notion of a child being your own only if you give birth to it. But I didn't see any difference. The way that I see it, what a child inherits is less important than what it gets while it's growing up. If it's a normal, healthy infant and you give it lots of love and encouragement, it will become a happy, productive person." Second, she had to be honest with herself about the kind of child she could parent. Could she raise a mixed-race child, a sick child, an older "difficult" child? She didn't have to justify her biases, just recognize them. "I decided that I didn't want to adopt a handicapped child—whether that meant a younger child with a physical handicap or an older child with an emotional handicap. And older children invariably have some kind of emotional handicap. You don't get taken away from your parents or moved from foster home to foster home without suffering some emotional damage. I wasn't trying to save the world; I just wanted a kid—a healthy baby."

During the course of her investigation, Jeanne learned that she would not be able to get a healthy baby in the United States. She was told about the lack of availability of infants and the policy of placing with couples the few who were put up for adoption. If she wanted a healthy infant, she would have to go through a foreign agency. "Either you give on the child's age or on its health or on where it was born. If you don't give on something, you don't get a child. I didn't want to give on age or health, so I started looking into international adoption."

In addition to resolving her own questions about adoption, Jeanne's research directed her to a locally based support group of adoptive parents and prospective adoptive parents. It was from a member of the group that Jeanne obtained a list of orphanages in developing countries. She started writing to them.

"I would write a flurry of letters to various agencies, most of whom never responded. That was kind of discouraging. Then I'd muster up the energy to write them another batch of letters so they'd get to know me and realize how serious I was."

Throughout a year of writing Jeanne kept attending the adoptive parents meetings. Talking with people who had adopted or were themselves trying to adopt made it a less lonely enterprise. The group proved to be an invaluable network; it provided moral support when she was discouraged and ultimately supplied a ready-made extended family to share her pleasure when she was successful.

But success was a long time coming. After a year of writing, an agency in Peru offered her a child. "I was floating. It was the happiest moment of my life. It was all I could think about. I called the airlines to make a reservation and called the social worker who would do the paper work on this side. I called my parents and all my friends. People started setting up showers. Teachers at my school offered cribs and changing tables. And then four days later I received a letter saying the child had died. I couldn't have been more hurt if she had been mine—because, you see, she was almost mine.

"I thought about giving up. That was when I talked to my mother about what she and Dad would think if I got pregnant. But she just confirmed what I knew—that was not an option. I kind of shelved the idea for a while, just stayed depressed."

After sitting out a couple of support group meetings, Jeanne returned to the group and met a woman who was in the process of adopting a child from an orphanage in Guatemala.

Using the woman as a contact, Jeanne wrote to the orphanage and almost immediately was offered a child. Again she let her hopes run free. Again she made plane reservations and called her family. Just before she was to fly to Guatemala to pick up the baby, the other woman returned from Guatemala. "She came back and said, 'I've seen the kid they have for you, and I don't think you should go. She's very sick and failing rapidly.' I cried all night.

"I could see this baby dying on the plane. I knew I couldn't handle that, so I wrote a letter saying I didn't think I could take the child because she was sick. It was hard, but I did it. And she did die a month later. I almost chucked the whole thing. I didn't think I could go through that again."

But her friend had seen another child at the orphanage and suggested to the administrators that they offer her to Jeanne.

Jeanne started corresponding with them about this particular baby in December, and in April she left for Guatemala to pick her up.

"I left April twenty-second and spent about a month there. In some ways it was like a short course in pregnancy. I threw up all the way on the plane and had diarrhea and was so sick by the time I got to the orphanage that I had to go right to bed. I rested in bed for a couple of hours, and they brought her in and said, 'Here's your new baby,' and she cried right away. She was nine months old, and all the people who had taken care of her were Spanish or Indian. All she had ever seen were people with dark hair and dark skin, and here I was—blond hair, fair skin— I must have looked kind of different."

Jeanne says the bonding to her daughter was immediate. "She was mine from the moment they handed her to me. She couldn't have been more mine if she had been handed to me on a delivery table."

Her daughter adjusted more slowly to her, but within a couple of days would smile at the sight of Jeanne.

After recuperating and getting acquainted with her daughter at the orphanage, Jeanne proceeded with the legal adoption. The people at the orphanage escorted her through the local procedure of filing. Then Jeanne and her daughter went to file at the national capital. Fortunately, Jeanne does speak Spanish, and the orphanage arranged a contact with a lawyer and a hotel for her, so she did not feel completely at sea. She spent a week meeting with the lawyer and having papers signed. Then it was on to the American embassy for a passport and home with her new daughter. Having invested a painful year and three thousand dollars, Jeanne became a mother.

ADOPTING A DISTURBED CHILD

Anita Lewis brings a unique perspective to issues surrounding single-parent adoption. She adopted Danny, age eleven, a normal healthy infant, and Jeffrey, age eight, an emotionally disturbed six-year-old.

Anita, stimulated by an article she read in the newspaper about an adoption agency that was placing children in single-parent homes, started thinking about adoption when she was twenty-eight. "It didn't take much after I realized it was a legal option for me to decide to go ahead and do it."

Anita chose to adopt rather than bear a child because of personal and professional considerations. On the personal side there was the question of who would be the father. As Anita put it, "If I was in love with someone with whom I wanted to raise a child, I would have married him. But that just wasn't the case. So if I was going to bear a child, it had to be with someone who would do it as a favor but not be part of child rearing. If the guy wasn't going to be a husband, he wasn't going to be a real and active father either. If I didn't love him enough to marry him, I didn't want him to be part of the child rearing."

She discussed this possibility with several men she was friends with at the time but found them unreceptive. "Men didn't like the idea of my having their child without being married. Most men who are pretty responsible are not going to think it's a great idea to father a child and then not have anything to do with it."

But even if she had found a man who was willing to be a biological father, her concern about the effect a single pregnancy would have on her career would have precluded that option. "My career's important, and that was the other big consideration. At that time I was a department head. It was a job where I was very visible. I had a great deal of interaction with the public and teaching and administrative responsibilities. I don't know if I could have pulled off a pregnancy as a single woman. I think it would have shocked too many people and ultimately hurt my possibilities for promotion. But it didn't matter, because adoption was never a second choice for me. I've always felt adoption was as acceptable as giving birth to a child. It isn't second best at all."

Anita contacted the agency cited in the newspaper article, and it agreed to conduct a home study to evaluate her as a prospective adoptive mother—a process that proved to be long, painful, and ultimately disappointing.

"The social worker assigned to me was a divorced mother, and she was raising two small children alone and not enjoying one minute of it. She spaced my interviews three or four months apart, so it took a whole year to get through the home study. And at every interview she would try to talk me out of it. She used to say, 'You know, you've got the world by the tail. You're young, you've got a nice career and a nice social life. Why would you want to do this?' Then at the end of the year the agency called me in for one last interview with a psychiatrist. He asked me about my relationship with my father—which had never been particularly close—and once he found that out, he went on and on about why my father and I weren't close and how I felt about that. He never let me get to the positive things about myself and my background. We never talked about my capabilities and interests. The whole interview centered around my father. Well, needless to say, soon afterward I got a phone call from the social worker saying that they weren't going to place a child with me. She said she thought I would be a wonderful mother and she had no concerns about that at all, but she knew I was a socially active person and I'd probably get married in a few years, so there was no need for me to adopt. I remember her saying, 'Now we're going to do you a favor, though you can't see it right now, and we're not going to place a child with you.' "

Some favor. More angry than discouraged, Anita contacted a lawyer who arranged independent adoptions. Within months Anita had Danny. (While independent adoption has become an increasingly viable alternative for would-be adoptive parents dissatisfied with public and private agencies, it should be pointed out that the prompt resolution of Anita's case was a function of its time; today there are fewer infants available, hence a longer wait.)

From the moment she saw Danny he was her son. There was never any question of attachment or bonding.

When Danny was three, Anita decided she wanted a second child—both for herself and for Danny. She thought they would both be healthier if Danny wasn't the only recipient of her love and if she wasn't the only one to whom Danny was attached. But she couldn't afford to raise a second child until she got a major job promotion. Danny was nine by this time.

Financially secure, she had another home study conducted and applied to the county adoption agency. Although she was approved on the home study, the county agency told her that infants were not placed with single people. She then applied with an agency that specialized in hard-to-place children. Seventeen days later she was given Jeffrey.

Jeffrey was six years old when he came to Anita. A veteran of fourteen foster homes, he was diagnosed as "unattached." Unattached children have never had a nurturing figure to become bonded to. They tend to be manipulative and destructive and to lack a social conscience. The social prognosis for them is very guarded.

"Jeffrey is like a Dr. Jeckyll and Mr. Hyde. His ability to take revenge is phenomenal, and there's nothing babyish about it. When he gets mad, he has really strange sick tantrums. Not just being angry and throwing things but saying really vile things and urinating all over my house—the walls, the curtains, the living room rug. That's been real hard to live with.

"That's the gross side of Jeffrey, but when he's OK, he'll get up in the morning and come to the kitchen to find me and say 'Hi' and make sure everything's OK with mom, and he goes back to his room and gets dressed and gets his bed made. If I tell him the grass needs to be cut, without a word to the contrary he'll go get the lawn mower, cut the whole yard, and if I give him fifty cents for doing it, he's real proud of that."

Jeffrey has improved immensely during the two years he has lived with Anita and Danny. His destructive periods are becoming less frequent, his general behavior more sociable. "Two years ago he was so disturbed that he had to have an aide hired by the school system just to get him through a day. That's how much support he needed. A separate room with a teacher just for Jeffrey. Now they have him in a regular classroom—so that's a huge amount of progress. And whereas anything academic used to throw him into a tantrum, now he tries very hard and brings his papers home for me to praise."

In the course of the two years Jeffrey has begun to experience attachment. Anita notes that if Jeffrey spends the night away from home he misses her "a little bit, not a whole lot." But he does care a great deal for Danny, so he is becoming emotionally more stable.

Not only has Jeffrey's attachment to Anita come slowly, her attachment to him has been difficult. "A parent attaches because a child is vulnerable. The parent protects and nurtures. If there is no vulnerability there, then that natural process is blocked. I really know what it means to have the frustration of a child who is never vulnerable. It doesn't matter what you're providing because he doesn't want it anyway. It's extremely frustrating. And when Jeffrey changes, I change too. I have a way of relating to Jeffrey when he's OK—there's love and commitment and everything else. But when he goes into a regression, my response is very disturbing because I don't feel that unconditional acceptance of him any more. I feel very, very conditional, and I feel a lot of resentment. But I also feel very committed. The commitment doesn't change. So it's a real uncomfortable thing. If you're going to feel negative toward somebody, you're better off if you can get rid of the commitment and let the negative feelings be complete. But I can't do that. It's real tangled."

The frustration and commitment Anita feels were tested when Jeffrey went into a regression. For three weeks he was hurtful toward Anita and Danny and destructive at home and at school. He broke lamps, hid keys, and tore furniture. By the time the siege ended, Anita was on the verge of giving him up. "A friend of mine offered to take Jeffrey for a week so I could think it through before I gave him up. I was that close. So she took him, and instead of having a wonderful peaceful week I had nightmares every night. I didn't miss him. I was glad he was gone. I was glad to have the break. But I had nightmares that I was killing him—over and over in different ways. You see, if I gave up on him, I would destroy him. I'm responsible. Whatever chance this kid has for any kind of life, it's all tied up in me. He's taken a risk with me, and if I give up on him, he'll never take that risk again. He won't have anything. That's why I dreamt that I was killing him, because his life wouldn't be worth anything. But I'm not just afraid of what he'll lose. Danny and

I will lose an awful lot, too. I do love him. It took a while because he's a hard kid to love. But the commitment's made. He's mine for better or worse, and I won't do anything to change that.''

So Jeffrey is her son "for better or worse." She doesn't know what the future holds in store, but she does know that in the last two years Jeffrey has become more of a person—he is more capable of expressing affection, less likely to be antisocial. Although adopting Jeffrey has certainly made Anita's life more difficult, he has also given it more fullness, and his presence has made Danny more responsible and more sensitive. But most important, adopting Jeffrey has given Jeffrey a chance at a real life—a chance to love and to be loved.

Does Anita recommend adoption? "I don't know about a child like Jeffrey. I think it's important to emphasize that he is pretty much at one end of the spectrum. There are children who are certainly nowhere nearly as disturbed as he was. But the truth is, I don't think many people could handle someone like him. I don't say that patting myself on the back. It's just a lot of stress, and you have to know how to find relief. But with a child like Danny I would heartily recommend it. You have to want it and you have to be a fairly independent person. I think it's a very viable option. I can't say how Jeffrey's going to turn out. I do know that he's going to turn out a whole lot better because of me. And Danny's going to be a very, very healthy adult—and he's going to make somebody a wonderful husband.''

FROM FOSTER MOTHER
TO ADOPTIVE MOTHER

Laurie Black became an adoptive mother through foster care. When she was in her mid-thirties, she experienced what she describes as a "nesting instinct," and she started thinking about adoption. She had never seriously considered getting pregnant as a single woman. As she explained it, ''I just couldn't justify bringing another child into the world as a single parent when there were so many kids who needed homes.''

After hearing about foster care from a social worker, she explored that as a means to adoption. Since foster children are often adoptable but are placed in homes on a temporary basis, Laurie saw this as a way to "double-check" on her desire to have children. She could take a child in, and if she liked being a mother, she would adopt the child. If she did not like being a mother, she would not have to make a commitment to it. She also saw it as a way to work part time and be home with a child. The state pays foster parents for the child's needs, and this would provide a supplement to her income.

Shortly after having a home study Laurie was assigned two children who were supposed to be long-term but who left in three weeks. "That's the way it goes; the short-term kids stay forever and the long-term kids leave in a hurry." Laurie wasn't hurt emotionally by having the children leave quickly, though she was hurt financially. "They were my first kids, and like most brand-new parents I did a lot of things with them and bought lots of clothes for them, and then suddenly they were gone. Most foster parents get stung that way—on the first child they go overboard. Plus you haven't accumulated a reservoir of clothes. After five years of foster parenting I have a veritable secondhand store in the basement."

Shortly after the first two children left Laurie was given three more children. They lived as a family for four months, but the situation was more difficult than Laurie had expected. "I couldn't cope with three. I had too many, too quickly, without any parenting skills. Chronologically they were ten, nine, and seven, but emotionally they were far younger. And I just didn't know how to cope with the bickering and squabbling. I got caught underneath, and I had the oldest one—the hardest one—removed."

Laurie had no qualms about choosing which of the children had to go. The oldest girl was extraordinarily difficult. She hid things, she stole, she sneaked out of the house at night. As Laurie describes her feelings at the time, "I just couldn't handle her. I did feel guilty when she left. I saw the light go out of her eyes. I knew it was me who couldn't cope, but it couldn't be helped."

A couple of months later Laurie decided to adopt the seven-year-old. Recalling the instant she made a commitment to her soon-to-be adopted daughter, she said, "It was during a flaming argument. We were screaming at each other, and I looked at her and thought, Yes, I want you, you're mine."

The nine-year-old was subsequently returned to her parents, but Laurie still had a series of five- to ten-year-olds in and out of her home. One of these she also adopted. "She is a quiet child and she quietly fit in. Without my really being aware of it, she became part of our permanent family, and since she was freed from her biological parents, I adopted her.

"Some kids just appeal. It's a very individual thing. Everybody has a different idea of what appeals. I don't like every adult I meet, and I think it's the same with kids. I started off thinking children are children and you should love every child. But that's not the way it is. If you talk to any teacher, he or she will tell you the same thing. With fostering an older child you have to be prepared to accept the possibility that it will be a bad match. It's not your fault; it's not the child's fault. It's just something that went wrong. But fostering does have an advantage: you can try children out and pick the one you want."

After she adopted her second daughter, Laurie told the agency she would be interested in fostering a baby. She knew she could not adopt an infant, but she wanted the experience of caring for one.

"Before I knew it, I had a three-day-old baby in my arms. I was petrified, absolutely petrified. She was this tiny little ball of nothing. She stayed with us for two weeks and went to be adopted. I was just overwhelmed. I didn't realize you could get so attached to such a ball of nothing. That was a gut wrencher. It was terrible. The following day I got a six-day-old who stayed for six weeks. When he left, that was a heart wrencher, too, but it wasn't as bad because I was expecting it. Knowing what was going to happen to me, I made efforts to go out and be active the moment I'd given that child up. But it still hurt. There was a gap of about a month, and then I got a five-week-old, Elisa. She is now almost two and a half, and I'm going to be adopting her."

Elisa hasn't been with Laurie continuously for the two and

a half years. When she was six months old, she went back to her biological mother, but within a month she was returned to Laurie. During the time Elisa was gone Laurie took a full-time job; when Elisa returned, Laurie was not home to care for a baby. "I told the agency that I would take her back if they would pay day care. They paid day care for six months, and then they said they couldn't do it any longer. So I had to make a choice. Was I willing to pay day care so she could stay with us until they placed her in a two-parent adoptive home—I knew they would never place her with me—or would I give her up and take the chance that she would go to a series of other foster homes before she was adopted and get messed up in the process? You see, I had visions of Elisa being moved from home to home, not because she was a problem but because she got the wrong families. And at that point I said, 'Yeah, I'll swing the finances somehow—even if I go into debt. You deserve it, even if you won't be ours forever.' "

So Laurie accepted the financial burden of Elisa's day care thinking that she could not adopt her. But a year later, when Elisa reached two, Laurie realized that it was becoming less and less likely for the state to place her with another family. She filed for adoption, and it looks as if it will go through.

In addition to the three children she has adopted, Laurie has had twenty-one foster children. Although Laurie describes foster parenting as "enormously enriching," she has stopped doing it. "The longer I've been in it, the more detached I've become, to the point that I don't feel I'm giving the children the emotional energy I should because I don't want to be hurt when they leave. I've had kids coming in and out so often that I've gotten burned out. The longer I've been doing it, the longer it's taken each child to get dug in. I hold off so I don't get hurt, and it's not fair to them. I'm also worried that it's not fair to the ones I've adopted. I was putting so much energy into having new children coming in, and shifting bedrooms and changing routines, that I was afraid the three I was keeping might be getting short shrift." When Elisa is five and the other children are in high school, Laurie says she will adopt a fourth to be a companion for Elisa.

But right now, she's willing to settle for a stable family—at least for a while.

TO ADOPT OR NOT?

We chose the stories of Jeanne, Anita, and Laurie not only because they illustrate the various ways of adopting but because they highlight a range of reasons women have for choosing adoption and of experiences they have with the children.

Jeanne's and Anita's concern about the social acceptability of a single woman adopting compared to a single woman getting pregnant is shared by many of the adoptive mothers. Over half note that they considered pregnancy, but fearing that parents or employers would not understand, they chose to adopt. The extent to which the question of acceptability can cause conflict is demonstrated by Debra Swanson's story. As the single adoptive mother of one Korean child, Debra was in the process of adopting a second when she found herself pregnant. Her first thought was to have an abortion.

"My daughter and I had lived with this man for two years. And basically we split because I wanted more children. He loved my daughter, but he didn't want more kids, more commitment. I did. A month after he moved out I found I was pregnant. I did not set out to be pregnant. I was in the process of adopting child number two. I immediately thought of having an abortion. It's very different to adopt a kid and to bear a kid. There is a big difference in the way people respond to the idea of your being an adoptive parent and an out-of-wedlock parent. I was going to make the decision myself, but I talked to people about it anyway. When I had talked to people about adopting, it was 'Brave old, courageous Debra. Let's do all we can to help her.' When I talked about *having* a child, it was a whole other thing. It was too far out. My close friends said they'd stick by, whatever my decision, but people I knew in that second layer of friendship were appalled. People, especially men, said it would ruin my career. But then I thought it would be ridiculous to have an abortion and adopt a second kid. That made absolutely no sense.

I wanted another kid, and here was a kid inside me. When I look at her now, I can't believe I even thought of it.''

But Debra didn't want to give up the child she was about to adopt either. She adopted a one-year-old Korean girl, and four months later gave birth to a daughter. "It was pretty hectic for awhile. What am I saying? It's still hectic. And I love it. The girls get along like sisters do. You know—they play, they fight. No one cares who was adopted and who wasn't. They're kids.''

For some women the issue is not merely that *others* would think them immoral; *they* would think themselves immoral. As one adoptive mother responded when asked if she had considered pregnancy instead of adoption; "Of course not. I'm not married.''

Morality can creep into the decision in another way: the question of the father. Anita noted that one of the reasons pregnancy was not an acceptable alternative for her was that she was not involved with anyone with whom she wanted to share a child and did not know any men who would be willing to father a child and not participate in raising it. Another woman phrased this concern as an ethical issue. "There was no one I wanted in my life as an active father to my child. But I strongly believe in things like fathers' rights, and I didn't see how I could ask a man to father a child and then insist that I raise it alone.'' As we have seen, artificial insemination eliminates potential ethical, legal, and emotional problems with the biological father, but for a number of women adoption is preferable.

Adoption is also desirable to women who regard pregnancy as impractical. One woman who began the process of adoption at forty saw her age as the determining factor. "Going through a first pregnancy at forty on my own was not a risk I wanted to take. If it was a difficult pregnancy, I couldn't really afford to miss work. If there had been another adult around or if I had been younger, I might have given pregnancy more thought. But since I didn't have an obsession about whether I experienced pregnancy or didn't experience pregnancy, and since I didn't think it would be any less my child if I didn't carry it, personally, for *me*, adoption made the most sense.''

An adoptive mother who is a lawyer also cited the impracticality of a leave from work. Her concern was not one of time lost during a difficult pregnancy but simply the time lost to postpartum recovery. "I have an established practice, and I could not take off six weeks to recover from birthing."

Laurie's reason for adopting—"I couldn't justify bringing another child into the world as a single parent when there were so many kids who needed homes"—is less frequently voiced. A woman who adopted a three-year-old boy with polio, however, did share Laurie's sentiment. "Everyone wants a baby, but children like Mike need to be loved too." But more often women agree with Jeanne's position. "I wasn't trying to save the world— I just wanted a kid." As Raya Moss put it, "I didn't assume that I was doing some poor kid a big favor. Quite the other way around—it was going to be an enrichment for me. Which in some sense is selfish but I think in an acceptable way. I didn't have a fantasy of rescuing some child, and I would be concerned about someone who did."

As suggested by Jeanne, Anita, and Laurie, the length of time it takes to establish parent/child bonding is influenced by the age and emotional state of the child. Attachments with an infant seem to be automatic. Echoing Jeanne's experience with her daughter, Anita's experience with her first son, and Laurie's experience with Elisa, every woman who adopted a child under one year of age immediately felt like a mother. Indeed, so immediate was the bonding that two women who discovered that the infants they were adopting might not be healthy took the children anyway.

Beth Conner, having completed all of the arrangements to adopt a child from Colombia, received a letter the day before she was to pick him up informing her that he had varicose veins on one leg. They said it meant he had a cancer of either the leg or the pelvis. "But I left to get him anyway. By that time he was mine. I had taken him sight unseen. If he had been mine by birth, it would have been the same deal." Happily, it turned out to be a skin problem that disappeared in a few months.

Sue Smith went to India to claim her son and found he had

no muscle tone. "His arms and legs were limp. I didn't know if it was malnutrition or a problem with his central nervous system." Did she consider not taking him? "Of course not. He was mine. All I could think of was getting him to the United States and into Children's Hospital." Sue was lucky, too. The problem was diagnosed as malnutrition, and there was no permanent damage.

BONDING

With an older child attachments tend to take longer. Laurie had her two older daughters for several months before she decided to adopt them, and Anita had Jeffrey for two years before she decided firmly that he was hers forever.

Carolyn Flowers describes a variation on this theme. When Carolyn adopted Anna, the little girl was two and a half and had known only one home—an orphanage in Calcutta. Carolyn flew to India ecstatic about becoming a mother. "My fantasy about what was awaiting me was very much like the old Clairol commercial on television where you saw this field of daisies. I'm running and my hair is flying, and she's running toward me with her hair flying, and the two of us meet and go into this wonderful, twirling embrace. But the reality was she didn't like me. She wouldn't come near me. She was like stainless steel, which, of course, is what it would take to survive two and a half years in an orphanage in Calcutta."

It took Carolyn a month in India to complete the legal aspects of the adoption. She spent that time trying to woo Anna. "I knew it was just going to take time. And the day we left she finally let me hug her. To this day—she's now seven—she's cold and it's hard—because I'm a very affectionate person. We've had problems. We've been in therapy twice, but we're making it. We've just had to work at it a lot harder than I thought we would."

Marsha Cusimano also recalls the lengthy time it took to make an attachment—for her and her daughter. Sara was six years old and the product of four foster mothers by the time she came to live with Marsha. "She didn't see me as a parent, and I didn't feel like one. When she called me 'mother,' I'd turn around to see who she was talking to. It felt more like baby-sitting for one of my nieces than like parenting. And I can understand why 'mother' meant so little to her. If none of her previous mothers had worked out, why should she expect me to? She was bound to be mistrustful." For the first several months Sara cried so much that she made herself physically sick. "I tried holding her and talking with her, but it wasn't working, and I was getting emotionally exhausted by the long periods of crying." So we went into counseling for five months, and it was sometime at the end of that first year that I started really being her mother and she became my daughter."

Adopting can therefore be a long and complex process in terms of getting a child and adjusting to being a family. Depending on the adoption route and the child adopted, it can be frustrating, expensive, and extraordinarily demanding. But the adoptive mothers we met are *mothers*. Indeed, they are among the most content, happy, enthusiastic mothers we met. As a group, adoptive single mothers do not equivocate in declaring their satisfaction with their course of action.

Single adoptive mothers may be a very special breed. Given the difficulty of adopting, it may be that all but the most committed, independent, self-directed women are weeded out. This is not to say that adoptive mothers are more committed, independent, and self-directed than birth mothers. The point is that one doesn't need this particular set of characteristics to get pregnant. They are essential, however, to the successful pursuit of adoption.

And there is another difference between single women who become adoptive mothers and those who become birth mothers. As noted in Chapter Two, few of the birth mothers we interviewed had a second child. Most adoptive mothers had two or three children. Adopting a second time is easier because there are established contacts with an agency, there is no problem with a father, and there is no physical and emotional strain from pregnancy and childbirth.

CHAPTER

4

PREGNANCY AND CHILDBIRTH

For the woman who conceives, a sense of mothering emerges well before the child is born. A mother-to-be is ever aware of the child growing inside her. She feels her baby moving and kicking, and if she has an ultrasound examination, she can see it on the monitor. There is even pleasure in experiencing the cramps that mean the uterus is gearing up for the main event.

A solid maternal comfort is derived from the activities of pregnancy—things a woman does for herself as well as for her baby: Doctor's checkups, eating the right foods, consuming those huge pink vitamins, taking naps, attending prenatal classes, doing exercises, rounding up infant furniture and clothing. All in all, it can be a lot of fun.

But how did it feel—physically and emotionally—for single women to be pregnant and give birth?

PHYSICAL WELL-BEING

The women we met described an enormous sense of well-being while pregnant. "I never really liked my body until I was pregnant,'' said one who had always been a bit plump, ''and I certainly never liked people paying attention to my body or touching it. But while I was pregnant I liked my body, my looks. I knew that when I'd walk through a restaurant or office that people were looking at me, and I was proud—even euphoric. I got a kick out of people—some of them perfect strangers—patting my tummy approvingly.''

This same sort of pride was described by a Los Angeles woman who works as a production assistant for one of the film studios. ''Every time I went on a set, people would turn and notice me. For the first time I didn't feel plain among all those beautiful people. In fact, I felt like the most beautiful woman there.''

''Everyone likes a baby, they say, but I think everyone also likes a pregnant woman,'' said a librarian who felt special throughout her pregnancy. ''People, especially other women, admired my ever-expanding body, and over and over again I found myself thinking that they *should* be envious of me.''

Of course, not everyone was delighted with the changes in body shape and size. Some women felt fat, dumpy, dowdy. Size-six Gail Jordan didn't feel proud when she was pregnant; she felt just plain fat. She says, ''You get such a weird body image about the fourth month. You feel ugly. In this 'body beautiful' culture, you think guys won't know you're pregnant and all they'll notice is that you're fat.''

But whatever her perceptions, Gail had no trouble finding dates. ''Some guys really like going out with pregnant women,'' she found to her amazement. Other women discovered the same thing; a couple of women who had no interest in or contact with the biological fathers began quite romantic affairs during their pregnancies. And even with those bothersome pounds, Gail says, ''I was wired to the wall. I was so high. I felt great. I never had so much energy in my whole life. I just felt good all the time.''

Only one of the mothers we talked to reported particular physical problems during pregnancy, some indication perhaps that women in their thirties and early forties can enjoy healthy pregnancies as much as those in their twenties. The one who did have problems was hospitalized five times for toxemia and as you might guess, she describes her pregnancy as "horrendous."

But others were able to work if they wanted to, right up until delivery. They continued to engage in sports and long-distance travel (including flying) and whatever else had been part of their usual routine. Indeed, some were quite grateful for their ongoing physical health at a point when they were emotionally vulnerable, for reasons we'll discuss later. "Emotionally, I was a wreck. Every day was a struggle," said one woman, "but thank God, my pregnancy was physically perfect. I never had one sick moment. And I think that was the key to retaining my sanity."

AVOIDING STRESS

Some women—clearly the most directed, self-reliant women—intentionally avoided stress because of its potential physiological ill effects. Beth Ryan, a lawyer in Boston, decided to cut her ties to her baby's father during her pregnancy because his anger was causing too much pain. "I knew I could have gone one of two ways. I could have gone downhill, getting all tense and upset. But that would have meant that my body would have been in a stressful position, which would not be a very good place for a child to grow. Or I could have gone the way that I did, which was to eliminate the source of the stress—him."

Micki Herlanger, a thirty-five-year-old bank manager who floated happily and serenely through the nine months, managed to do so in part because she took great pains to protect herself from anxiety once she was "conspicuous." She dropped outside activities and avoided going places where she was not already known or where she thought she might face rejection. "I didn't run around as much as I had before I was pregnant. Not that I didn't feel up to it. I felt fine. I was more comfortable either being with old friends or being at home alone. I didn't want to have to explain myself to anyone or to put myself in awkward positions. I just wanted to be calm and peaceful and enjoy the pregnancy."

This intentional self-protection from stress may be significant in light of some recent medical research suggesting that attitudes about pregnancy and childbirth affect the health of a pregnant woman as well as the health and well-being of the fetus. Women with negative attitudes, this research claims, are statistically more likely to have premature or underweight babies or babies with abnormalities. One might add that some people believe that in some primitive way a fetus experiences—tastes, hears, feels—and more importantly, that persistent patterns of the parent during pregnancy can affect the personality and character of the child for years after. Dr. Thomas Verny, for example, does not claim that the fetus is affected by each passing feeling but that it is affected when the mother experiences, over a long period of time, either "life-enhancing emotions" like joy and elation or, on the other hand, chronic anxiety and wrenching ambivalence.[1] While the women we talked to do not make explicit reference to these lines of research, they intuitively understand the wisdom of protecting themselves from stress or pain for the sake of the child.

THE SENSE OF WE-NESS

Some of the women we interviewed not only felt that their own experiences and emotions were being communicated to the fetus but also that they were in some sense communicating with the fetus. They breathe deeply and slowly, perhaps singing or talking out loud to the as-yet-unborn child, delicately massaging the stomach.

For women who had amniocentesis, the sense of we-ness was delayed until it was determined that the fetus was healthy. In the period of waiting, women distanced themselves from the fetus. But after the amniocentesis report (verifying, in addition to health, the baby's sex) the sense of communication was even stronger. Carol Mead, who talked to us during her seventh month of pregnancy (after the amniocentesis report), was very much struck by this sense of "we-ness." "The feelings are just amazing. I'll just sit here—that is, we sit here. . . . It's a feeling about me

[1] Dr. Thomas Verny, *The Secret Life of the Unborn Child* (New York: Summit Books, 1981).

not being by myself. All the time I wonder, Does she know? Is she having fun? Does she hear me talking? Does a pat on the belly get through? I don't think there's very much of my day that I'm not aware of her being there.''

Many women want calmness and solitude for this ''communion'' with the child; they appreciate certain periods of ''aloneness.'' Some of the women we met thought they had an advantage over married women because they had plenty of such times, for contemplating and preparing, for tuning in to self and child. As one woman said, ''I felt so alone. But it wasn't that I regretted my decision. Oh, no. I felt closer to the baby. It really made me feel close while I was pregnant. I'd just sit and rub my stomach and talk to her and tell her how much I loved her. I'd say, 'We're going to do this and we're going to do that.' ''

Unfortunately, for some of the women, communion with the unborn child has an element of pathos. Kate Marley, for example, recalls a Father's Day during her pregnancy. ''I had gone to church, and the whole sermon was about fathers, fatherhood, fathers' participation. I just had to leave. I sat in that rocking chair, rubbing my stomach and telling the baby inside, 'We don't have anyone' and 'I've got to be both father and mother to you.' I was very lonely and I cried a whole lot.''

EMOTIONAL WELL-BEING

If nearly all of these women enjoyed physical health during pregnancy, many of them still experienced a certain amount of ''neediness.'' For some this was expressed as a need for pampering, for others as loneliness, and for still others as a need for support or a need to resolve the relationship with the father.

THE NEED FOR PAMPERING

Most women said they wanted to be pampered a bit more; they wanted more attention. As Lucy Kramer told us in her eighth month of pregnancy, ''One thing I really miss is having someone around to make a fuss over me. And I do think that makes a difference in pregnancy. You know they talk about how pregnant women are angelic. Well, I think that comes about when someone says, 'Oh, you look so beautiful,' and 'Let me do this for you.' But nobody does that for me. My friends do say I look wonderful, but it's not the same. When I can't breathe, when I get indigestion, when my ankles swell up, when I walk like a cow, when I'm horny as hell and there's nobody here to make love to, then I think it would be nice if a man were here. I want someone to give me massages, to make love to me, to appreciate my body. Here I have to surrender my body—it's gone—and there's nobody to pamper me.''

Likewise, another woman had always thought of herself as ''one of those strong women that you read about in history that can handle it and never go under.'' She regarded the biological father as having done little more than provide ''stud service'' and refused any involvement with him ''because it might put stress on me and that might damage the baby.'' But she admitted that she missed male companionship—indeed, resented its absence. ''The nurturing I was getting from women friends was not enough; I suffered from not having the male support that I had always visualized would be around if I were pregnant. So I felt I missed half the boat—the touching and the cuddling and all that. . . . I felt gypped.''

Most pregnant women seem to expect cuddling and a certain amount of pampering. Besides wanting their backs massaged, they want their egos soothed. Part of it may be that they inevitably feel vulnerable, emotionally and physically; and part of it may be that they know that this may be their last chance to be cared for. Soon they will have to do all the caring, all the giving. One woman who, in fact, found it difficult to accept her own neediness quite plausibly suggests, ''All of this nurturing that goes on in your body—your body is just building a baby and building and building, and that is all that is going on—but meanwhile I felt really uncared for myself. I felt that I was doing this thing for this other person and that I was getting nothing.''

But not everyone felt gypped. For some the baby showers, the gifts, and the luncheons satisfied that need. For Sharon

Greene, who was teaching high school during her pregnancy, it was the attentiveness and compliments of her students. "I was really involved with the kids, and the kids were really involved with me. They would rub my back, and they would bring me things, and they would tell me how pretty I was. Oh, it was lovely. It was really great. It did me a whole lot of good to have them tell me, 'Oh, you're just beautiful.' I felt really, really good. I had a fine time."

LONELINESS

We've already made some reference to some "down" moments. Kate Marley was not the only one who was lonely and cried. Nearly all of the women remembered their pregnancies as marked by loneliness ranging from intermittent bouts of "the blues" to a profound sense of isolation, although there were some notable exceptions. In fact, it never "occurred" to a few women to be lonely.

Dorothy Wold, one of those who chose to become pregnant through artificial insemination, reasoned, "I think if you've just come out of living with somebody and are used to having somebody there, it would be tremendously hard. There would be the added stress that being alone would bring home to you—on top of being pregnant. But if you're used to living as a single person and are happy with that, you don't mind. And I didn't see being pregnant—with the exception of a couple of down times—as that different."

But Dorothy is not typical. Most women—even those used to being independent—were bothered by loneliness. Indeed, perhaps precisely because so many of these women were so independent and so accustomed to living on their own and taking care of themselves, they were often quite bewildered by this penetrating loneliness. Many of them were upset by their own reaction, angry at their tears, especially when it indicated some yearnings for the father of the child. We heard over and over again: "I didn't understand myself." "It was so unlike me." "My God, what is happening to me that I'm so lonely?"

For some the loneliness was no more than the frustration of not being able to share the sheer happiness of the various landmarks of pregnancy and childbirth. Lois Silba, interviewed shortly before her baby was born, said she was "really happy for more weeks in a row than ever before" (except perhaps during the time when first falling in love with the man who turned out to be the father of her child).

"But the only negative feeling I have—and that negative feeling doesn't usually last long—is that I don't have an intimate relationship so I could share all this happiness. It's Gee, this is so wonderful—I feel great, but I'm alone. That hurts. And my best friend's lover [a woman] is a little threatened, so I don't feel welcome to just drop in when I need to be close to somebody. I don't want to shove my own happiness into somebody else's face if it's hard for them to deal with."

Another woman enjoyed a tremendous amount of help, support, and companionship from the church group with which she was involved. Ironically, friends from the church extended more help than she says she wanted or needed. That sort of help solved one kind of loneliness—the kind that can be erased simply by having someone, anyone, there. But that sociability did not cure another type of loneliness, the kind that, as Renee says, can be soothed only by being with someone you love. "There was a certain feeling of sadness because he [the father] wasn't here, wasn't looking forward to having the child, would never know what a beautiful child he would have."

Some women tried to find a substitute to be emotionally involved with during their pregnancies. Cheryl Valin, who was living with a friend, was terribly disappointed that her friend wasn't more interested. "My roommate would come home after working twelve hours at her office, and I'd say, 'I saw a picture of the fetus today on an ultrasound machine.' But she wouldn't be excited. She was just too tired. But I needed to talk to somebody."

Instead, Cheryl took unusual interest in appointments with her obstetrician and depended on that relationship, "probably because it was a man being involved with the pregnancy. He was real excited and real supportive and real encouraging. I wondered if I was getting too dependent on him.''

One hears over and over again references to the need for intimacy, closeness. Cary Adams is a case in point. Having been told at twenty-eight that she might be sterile, Cary was ecstatic to find herself pregnant. But even though she was immensely happy that she would be able, after all, to have a baby, she wanted to share the child growing inside her. She yearned for someone to touch her stomach and say, ''Wow, that's terrific. Let's read about how the baby is growing.'' Cary had plenty of casual friends, but no one to whom she felt really connected. Having recently moved from Chicago to New York, she had no one close who she felt cared about her.

Cary explained how depressed she got. ''At five months I was just consumed with self-sorrow. I thought, Oh, I'm alone, my heart is breaking, I can't stand it. My self-esteem was on edge. I had problems with the father; my New York friends said they were not interested; my family said I was shaming them. That stuff started taking its toll. I sat here and thought, Now, I can go on crying all night, which will make me sick, or I can take hold of the reins and do something.''

Fortunately, Cary had a solution, albeit an expensive one. ''I thought to myself, What do I want the most? I wanted to be surrounded by loving, caring individuals, but they were in Chicago. Well, I thought, get on an airplane, girl; use your plastic and do it. And I did. I picked up the phone that minute and made reservations. The phone call put me back together again. It really helped. I could have just gone on crying and being miserable. But rather than endlessly mope around in self-sorrow, I did something. And it worked.''

Ironically, fighting the neediness by trying to conform to some impossible self-image of independence may make resolution of the problem even more difficult. Eleanor Gates's situation is instructive. For fifteen years she had thought of herself as countercultural, apart and different. ''I never realized that I had been influenced,'' she says. ''Even though I was living a life that was in a sense outside the culture, when I was actually doing something that was countercultural—having a child alone—I found I wanted certain traditional things, like a man to rub my back.

"I had unrealistic expectations of myself, and it was really hard to let go of those expectations and interpretations of my life and my way of being. There was a tremendous conflict between how I wanted to be in this situation and how I actually was. I wanted to be able to go ahead and be some fantasy person who could just handle it, who was completely strong. But instead I felt abandoned, and I felt lonely, and I felt unbelievably needy, more needy than I ever felt in my life."

Another woman, with an image of herself as a "courageous, really strong, new-age feminist" can laugh now, although she could not then. "I was fantasizing about our being this little unit—him and me against the world. I think I was influenced by movies. I remember a Brigitte Bardot movie about a woman and her lover who were revolutionaries. At the end he was gunned down, but she was pregnant with his child, so the revolution went on. . . . I got into therapy in the fourth month of my pregnancy, I was so miserable."

GETTING SUPPORT

One woman confessed that she was "jealous of women who are single and who are doing it handily, doing it cheerfully, don't seem to be needing much." But in fact, she envied a phantom. Pregnant women have needs, and it is unlikely that they can "do it handily" without some support.

Some women, especially ones who had given single parenthood somewhat less analytic consideration before their decision, also experienced a rather stinging sense of isolation in not being able to talk to other single mothers about their common situation. Said one West Coast woman who had two close—but married—friends who were pregnant at the same time she was, "I wouldn't have felt so lonesome if I had known other single pregnant women. I knew I wasn't the only single pregnant woman in this town who was not a teenager, but where were they? How do you go about meeting them? I needed to talk to someone with the same interests and problems. I just wanted to know someone who was doing the same thing I was.''

Indeed, this woman, when her daughter was one year old, formed a support group for single pregnant women, a group still going strong, which provided precisely the context and support she would have liked for herself. Similar self-help groups have been organized in other cities, and many women take great satisfaction in providing comfort and advice to others—or in receiving it.

It should be noted, on the other hand, that other women we interviewed regard it as important to maintain contact with pregnant women, single or married, to compare notes, commiserate, reassure. All pregnant women invariably become part of a huge sorority, with new mothers treated as ex-officio members. Many of the problems are the same: married women may suffer the same loneliness, self-doubt and fear as well as the same aches, heartburn, swollen ankles, tiredness, muscle cramps. And their husbands may snore away the night, unsympathetic and unimpressed. Furthermore, it may be that many husbands do not regularly accompany their wives to routine doctors' checkups, do not look forward to buying sleepers and booties, do not "ooh" and "ah" over baby books.

One woman observed, "My sister was pregnant the same time I was, and I would talk to her on the phone and say, 'God, Terry, I feel so lonely.' And she would say, 'Me, too. Bill comes home from work and he wants dinner and then he goes to bed. Sometimes in the middle of the night I want to say, "Bill, wake up, honey. Wake up, sweetheart"—and he doesn't even turn over. And I get so lonely.' So there's a married woman with a husband who's excited about his baby, and she's lonely in the middle of the night, too. So I don't know how different it is for single women. It's different not having a mate, but I don't know how different.''

Perhaps even much of the emotional upheaval, irritability, and sudden, radical shifts in mood for which pregnancy is notorious have some physiological basis. As Cary Adams put it,

"When you're pregnant, you're up a lot, either peeing or walking around because the kid's kicking and you can't sleep. Your entire time clock is different. Your hormones are in gear; your chemistry is like firecrackers. You're up, you're down, you're emotional. It's like a nine-month premenstrual thing."

Thirty-seven-year-old Lucy Kramer, eager to have a child after years of ambivalence (and four abortions), can list a number of the fears that plagued her in the early months of her pregnancy. "I had the most weird, outrageous fears: I smoke too many cigarettes; I'm too old; I'm going to die of a stroke; what did I do this for; the baby's not going to be healthy; the baby will be a freak." Her married sister, however, reassured her that the fears were normal, that she had experienced similar fears. And certainly no one now could think that her blond-haired, blue-eyed daughter, who at three is doing commercial modeling, isn't healthy and normal.

However, the single women we talked to seemed unusually wracked by doubts at different times during the pregnancy, although the frequency, duration, and intensity varied. Again, a very few—the most confident and independent—maintained their composure and stable disposition. But the rest cried not a little as they questioned their decision, their ability or desire to cope with that decision, or both.

Judith Lawrence, a committed feminist who wanted a child in part to pass along some of what she had learned as a woman, is typical of those who suffered a rather mild bout of self-criticism and then recovered. She recalls sitting on her bed one day, crying for hours, and thinking, "My God, what have I done to my life? What have I done? Where was my head when I made this decision?" But she was able to think it through and reaffirm the rightness of her course.

Another woman explains that at early stages of pregnancy she suffered only fleeting doubts. Later she grew more uneasy. "At about seven or eight months there were times when I thought, God, this is scary—taking this on alone. Can I really do this?" She could, she decided. And she did, with the help of friends.

CONTACT WITH THE
BIOLOGICAL FATHER

As we know, some of the women embarking on the course of single parenthood had thought or hoped that the child's father would be around or might even be actively involved during pregnancy as well as child rearing. Some anticipated richer, deeper relationships (outside marriage) with the father. Many of them were bitterly disappointed to be essentially "deserted" or "rejected," and this made for rather severe emotional upheaval during the pregnancy.

Other women suffered more because of the on-and-off relationship with the biological father. Either way, the fact that the relationship was not stable or satisfying made for rocky pregnancies. One woman, disappointed by her lover's lack of support and enthusiasm (he was, after all, involved with another woman), moved out of town, but the resentment continued. "When I was pregnant I just stopped believing in the existence of nice, supportive, stable relationships with men. I saw other women having a real hard time in relationships when they were pregnant, too. I thought that the time is too devastating to deal with another person. I got awfully cynical about it all."

For some women pregnancy provided a catalyst—indirectly or directly—for ending the relationship with the baby's father. For instance, one woman intentionally distanced herself from her lover (whom she described as compulsive and neurotic) because "he'd be impossible to be with and he'd drive me crazy, when what I wanted was to enjoy my pregnancy. He's not the person I would choose to spend that time with and share what goes on with my body."

Another woman, who had deliberately set out to have a child despite her lover's lack of interest, believes that pregnancy-related hormonal and mood changes contributed to the deterioration and dissolution, during her pregnancy, of the nine-year relationship with the biological father. Other women believe that it was only while pregnant that they realized the problems in the relationship or the glaring faults of the man. Apparently, pregnancy gave them the courage (or at least the opportunity) to come to terms with sometimes radical differences in values, moral systems, and long-term expectations and aspirations. The women involved with married men finally saw these relationships as futile or unsatisfying. In some cases decisions about the father's involvement with the child—his financial support, legal responsibility, participation in child rearing, and so forth—simply forced the couple to square off, understand their ultimate incompatibility, and say farewell. For many of the women, then, pregnancy was the ultimate test of the relationship and the degree of commitment of both parties.

As painful as the process of breaking up was, in the long run it was probably less hurtful and demoralizing than the up-and-down, back-and-forth relationship with the father. These attempts at reconciliation rarely succeeded.

One woman succinctly describes the agony involved in trying to work out a relationship, an attempt she made simply because she had spent so many years with the child's father. "It was more effort for me to try to piece it together just so we would have a family—mommy, daddy, baby—than to be alone and cope. It was a tremendous drain to try to put it back together again, when all the king's horses and all the king's men couldn't do it. We were highly emotional, and I was torn apart. It was oh, no—oh, maybe—back and forth. I was miserable." And so it went until she asked the biological father to leave the birthing room, where he had appeared by surprise, and not to come back.

A CAUTIONARY TALE

Norma's story all too poignantly but instructively dramatizes the debilitating strain and trauma that accompanies an unresolved relationship and unstable situation, precisely at a point when one is vulnerable and needs to build emotional reserves and a secure haven—a nest, as it were. On the face of it Norma's case is not typical. Yet it illustrates a terrible scenario come to life—what can happen when one is ambivalent or when one relies on untested assumptions and fantasies. Norma, an independent twenty-nine-year-old, might have been somewhat unnerved by the emotional neediness associated with pregnancy, but the haggling with the father, a man she had known since she was twelve, was enough to undermine her confidence in herself and her decision-making ability to the extent that she succumbed to emotional blackmail.

As late as her twelfth week Norma and John—who was quite in love with another woman, who did not return the affection—were still debating whether she should have the child. Once Norma decided that she would not be dissuaded, she also decided she must quit her job (which she had held for only six months and which involved considerable traveling) and return to Denver to friends, family, and John. Having neither strength nor money for the move, she relied on John, who made it known that he resented the imposition. Furthermore, despite his involvement with the other woman Norma temporarily moved into his apartment.

"I was never a crier, but during the pregnancy I cried all the time. I'm a very independent person, and suddenly I was so needy and dependent. I wasn't myself—this had never happened before. I couldn't believe I was staying at John's—it was so unlike me. I would never normally do this, but I felt like I couldn't stand on my own feet. It was bizarre, weird. I think it was partly being pregnant—the hormones kicking into gear—and partly everything that goes along with pregnancy mentally, in terms of society and society's expectations.

"I was so upset and lonely and depressed, I could barely keep my wits about me. John was giving me such different signals. One minute he was very compassionate and warm, and the next minute he was kissing me off, not wanting to have anything to do with me, accusing me of ruining his life. It was hot, cold, hot, cold. It was horrible for me, but I was so needy I just let it continue. And my whole family is telling me to kiss the shithead good-bye. So I spent a lot of time crying.

"And then there is the issue of whether we should get married. I didn't love him and didn't want to be married to him. I don't want to be married. I wanted to have this child and keep living my life the way I'd been living. He didn't want to get married, but his family said we shouldn't bring a bastard into this world—society will ruin him. 'What is going to happen,' he said, 'when he is five years old and kids at school find out and say, "Na, na, na, na, na, you are a bastard"?'

"A couple of weeks before my due date he really leaned on me. I thought and thought and thought. I even saw a counselor. The bottom line was that I did get married the day before my due date because right at the end I decided I did not want to take responsibility for inflicting discomfort on my child about being illegitimate. Why not say 'I do' to avoid one chance out of a million of somebody saying 'bastard' to him?

"That was what pushed me over, but it was also John's persistence. If he had not persisted, I wouldn't have continued thinking about all this. The agreement was that we would get married and then get divorced a month later.

"The marriage thing was disastrous. It was the most depressing thing about both our lives. It's not as easy to get married and unmarried as you think. And he was still going away for weekends with his lover—and I was pissed because he was my Lamaze partner."

At this point Norma interrupted herself. "I forgot to tell you one of the most important things. In my seventh month I decided to give the baby up for adoption. Now, when I decided to have the baby I created a positive scenario: I'd be working and raising the baby by myself with John's support. He would help with money and with child care. But no longer could I visualize a positive scenario for when the baby came. Every option seemed like doom and gloom. Everything was screwed up. I couldn't think of anything positive. I really felt suicidal. I had never felt that kind of despair. That's when I thought adoption was the only way out, as hard as it would be. I thought I could never be happy having the baby, but I cried hysterically at the thought of giving the baby up. So I called all the adoption agencies and met with them and got all the details, and I made up my mind that this was the only way to go. Then I called John and said the only thing to do is give this child up for adoption.

"John went insane. He said that he would never give up his child for adoption, and that if I tried, he would adopt him.

"That's when I felt the most despair, because I thought, I can't even get relief by giving him up, because John will adopt him. There's no way he could have the baby without my being involved. And if I'm going to be involved, I want the baby. It was terrible. At that point I knew I had to keep the baby.

"Then I got afraid that the baby would think he was not wanted. I'm a little superstitious. I remember sitting here and thinking I had to tell the baby he was wanted, because I didn't want something to happen to him. I would sit and talk to the baby. I'd put my hand on my stomach and say, 'Now, this is very hard and I really really love you.' I believe that the fetus can sense these things. So the whole time I am feeling this terrible responsibility because I don't want the baby to feel unwanted."

Reflecting on her experience, Norma offers some excellent advice: "If I knew then what I know now, I would still have had the child, but I would not have encouraged the fantasy. I would not have suffered the emotional upheaval with that man. I would have finished it. I would have written it off the best that I could. It's a huge effort to break those fantasies, but I think you have to try."

SOLUTIONS

Cary provides equally serious advice in dealing with the loneliness, advice that she took with admirable results.

"Maybe you are feeling lonely, but try to reach out. Do reach for others. Take a trip, be with friends—anything—but don't sit in self-sorrow, although it is easy to feel sorry for yourself. There are lonely times and it's hard, but that is the game, that is what you chose to do. And sometimes it does [you] good to talk to married pregnant women to see how similar their feelings are. Get ready for those feelings and have some alternatives planned, whether . . . gardening or visiting friends. Push yourself out of the doldrums. Have a special person—some friend or relative—

to whom you can say, 'If I get scared at three o'clock in the morning, can I call you?' ''

The other effective solution seems to be the exercise of will-power. Martha Stevens, for example, simply did not let herself get depressed. ''I just never let myself think, If only things had been like this or that. Because everything was proceeding according to plan, and the most important thing was having a healthy baby. I never had any illusions about pregnancy, and I never thought my relation with the father was significant or long-term, so I never had expectations.''

Martha adds that her friends criticized her for being so cool; they assumed that she was not ''in touch'' with her feelings. She doesn't look at it that way at all. Her position was that her life was going just the way she wanted.

These women add that if it's hard to think positively, hard to exercise that willpower, then at least *act* as if you're thinking positively. The rest may follow. Said one, ''I'm the sort of person that believes that when you're going through something, no matter how you feel, you have to appear 'together.' And the more you appear together, the less likely you are to *not* be together. Because you will be together. At least I was.''

PRENATAL AND
BIRTHING CLASSES

Nearly all the women in our study enrolled in a Lamaze course, with some taking additional prenatal courses, such as those sponsored by various hospitals and Red Cross agencies. They found these classes instructive and the exercises helpful. Naturally, the difficulty and painfulness of labor varied from woman to woman, but in general their experiences bear out Fernand Lamaze's theory that a woman who knows exactly what is happening and why will be able to relax, and a woman who can relax suffers less discomfort. These prenatal and birthing classes helped make pregnancy and childbirth a more deeply satisfying and exciting experience.

Many women found these classes an additional and much

appreciated source of support. Pam Wood, whose Lamaze teacher agreed to be her labor and delivery coach at the hospital, found that by sheer coincidence all of the women in her prenatal class were over thirty, and all but a few were single. She became friendly with three of those women, and they remain close. In fact, it was in talking with these women that she made her decisions about what to do after the baby was born.

Most of the women we interviewed asked sisters, roommates, or close women friends—these were not necessarily women who had children but more often single women who were considering motherhood—to go to the classes with them and serve as their labor coaches. Two single mothers-to-be managed to attend class together and served as each other's coaches. This worked out very well for both partners. The coaches apparently were not only happy to help but were moved by the experience. They were excited about their participation in the birthing process and even joined in the exercises.

Cary initially did not have a Lamaze partner. "My mother was not very supportive, my sister was too far away, my lady friends had decided they couldn't be around me while, as they saw it, I 'ruined my life.' I thought and thought and finally I called a divine friend—a gay man. Ted said he'd be honored, and for the next three months he was right there. During my last month whenever he and his lover would go out, they would call and tell me where they were going, what the phone number was, when they would be home. And Ted gave me love and support and hugs whenever I needed. I only wished I had asked for that earlier. And he made me do my exercises. There were nights when he'd say, 'Now stretch, Cary,' and I'd say, 'Damn it, Ted, I'm not going to. I'm tired. Don't make me do this.' But he would answer, 'You're going to do it, dear. You're going to do it.' He was great."

Cary adds that the child's father appeared in the birthing room, but by then she did not want him there. "I had shared the pregnancy with Ted. Ted and I had the intimacy, not this man. I felt guilty, but I asked him to leave."

Ann Parker, despite her resentment that her lover was dating a much younger woman, asked him to attend the class as her partner. But when he started missing classes, she was furious and canceled the class—until a good friend offered to go with her. A couple of fathers who had maintained contact through the pregnancy were reluctant to go to the classes and were fearful of the entire birthing process, but later they regretted "missing out."

A few independent, strong-minded women attended Lamaze classes without partners. While they enjoyed the class somewhat less than the others, they still found the techniques useful. Most obstetric nurses are trained in Lamaze, so women without coaches may receive adequately helpful attention from nurses at the hospital. If, however, all the nurses are busy, they will not be able to provide continual care and attention.

One woman had arranged for her sister, a nurse with two children of her own, to be her coach. Since the sister could not arrange her schedule so that she could attend the classes, Marianne first went to class alone. But Marianne claims that the teacher gave her a hard time about her sister not being there. Besides, as the only unmarried woman, Marianne felt not only out of place in class but suddenly annoyed that the baby's father was not there. So after attending three of the eight sessions she stopped going to Lamaze. "We can do it," she told her sister. "I have confidence in you."

Unfortunately, Marianne was not the only one to feel odd about attending Lamaze alone. Although Lamaze teachers often go to great pains to restrict their references to "coaches" and "partners" or even "lovers," occasionally they slip and talk about "husbands" or "spouses." The Lamaze movie often shown at an early session presents, as one example, a single parent, but the other births depicted involve two-parent families. So Dorothy Wold says, "For me, the only negative thing about the course was the night they showed the childbirth movies, with that whole emphasis on the family and the husband holding the baby and the togetherness thing. Plus, they showed a fairly difficult delivery, a cesarean, a forceps delivery. So it was scary, and there was this sense of 'You can deal with anything with your husband there to hold your hand.' I went home crying, thinking that I wanted someone there with me, that it was going to be really hard, that I didn't want to do this by myself. . . . But the moment passed.'' Dorothy, who was forty at the time, had a cesarean delivery.

Another woman adds, "It really hit me to the core, reading 'Now that you and your husband are going to have a child . . .' and 'Now that you and your husband are taking Lamaze. . . .' At times that hurt. Even the organic natural books are the same— except that they say, 'Now that you and your old man are having a kid. . . .' "

Cheryl Valin had become fairly cynical about men—both about relationships of men and women and about men's concern for children. But she was still lonely, and on the way to the first night of Lamaze she felt particularly alone. "I was listening to the car radio and Helen Reddy was singing, 'You and Me Against the World' to her baby. I started to cry. I was driving down the street bawling. It surprised me that I felt so bad. When I got there, I hated it. I wanted to leave. They were showing diagrams and pictures of babies, and I didn't want to hear about it. And I couldn't believe all these men in the class—that they were really concerned, that there really were men who were involved, who wanted to have children. Two other women there were also alone, but I felt too bad to even look at anybody. But during the break I started talking to people and feeling better. After that it was much easier.''

THE BIRTH ITSELF

A few women allowed the father to be present during labor or delivery or both. Of course, some hospitals allow only one designated "coach" to accompany the mother. But many hospitals now have birthing rooms where, in a more informal, cozy, homelike atmosphere, both labor and delivery are accomplished in the presence of any number of friends and relatives.

Certain women, who wanted father and child to be close despite their own feelings for the father, pushed for the father to witness the delivery, to hold the child in the recovery room, and so forth, to promote bonding.

Eleanor Gates, for example, was disappointed—or more accurately, angered—by the indifference of her lover, but she did encourage him to be present at the birth. "I told him that I wanted him to be there, that it was the most important thing he could do. And I still think that's really critical to the success of a relationship between father and child." In a sense it worked: A few years later the father admitted that he wished he had married Eleanor and that they had been "a family." Apparently, he regarded his lack of interest as a major mistake. "Too late," Eleanor replied.

To Stacy Small, bonding with a grandmother was much more important than bonding with the father. Stacy attended Lamaze with a close, long-time friend as her coach, but she also went to great pains to involve her mother, not only in the pregnancy but in labor and delivery. Having seen her mother respond somewhat coolly to the adopted child of Stacy's sister, Stacy reasoned, apparently correctly, that her mother would feel closer to her grandchild if she were there from the first contraction on.

Bonding aside, it's nice to have someone there, to share both the pain of labor and the joy of delivery. The flip side of this is evident in the story of Marsha Balen, who, although she thoroughly enjoyed her perfect pregnancy, found birthing "the worst thing I ever went through." Marsha not only had not taken Lamaze (one of the few) but was alone during labor. She went into labor three weeks early, and the friend who had planned to be with her could not leave work. "Nobody was there. There wasn't even a nurse. They were all too busy. Loneliness is the one overwhelming feeling that I can remember, besides the pain . . . which was unbelievable. I felt very sad, very abandoned, very alone. I was changing from an old life to a new life right there and had nobody to talk to about it. I cried, not because of pain, but because I felt so alone."

After Marsha's little girl was born, however, that sadness disappeared. Except for an hour of postpartum depression, Marsha reports, "I've been on a cloud ever since."

Nearly all of the women we talked to had routine deliveries

and, more importantly, healthy babies. Two women delivered prematurely; as a result their babies stayed in the hospital for a few weeks.

One mother, however, had a sad experience, and she links the tragedy directly to her status as a single woman. In fact, Doris wanted to talk to us specifically to be able to share what happened. Doris had identical twins, delivered two months prematurely. One twin died.

Apparently, the twins came as a surprise to both Doris and her doctor. Of this Doris says, "They should have known I was having twins. Although I went to see one of the best doctors in the city, he didn't do all the tests he should have. I got treated like a second-class citizen because I wasn't married. I think back then—this was the sixties—they had a 'we'll teach her a lesson' idea.

"I think that had I been married, I would have been treated a little bit better, and probably the other one would have lived. I really think the other twin would have lived had he been checked closer. But I had no husband to back me up. I suppose that gave me somewhat less authority.

"I had gone to the nursery window, and there was a nurse giving one twin an injection. I had no idea what was happening. I went back to my bed, and then later that evening I went back to the window and one incubator was empty. I couldn't believe it. It was so terrible. They should have told me.

"Perhaps it would have happened anyway, but it would have happened differently."

Doris and her son, now fourteen years old, are doing fine. But she still thinks that what happened would not have happened to the typical couple where "the new father waltzes in bearing flowers and candy for his wife."

Pregnancy and childbearing are fraught with potential problems. The inherent possibility of stress and loneliness experienced by all pregnant women—married and single—is compounded for single mothers by the unresolved quality of their relationship with the biological father. And yet in spite of this, most of the women we talked to managed to enjoy their pregnancies and birthing.

CHAPTER

5

WHAT WILL PEOPLE SAY?

One woman who was thinking about getting pregnant told us the only thing stopping her was a fear that her parents would disown her. Our survey indicates that unless her parents are very unusual, she needn't have worried. Parents come around—perhaps hesitantly—but come around they do. Brothers, sisters, friends, and acquaintances vary. Some are accepting, some are rejecting. But it appears that even in the face of the least ideal of circumstances, grandparents can't resist a grandchild.

PARENTS

Breaking the news to parents about a pregnancy is often harder than breaking the news about an adoption.

Gail Jordan's story shows how sensitive a woman can be to her parents' evaluation of her when she is about to become a parent herself. Gail, a freelance journalist who's been on her own since college, has worked for major dailies, been editor of a magazine, and reported for a wire service. She's traveled to Alaska to write about the pipeline, to Australia to cover film-making, and to Kuwait to interview sheiks. Yet with all her confidence, poise, and sophistication, she clammed up when it came to telling her father that she was pregnant.

Gail intentionally got pregnant, but worry followed delight when she skipped her period. "A few weeks after I got pregnant I went into an awful slump, wondering how my dad would take it. He and my mom are divorced. I wasn't really worried about telling her—she's a very 'with it' lady—but he's reserved and conservative and I was so afraid he'd be hurt or angry or I don't know what. I kept having these imaginary conversations with him. I'd practice what I'd say and how he might respond, and I'd just get more and more depressed. I finally decided imaginary conversations weren't going to do it, and I had to get the real thing over with. So I called my dad, and I told him I had the blues real bad and asked him if I could come visit the next day.

"I was going to tell him as soon as I saw him, but when I got there, he was so flattered that I would call him when I had the blues that he flipped out. He started telling me how close we were and how proud he was of me and how much he loved me. He'd never told me those things before. All my life I wanted to hear that stuff, and here he was doling it out in big lumps. And, well, I didn't want to spoil it. He told me how of all the children I was the only one who never let him down. And I just couldn't tell him.

"Anyway, I went back home and realized he had to know about my being pregnant, so I wrote him. And I was real worried about how he'd respond. And he wrote back, 'Well, you waited so long, I never figured you'd have children, but if that's what makes you happy, I'm all for you.' It was wonderful."

Lucy is another independent, self-confident career woman. As a bank loan officer, she has no difficulty telling applicants that they can't have money, but when careless use of birth control resulted in the pregnancy she had always wanted, she couldn't bring herself to tell her parents. Not only couldn't she face telling them in person, she couldn't even face writing them. Instead she had her sister break the news for her.

As Lucy tells it, "My parents are Fundamentalist Christians, and I knew they'd just think this was so sinful. I thought about telling them all the time, but I couldn't bring myself to do it. I didn't know how they'd react. I was telling my sister how worried I was—I had told her about the baby as soon as the test came back positive. We're real close, and she was a hundred percent supportive; she offered to tell our folks for me. At first it sounded like a cop-out, but then I started thinking, I don't have to prove anything, and she might be able to tell them better than I would. So she told them. She made them understand that I wanted to have a baby, that I didn't really love the man who got me pregnant, and that we didn't want to get married.

"The next night they called—I guess they needed a day to let it sink in—and they said they thought I'd make a terrific mother, but why couldn't I be married? It was immoral, and it was a sin, and I should be married. The baby was not a problem; that I wasn't married was the problem.

"So they ended up being more angry with Jeff, the baby's father, than with me, even though I kept telling them I didn't want to marry him. But they got real excited about the baby—started calling all the time, asking how I was doing. And after I had her, they came out, and they adore her. They just adore her. They're still preaching to me about my morality. They can't help it. But they love her, and they still love me. In fact, I talk to them more and see them more now than I ever did before I had her, and I feel so much closer to them."

Marsha Baker's two-part approach was somewhat different. Instead of fearing telling her mother, she manipulated her mother into supporting her. First, even though she had intentionally gotten pregnant, she decided to tell her mother it was an accident. "Certain people will be less offended by an accidental pregnancy than an intentional one—like my mom."

The second part of her plan was to time telling her mother to gain the greatest sympathy. "I called her when I was in my fifth month, right after the amniocentesis. I told her that my periods had been so screwed up that I didn't realize I was pregnant until it was almost too late. And I said, 'Now I've got a week to decide, and I can have an abortion, but I have to tell you that I've had the test and I know it's a girl.' So I told her I needed her advice. That way she could tell other people, 'Well, my daughter did come to me.' So I called her back at the end of the week, and I said 'I think I should have the baby, what do you think? I don't think I should have an abortion, do you?' It really kind of locked her in, and she said, 'Yes, dear, that's the right decision.'

Julie Holmes was one of the few women who discussed her intention to have a child with her parent prior to getting pregnant. Julie had always been very close to her father. Her mother had died when Julie was a child, and she had no brothers or sisters. Her father had always given her unconditional support; his attitude was "whatever makes you happy, baby."

The first time Julie talked to her father about having a baby, she brought it up as a hypothetical question. "I said to him, 'Say, Dad, what do you think about grandchildren?' and he said, 'Is there anyone in particular you're thinking about marrying?' And I said, 'Well, what would you think if I had a child and I wasn't married?' And he said, 'Hmm, I want to think about that a little bit.' "

Once she made her decision to have a baby, she discussed it with him more frankly. Although he expressed concern about the practical difficulties of single parenting, his response was, as always, "If that's what you want, it's what I want." As Julie tells it, "When I did get pregnant and I told him, he was elated. He cried and we hugged. The only thing he didn't like about it was my choice of the baby's father. He knew him, and he thought I could have chosen better genes."

For at least two women initial rejection turned into more support than they wanted. Norma told her mother that she was pregnant first. "Her response was deep concern and then complete support. Then I told my father, and he became a maniac. He started screaming that he wanted nothing to do with me. 'You either have an abortion or you get married, but you don't do this, and if you do, I will never speak with you again.' I was so hurt, I can't tell you. Then he called back half an hour later—I think my mom talked to him—and he said he didn't mean what he had said, and they would support me emotionally, but financially I was on my own. I think it was his way of, if not discouraging me, at least making me recognize what a responsibility having a child was. Then the first time I saw him after the call, he just fell apart. He saw that I was the same person I had been, and he became so protective of me that he threatened to kill John, the baby's father. In fact he went to talk to John and told him 'You either take a walk and never see her or the baby, or you give them the financial support they need. If you want to walk away from it completely, I would understand, but as long as you want to have anything to do with them, you better take care of them or I'll send somebody to break your arms off.' That's my dad's way of being protective."

Cheryl Valin also found her parents too supportive. When we arrived at Cheryl's house, a woman in her fifties carrying a pudgy one-year-old greeted us. "I'm Cheryl's mom and this is Billy," she announced with a broad smile. "I'm here visiting from San Diego. I wanted to spend some time with the baby." It was obvious that whatever the initial response of this grandmother, she was not merely accepting but thoroughly devoted to her grandchild.

Cheryl came to the door holding her hands out to take Billy. "I can take him now, Mom." "Oh, no, you girls have your talk and I'll take care of Billy. And I'll make you some coffee and a snack." Cheryl put her arms down, rolled her eyes to the ceiling, let out a long sigh, and invited us into the living room.

Considering how her mother doted on both the baby and Cheryl it was surprising that Cheryl was also one of the women who had been afraid to tell her parents she was pregnant.

Cheryl's pregnancy wasn't consciously planned, but it was wanted. She never considered an abortion. She had no ethical, practical, or social concerns about single parenting, yet she couldn't tell her parents.

"I meant to tell them, but I just couldn't. Every time I talked to my mother on the phone, I knew I should tell her, but I just couldn't. And I felt terrible for not being able to. When I was four months pregnant, I finally wrote her a letter. She called when I wasn't home and got my roommate, and she told her she thought it was terrible and immoral and all that. Then she called back the next day, and I was home, and she apparently had gotten used to the idea. She had told my father, and the way she put it was 'He didn't fall out of his chair.' In fact, they asked me to move back home. My father got on the phone and said, 'How can you raise a child without a father?' And I said, 'Well, he'll need only me for a while.' And he said, 'Well, if he doesn't have a father, he should at least have a grandfather, so you come and live with us.' "

Cheryl pointed to the dining room where her mother was setting the table with coffee and cookies for us while holding Billy to her grandmotherly bosom and singing a little tune. "I couldn't live with them. Just look. They want to take care of me and take care of him. They're real supportive, but in an 'oh, you poor thing' sort of way. When my mother comes to visit, I start feeling incompetent. If I lived with them, I'd forget how to feed myself after a couple of months."

Of all the women we interviewed, Martha Stevens had the worst time with her parents.

Martha comes from a very upper-class family. She went to school in Switzerland, where she played tennis and rode horses. Her father is a corporate lawyer, and her mother is a professional volunteer.

Martha knew her parents would not be pleased when they found out she was pregnant, but she was unprepared for an overwhelmingly negative response.

"It was terrible. I wrote them and told them that I was pregnant in my fourth month, so they couldn't tell me to get an abortion. I told them the facts—that the father was married and that he wasn't going to have anything to do with the baby. My mother's response to me was 'Well, obviously this is what you intended to do, so you are the worst scum of the earth.' She really let it fly. Absolute condemnation and complete rejection. She told me I had ruined their lives, that I had taken all of the joy out of their having had me as their child. That there was no room in their world for a slut like me. Everything imaginable. And then I didn't hear from them again for the rest of the pregnancy.

"After I had Rhonda, I sent them a birth announcement and I wrote on it that even though the circumstances of her birth were not ideal, I hoped the time would come when they would recognize that they had a beautiful granddaughter. Then about two weeks later the phone rang. It was my father. He started asking about the baby and being real chatty, like the seven months since I'd heard from them had never happened, like they still had been calling every week. The connection was staticky, and I figured he'd gone to a gas station to call so my mother wouldn't know. And we talked for four or five minutes, and then my mother, who had been on the extension the entire time, asked in a very subdued voice, 'How's your little girl?' I couldn't believe she was actually on the phone. From then on they called every week and acted like everything was fine.

"Then my mother decided she was coming to visit. She came out and was absolutely doting on Rhonda. She bought her presents and played with her all the time. Then the night before she left she let me have it again with both barrels. She said I lived my life like vermin, and I had no place in her life. I should go live in the gutter. I had the morals of a cat. And I was furious, but I didn't yell back. I just let her yell at me.

"The next day she left, and that night my father called and said, 'Don't pay any attention to anything she said.' He said that the fact that she came meant that she was trying to deal with it, and it was unfortunate that she lost herself the day before. He said I should pretend it didn't happen because she was really trying to be good.

"Well, they kept calling every week, and a couple of months later Rhonda and I flew out to visit them. They were both very sweet. And at different times they each made comments about 'you better never do this again.' It was like 'The oak has bent for this little kid, but don't think that it would again.' They really do love her."

It's not just the moral questions surrounding pregnancy that make grandparents blanch. Parents of women who adopt are also often initially tense about the prospect of nontraditional grandparenting. But they too come around.

Raya Moss, who adopted at forty, describes her mother's immediate response as "hysterical." "And I don't mean good-hysterical. There was something outrageous about the idea of a single woman being a mother. I think they had gotten used to the idea that I was a career woman, but the fact that I wasn't married was always a source of embarrassment to them. And this doesn't seem very logical, but I think part of her hysteria was that she thought if I could have a baby without a man, I surely would never get married now. That was part of it. The other part was somehow it just wasn't right. It wasn't the way you did things. It was sort of unheard of. Her arguments were so irrational that at one point she said that at least if I had a child biologically, she would have known one of the parents. But that was almost comical, because if I had gotten pregnant she would have been even more upset.

"My father's response was more sedate, but to me also comical. He said, 'Well, why don't you just get a dog or a cat?' He had trouble understanding why anybody would want to take on the responsibility of a child alone. So while she was outraged, he was mystified.

"That was before I got the baby. Afterwards everything changed. If you saw them now, you'd think it had been their idea that I adopt."

For other women who adopt, the issue for their parents is not adoption per se but the child's race.

For one adoptive mother, "My parents were a little tame about the baby for a while because she's Chicano. I could hear it in their voices. But they've warmed up. I don't know how they would have responded had I adopted a black or very dark colored child."

Another woman's parents had trouble accepting the idea of international adoption. "They've had a hard time with it. They're a very traditional New England family. But I told them from the beginning about trying to adopt. And it took so long that they'd been hearing about it for years, so at least they had time to get used to it. If I had been able to adopt right away, it would have been harder. And if the baby had been a lot darker, I think they would have had more difficulty accepting her. As it is, she's very fair-skinned, and they think she's fantastic. My father even commented, 'Hey, look, I'm darker than she is.' "

Race was a more subtle issue for Ruth Sohn. She adopted her Korean son, Brian, when he was an infant. And while her parents saw the baby often, there was no sign of tension about Brian's race until he was three years old. "Brian and I were visiting my folks, and a neighbor of theirs stopped by, and my dad introduced us saying, 'This is my daughter and my adopted grandson.' I was terribly upset, but I didn't want to say anything in front of Brian. So I waited until we got home, and then I pulled my father aside and I said, 'I don't want you introducing him as your *adopted* grandson. He's your grandson period. You don't have to let people know I wasn't part of a biracial marriage by saying he's adopted. He's ours and that's that.' And he never said it again. It was a slip. I know. He loves him terribly."

For other grandparents the problem is what other people will say. These grandparents, much to the dismay of their daughters, often choose to lie.

Cheryl Valin's parents, very much against Cheryl's wishes told her relatives a lie. "My mother told the relatives that I was married and divorced. I tried to talk her into telling them the truth. I'd rather they thought I was terrible than thought I was stupid. But she did it anyway. I told her if anybody asked me, I was going to tell them that I never married, but no one has asked. I think they all know, but they'd rather not hear it."

Marsha Baker's mother decided she would tell people her grandchild was adopted rather than saying Marsha bore her while she was single. The only problem inherent in this strategy was that since Marsha and her mother lived in the same city, Marsha's pregnancy had to be hidden. In her seventh month of pregnancy, Marsha explained, "Mom is extremely active in this senior citizens group, and she's always been very concerned about what other people think. She said if the people in her group found out about me, she'd have to quit. So my pregnancy has to be a secret. I haven't been allowed to get out of the car at her house since I started to show, so the neighbors won't see. I have to honk the horn and she comes out. And if we go to the grocery store or a local restaurant together, I have to call her Mrs. Baker. I can't call her Mom.

"That's how she's handling it. I go along in order to not upset her. When she's old enough, my kid will know that I wasn't married. But if that's what my mom needs, I'll go along. It's really a lesson in adaptation."

Another set of self-conscious grandparents managed to skirt the issue. Here's the birth announcement they sent out to their friends:

The Proud Grandparents
Frank and Pauline Lash
proudly announce the birth of their granddaughter
Daphne Ann

As Daphne Ann's single mother puts it, "It was ridiculous. It didn't mention my name and it didn't mention Daphne's last name which is Lash—same as theirs, same as mine."

SIBLINGS

Responses of brothers and sisters are mixed. In most cases single mothers describe their siblings as "accepting." In several cases siblings are outright "enthusiastic" and become the woman's main emotional support. In each of the cases of exceptional support, the sibling is an older married sister with several children of her own. There are also cases of extremely negative responses, from either very conservative brothers or very religious brothers or sisters.

Gail Jordan was one of the women who received her main support from her sister. Gail intentionally got pregnant, and her older sister was the first one she called. "And, oh, she was delighted for me. Just delighted. She told me the things that were really the true stuff. She told me, 'Gail, you won't believe it. You'll never regret having done it. You will find out that it is the most absorbing love affair that you have ever had.' She said when her son was born, a smile came on her face and it hasn't left it yet.''

Yet in spite of this unqualified endorsement, as Gail approached the end of her third month—the end of the time when she could still have an easy abortion—she started questioning her decision. ''I was sitting there crying and wondering if I should go through with it, and my sister called. I told her I was worried that it was a mistake and I should just undo it, and she said if there was any question in my mind, I shouldn't have an abortion. She told me, 'You won't believe how hard it is to live with an abortion. You know you want a child, and you're happy with the choice of the father, and you made the right decision. Remember why you did it.' And I knew she was right. She was so right. I can't believe now that I ever considered not having my daughter in my life.''

Another woman also listened to her older sister when she was considering an abortion. ''All my friends tried to talk me out of having the baby. My sister's the only one who encouraged me. She has three children. She said, 'It's very hard, but it's very rewarding and very exciting.' And knowing me and the way I am and my ability to cope with situations and my resourcefulness, she felt that I could handle it.''

The negative responses from siblings, frequently a result of conservative viewpoints, were in some cases rural traditional and in others urban elitist. For Anita Lewis rejection came from her sister in rural Kentucky. When Anita announced that she was trying to adopt, her sister wrote her a series of letters saying her adopting would ruin both Anita's life and her parents' lives. ''I remember in one letter she claimed this would kill my parents because they were going to worry themselves to death about me. I didn't see much logic in her reasoning, but she's from a very small community in Kentucky where the idea of adoption would be very risky and definitely deviant.''

Judy Ford's rejection came from her oldest brother. ''He's

in Boston, and he's very well known and very socially promi-
nent. His sons are in the finest prep school, and I think he was
afraid I would be an embarrassment.'' Judy's brother never actually confronted her with his concern. Instead he wrote to her
mother. ''I saw the letter, and he said things like I was 'irresponsible and stupid' and what was I trying to do, wasn't I old
enough to have outlived my college girl need to go against society? And I really got upset. But what I resented most was that
he couldn't tell me face-to-face. He did call once, right after
Shelly was born, but he didn't even ask about her. He just asked
to talk to my mother. So I told my mom I never wanted to see
him again. But she lives in Boston too, and I like to spend
Christmas with her, so I didn't do anything final. I've seen him
since, and we pretty much disregard each other.''

Sally Kohn received a similar cold shoulder from her brother,
but the hostility was communicated by a third party. It was Sally's mother, not Sally, who told Sally's brother and sister-in-
law about the pregnancy. Sally had never been close to her brother
and his family. Their life-styles were very different from hers.
Sally liked the simple life: an adequate-paying but low-powered
job, gardening, bicycling, camping. Her brother and sister-in-
law were far more attuned to wealth and what it could buy: a
Mercedes, a swimming pool, trips to Europe, live-in help.

After her mother told them, Sally's sister-in-law called her.
''She said, 'Oh, we're so shocked. Your brother's speechless.'
And I said, 'Does he want to talk to me?' and she said, 'No,
he's speechless.' Then a few days later she sent me a letter that
was just devastating. It was so nasty. She said I was going about
my life all wrong. She said that I couldn't get along well enough
with a man to get married, so I was going to have a baby and
get all my emotional needs met by it. She said she felt sorry for
the baby.

''I just fumed. I wrote her back and told her that I was angry, and I was glad to find out how she felt about things, and I
didn't want to have anything to do with her again.''

Sally didn't talk to her brother or sister-in-law for another
year. When she went to Dallas to visit her mother, her brother

came for dinner and Sally didn't speak to him. But afterward she realized she seldom spoke with him at family get-togethers anyway, so "it was no big loss."

It's worth noting that not all conservative siblings dish out rejection. Martha Stevens expected a curt note from her "politically right wing" brother but was met with a lovely surprise.

"My brother and I never got along. He's very conservative and I'm very liberal, and we just never clicked. I did write to him when I had the baby, though. It was the polite thing to do. And he wrote back this real nice letter saying he had spoken with my mother, and she kept talking about 'my problem,' and he had thought I had cancer or tuberculosis or some life-threatening disease, and he was so relieved to find out I was only having a baby. He enclosed a check for a thousand dollars and said I should use it for things I needed for the baby. That took me totally by surprise. It was the last thing in the world I expected. It was wonderful."

The rejection that comes from very religious siblings is regarded more as annoying than devastating.

Georgina Leone wrote to her sister, whom Georgina describes as a "Jesus freak," to tell her she was pregnant. She got a letter back that "really set me off." "She said, 'Of course I love you,' but then she got all preachy and righteous and said the situation was sinful and so was I and so was my baby. Listen, I don't believe what she believes, but who needs the aggravation of hearing someone say my baby is sinful."

Another woman got a somewhat more tempered response from her minister brother. "To this day I don't understand. It had something to do with creating a problem where there hadn't been one before. He thought I was being selfish, but that's what I think essentially motivates all people to become parents. Later I found out from my mother that his real concern was that I was not following a Christian life-style, and the baby would be one more child born into a non-Christian home. And Mom told him, 'You cannot sterilize all non-Christians.' "

He ultimately came around. "He's been out to visit us, and he really cares for Bobby. He still thinks it was the wrong thing to do, but Bobby is in fact his nephew, and they have a very nice relationship. It seems he's been able to separate out the ethical issue from how he feels about Bobby as a person and a relative.''

FRIENDS

The reaction of friends is also mixed. Some friends give women "total loving support"; other friends "disappear." There are, however, patterns of who is supportive and who disappears, and these patterns coalesce around factors of gender and marital status.

Least accepting of single parenting are men, married or single.

Several women suggested that men seemed threatened or resentful that a woman could have a family on her own. Dorothy Wold, a social worker, describes conversations she had with male friends and colleagues about her decision to have artificial insemination. "The response I kept getting from men was 'Well, I guess you proved you don't need men.' And I'd say, 'Oh, yes I do. Not for this baby, but I still need men.' I think they thought they were putting me down, but they were really putting themselves down. The ones who weren't flippant and really wanted to discuss it, I'd tell, 'You know, you're selling yourself short. When you say I don't need men just because I can get pregnant by artificial insemination, you're saying that all men are is a source of sperm. You don't believe that and I don't believe that.' But they would still come back with something about men being unnecessary.''

Similar to statements about being unnecessary were after-the-fact offers to do the fathering. Several male friends and former lovers said things like "Why didn't you ask me? I would have done it." Though as one woman notes, "That's what they say now. Who knows if they really would have."

A third response was more blatantly sexual. "If you want to practice having another one, I'm available." While this kind of response may be another way of creating a necessary role for the males, it also confuses conception without marriage with sexual promiscuity. That bothered and insulted the women we interviewed as none of them considered themselves promiscuous.

Male response was not limited to innuendoes about the process of getting pregnant. From one woman we heard, "The only man who didn't tell me to have an abortion was my father." And from another, "When I adopted, some of my friends disappeared—boyfriends."

A couple of women also lost women friends over their decision to have the baby. Cary Adams lost her two closest friends over her decision to not abort. Cary was one of the women who had been incorrectly told by her gynecologist that she could not conceive. She was not going to let this unexpected "miracle" pass by. When she told her two closest women friends, they were appalled. "They told me I was going to ruin my life and ruin the baby's life. I tried to make them understand, but they just thought I was immoral and crazy and selfish and tried to get me to have an abortion. But I knew I couldn't give up what was probably my only chance to have a kid—ever—so I didn't, and they just left my life. They said they couldn't bear to watch me make such a mistake. I guess I wouldn't want to be friends with someone I thought was immoral and crazy and selfish either, but God, it hurt to be deserted."

Another reason given for women friends disapproving and disappearing was their own conflict about motherhood or bad marriages. Margaret Richards describes one woman with whom she had once been very close. "I have not seen her since I was five months pregnant. She herself had a painful history of forced-marriage pregnancy and several abortions, and she has had nothing to do with me."

Dorothy Wold reports that one of her friends told her she was crazy, and if she was lonely, she should get a dog. But Dorothy notes, "I had a feeling that her response was at least in part due to the fact that she had given up custody of her children to their father, from whom she was divorced."

And Cheryl Valin lost a friend who wanted a baby but who herself had had an abortion. As Cheryl put it, "I think she came to terms with the abortion, but she couldn't come to terms with the fact that I was making the choice she had passed by."

Not all women friends who are conflicted about their own mothering status desert. One woman told us of her best friend, "I told her I thought I was pregnant. She began to act so ugly to me you would not believe it. She was being a super-bitch. I couldn't say anything without her trying to bite my head off. And we're very close. We never fight. One night we got drunk, and I finally said, 'What on earth is going on? I don't understand why you're so upset.' And she said that she was jealous. It never occurred to me. She said, 'I'm not in the position to get pregnant. I only want to do it if I'm married, so I can't do it and I'm jealous.' As soon as she said it, it cleared the air for both of us."

Lest it sound as though the responses of women friends are basically negative, we should point out that many of the women reported overwhelming support from their women friends. One woman said, "I think the response was about ninty-five percent positive. Almost every woman who knew me responded, 'That's fantastic, you'll make a great mother.' " Another woman reported, "I got tons of support. Friends wanted to be my Lamaze coach, 'the Japanese godmother'; 'the Filipino aunt.' " And another recalled, "Friends are terrific, fabulous. Everybody thinks it's a great idea. There were a couple of friends who told me in the beginning they thought I was crazy and I didn't know what I was getting myself into, but they've all come around." And a pregnant woman reported, "All of my single friends are so excited. This is going to be the single person's baby. They all have a stake in it."

Perhaps the most striking instance of support came from Debra Swanson's five best women friends. Each of the five contributed two thousand dollars, giving Debra a cash gift of ten thousand dollars so she could take six months off from work after the birth of her new baby.

THE WORLD AT LARGE

We also asked the women how people outside their intimate circle of friends and relatives responded to their becoming single parents. But before we look at those, it's worth noting how some women managed to avoid the issue so that they do not deal with responses at all.

Irene Sullivan got pregnant by passive choice; she wanted to have a baby, stopped using birth control, and "accidentally" got pregnant. She did not acknowledge to either the man nor to herself what her intentions were. And while she was delighted when she found out she was pregnant, she was also beset with doubts. For one, she was concerned about how people would respond. Her parents rallied. But she was so self-conscious that rather than telling the people at work that she was pregnant, in her fourth month she took a one-year unpaid leave of absence for "personal reasons."

Not everyone can afford a year's leave of absence. Other women avoided the issue in various ways. Two women gave the impression to people at work that they had gotten pregnant by their ex-husbands. Both had been divorced for years before they got pregnant, but apparently people who knew they had been divorced for a long time disregarded the inconsistency. Those who did not know assumed they had gotten divorced some time after getting pregnant.

Several other women pursued what could be called the ostrich strategy. Uncomfortable about their status, they chose simply to not talk about it with people at work. As one woman put it, "I felt real defensive. I kept worrying that I'd have to explain myself all the time. Then I finally realized I didn't have to explain to anyone. I just didn't say anything about it and no one asked. I'm sure they talked about me behind my back, but I didn't care."

Most women, on the other hand frankly discussed their status and were met with just about total acceptance. A woman who taught at a junior high school in San Francisco described the response of parents, teachers, superiors, and students as "fantastic."

"I told the students I was pregnant shortly after I found out. And they were terribly excited. We discussed the difference between getting pregnant as a single woman when you're a teenager and getting pregnant as a single woman when you have your master's degree, and a good-paying job, and you already own your own house. I have made certain they understood what you could offer a child when you had money and security and a profession. The boys were worried that if the baby was a boy, there was no one to teach him to ride motorcycles. But I told them one of them could do that for me, and that seemed to cheer them up.

"We talked about amniocentesis, and I showed them the polaroid I took of the ultrasound when I had the amnio done. Thinking back on it, that probably wasn't wise, because if the baby had turned out to have Down's syndrome, I would have aborted, and I think that would have hurt some of the kids terribly. But as it was, everything was fine. I received the report on the amnio when I was at school, and I announced to my class that it was a girl. They were so excited. They all felt a part of it.

"After the amnio report the kids did the nicest thing. Each one gave me a piece of children's clothing they had worn when they were growing up. Their parents were great, too. They gave me hand-me-downs and little tips, and five of them gave me a shower. Then the entire teaching staff threw me a baby shower. Between the kids and the parents and the staff, there was nothing I had to buy for the baby.

"The first person to arrive at the hospital when I had the baby was the principal, and then every staff member but two visited me in the hospital at some point during my stay. They were all just lovely."

Other women had less dramatic stories but received far more support than they had anticipated. A woman who worked in a very conservative bank found people "really went out of their way to be considerate." She was most surprised by the response of her superiors. "My boss, a new father himself, was extremely supportive, and the most senior woman executive in the organization really went out of her way. She took me out to lunch at a private club, and she bought me a very lovely baby gift and has invited me to her home several times. We had no special relationship before my pregnancy—in fact we hardly knew each other—but she's been exceptionally thoughtful. Actually, everyone has.''

An electrical engineer in California received strong support from the secretarial staff. As she describes the response, ''The men didn't say anything, but the the secretaries totally rallied around me. I never had so many girl friends before. I'd always been a loner—a woman in a man's field. As an engineer, I was always the boss among the secretaries. But that broke down. They listened to all of my complaints about the aches and pains. They laughed when I ironed my stomach accidentally. It was more than I had ever hoped for.''

Several women were told that they were "brave." One recalled, "People I really didn't know well would stop me in the elevator and say, 'Oh, you're really blazing trails.' And I'd think, 'Is that how they see me?' " Another told us, "One comment I get a lot at work is 'I didn't know you were married.' And I whisper, 'Did anyone ever tell you you don't have to be married to get pregnant?' And then they tell me, 'God, you're courageous.' Though I don't think that it takes any courage to do this.''

While some women told us they had feared negative responses from colleagues and were pleasantly surprised by support, other women told us they hadn't even considered an evaluative response from their doctor and were shocked by criticism.

One woman who was considering single parenting told us, "I talked to my gynecologist about it, and he said, 'Don't.' He said, 'I would be glad to help you through it if you make the decision, but I would advise against it. It's hard enough when there are two parents.' "

A woman who became pregnant intentionally reported, "The only time I really dumped was when my obstetrician set up an abortion for me. He said I hadn't considered what I was doing, that I had been too arbitrary. So he set up an appointment for an abortion, and if I didn't want to have it done I could call and cancel it. He thought getting pregnant if you weren't married was a dumb thing. And part of the evidence of how dumb it was was that I hadn't considered an abortion. So he made me consider it. I really got depressed. I thought about it and thought about it, and then I decided I knew what I wanted and I knew what I didn't want. I wanted my baby. I didn't want an abortion. And I didn't want him to be my gynecologist anymore.''

And there were also negative experiences with pediatricians and psychiatrists. One adoptive mother had moved with her son from Los Angeles, where, she says, "people let you live your own life," to Tulsa, where the general feeling she received from people was anger. But she singled out her son's pediatrician as a key source of negative response. "I remember our pediatrician was horrified. I was the only single adoptive parent he had ever run into. He was always very cold, and finally I asked him if my being single bothered him. And he let loose a tirade about how I was depriving David of a normal existence, that I was ruining his life. It was really horrible. Needless to say, I changed pediatricians.''

And a woman who was artificially inseminated recalls that of all the people with whom she discussed her plans, "the only person who was opposed to it was my former therapist. I went back to see him when I was thinking about getting pregnant. Since he knew me as well as or better than anyone else, I thought he might have some points for me to look out for. Perhaps knowing me, he would be able to tell me if there were certain times or certain issues that I should be alert to or extra cautious about. Well, I went to see him, and we never got to that. He wanted to know why I was even thinking about having a child. He had two suggestions: that I go into deep analysis or that I get a dog. I left furious. I went back to work and burst into my boss's office and said, 'Do you know what that son of a bitch said?' Fortunately, my boss was very supportive.''

When she ran into the therapist at a social occasion several years after her son was born, he apologized. "He said that he just had trouble thinking about it, but it was his problem, not mine.''

This is not to say that all doctors were negative. Indeed, several of the women were delighted by their doctor's caring and felt wonderful after their visits. One woman told us her doctor offered to do "everything she could to help her get pregnant" from running fertility tests to finding a sperm donor. Another told us her psychiatrist's response to her discussion of single motherhood was "Do it. You'll make a great mother." And yet another woman told us that every time she came out of her obstetrician's office she felt like "the greatest person in the world: brave and terrific and strong and beautiful."

It is likely that people sense our own fears and joys and respond to us accordingly. That's not to say that if you're ecstatic about your pregnancy and you encounter people who think you're positively sinful that they will change their minds, but they may be less likely to voice their opinions. And if you question what you are doing and you encounter people who might otherwise be accepting, you raise some doubt in their minds that otherwise would have not been there.

One of the women we interviewed put it this way, "You get back what you give out. So if you're positive and you're happy and you're thrilled to death, that's how people feed it back." Another said, "I accepted my pregnancy without any hesitation, so other people did too. I was consistent and I knew what I wanted. Basically, I think if you feel good about what you're doing and you feel it's right, people are much more willing to accept it. That doesn't mean people weren't concerned. Some people worried about whether I could afford to raise a child and some were concerned about my age. I allowed them their concerns, but I let them know I felt great about it and they did too."

CHAPTER
6
BRINGING UP BABY

Finally, after all that planning and waiting and wondering, mother and child come home. And even with all that planning, waiting, wondering, whoever thought motherhood could be so much fun— or so much work? One simply cannot describe or anticipate the elation or exhaustion of being a new mother. What else produces as much anxiety or as much satisfaction? As one mother told us, "The reality of having a baby is mind-blowing."

The women we interviewed enjoyed motherhood, whatever the problems and hardships. Some described themselves as drunk with joy, "high" on cuddling. They were enthralled with their children, fascinated by seeing them grow and prosper. As one woman put it, "Who cares about going out when I can stay home and watch the baby gurgle?"

Similarly, one highly "cerebral" professional had expected motherhood to be "so strained, so confining, so restrictive, so overwhelming. I thought it would be miserable until my daughter got to the part that I really like, which is when they are seven or eight and they can talk and read. But it's been a daily treat from the beginning. It's been infinitely better than I anticipated.

It's the most absorbing love affair that I've ever had—and I wasn't expecting that at all.''

NEW MOTHERHOOD

But motherhood is a lot of work, even with disposable diapers, washing machines, TV dinners, and ready-mixed formula (although most of the mothers breast-fed if they could, finding nursing easier and more satisfying). Moreover, a woman needs time to recover from even a problem-free delivery.

The first-time mother worries endlessly and bemoans the fact that the now liberated and gender-free manual by Dr. Spock raises more questions than it answers. Why is the baby crying? Is it colic? Do I have enough milk? Is this normal spitting up or projectile vomiting? Is this normal tearing or an eye discharge? Is this bath water too hot? Too cold? Too little? Too much? Is this normal stool or diarrhea or constipation? And what is this redness, this pimple, this brown spot by the ear? Did the kid from next door who came over to visit have chicken pox?

Being single has little to do with the anxiety and nervousness of first-baby syndrome, but it *may* make resolution a bit more complicated. With whom does one share concern about problems, real or imaginary? Who can a mother trust to have as much concern for her baby's welfare? This lack of another caring adult with whom to share responsibility is keenly felt, a point we'll come back to again.

Furthermore, the new, nervous, and single mother faces a considerable dilemma when it comes to doing routine chores. What does one do with a newborn infant while emptying the garbage or transferring clothes from washing machine to dryer? One woman we talked to bundled her newborn son off to a neighbor's house whenever she wanted to shampoo her hair. That's probably unnecessary; instead, it may be convenient and reassuring to plug in a portable intercom system so that the mother who has to be downstairs can hear when the baby cries upstairs. But how does she get to the post office or pharmacy? And how does she shovel snow, or mow the lawn?

MOTHERS' MOTHERS

Many of the women we talked to—many of them ferociously self-reliant—had not expected to need help. They knew they'd have questions but had not anticipated the kind of exhaustion and even frustration that overtook them. For many, their own mothers turned out to be indispensable, at least for the first week or so, and in some cases, longer.

Eleanor Gates, a thirty-five-year-old who prided herself on her independence, was ambivalent about asking her mother to help out. Two months before the baby was born, her mother volunteered to stay for a week after the birth. Eleanor recalls, "At the time, I had no idea what was coming, what postpartum was like. So I just said, 'Oh, yeah, maybe you can come for a few days.' I just didn't realize how much I would need and want her help, how much I would depend on her. So she arrived with the idea of staying a week—and wound up, at my request, moving in for a month."

If some women hadn't realized how weak or anxious they would be, others were reluctant to make demands on their parents and were concerned about exploiting their mothers. They were embarrassed to be so dependent after ten or fifteen or twenty years of independence—although apparently the grandmothers didn't see this as problematic. Ellen Sawyer says she was initially mortified to think of her sixty-year-old mother doing all that work. "I mean, she was on her hands and knees, scrubbing. She would take the phone off the hook so I could nap and then she'd do the bathroom. But funny, I learned a lot about a mother's love. I never really understood that before. It was only when I understood how much I loved my child and knew I would do anything for my child that I could see and accept that fiercely intense and protective love from my own mother. So now I am appreciative—I don't feel guilty about letting her do that work. And—though I don't know if she agrees with this—I think this has brought us closer. The baby has brought us closer together. I'm still her daughter, but she sees me as another mother, too."

Another woman, who had cheerfully described her problem-free pregnancy, recounted: "I told myself that I was going to give myself fourteen days of relaxing after Stacy was born. I let my mother do everything short of breast-feeding. I did a lot of sleeping, and on the fourteenth day I felt great."

Mothers' mothers provided not only help but reassurance and encouragement. New mothers inevitably doubt their abilities. One remembered: "I was so scared. Here all of a sudden I was a mother and I really didn't know what I was supposed to do. But my mother kept telling me I was doing fine. She kept reminding me that after ten days under my care he still had ten fingers and ten toes. And by the time Grandma left, I knew everything. I quickly became an expert."

Mothers may even help keep new mom on a diet—or get her on one. Some mothers we talked to gained twenty-five to thirty pounds, but others gained forty and even fifty pounds and were very discouraged about the weight they *didn't* lose with the birth of the baby. "As soon as my mother left," admits Ellen, one of those significant gainers, "I cheated on the diet, but my mother made me stick to it while she was here. And the fifteen pounds I lost those two weeks while she was here sure went a lot easier than the next fifteen pounds."

Moving in with one's mother is also common. One woman who couldn't handle the stairs in her townhouse chose to go to her mother's ranch house instead. Dorothy Wold was grateful that her mother stayed with her for a week after she came home from the hospital; however, when her mother had to return home to Virginia, Dorothy and her son went with her and stayed a month. "I hadn't recovered from the Cesarean yet, and I just couldn't get up and down to take care of the baby. Mom followed the routine established by the nurses at the hospital. At night, when the baby cried, she would bring him to me to nurse and then take him back to her room and rock him to sleep. That was important. I don't know how I would have managed if she and my dad hadn't helped me. There's just no way to recover from a C-section on your own."

A few women managed with considerably less help from their

families. Judith, for example, was one of those essentially on her own with the baby. But her son Ethan never slept more than 1½ hours, so Judith hardly slept during the first week at home. On the second weekend she called her mother—who had been very supportive once she recovered from the initial shock—and cried, "I can't stand it. I've got to come home. Can you help me?" Grandma then stayed up through the night, and Judith slept.

A woman who had spent a few weeks with her parents admits that she was a little nervous when finally left to her own devices. "It was scary to be all alone finally. 'Oh my God,' I thought, 'I am really on my own with this baby.' On the other hand, by then it was really nice to be in my own home after having been away. It was nice to be back in my own house on my own routine. After all those weeks with my parents I had confidence in myself. It was summer, and after the six A.M. feeding I'd go out and sit on the porch, burping little Grady and watching the birds. And all was right with the world. What a delightful time."

Of course, the main reason for grandma's being there is assistance: to serve and help as necessary and to advise when consulted—and *not* to take over, monopolize the baby, and be entertained. Some women found they had to be firm with their mothers and communicate their needs clearly. Otherwise the presence of the so-called helpers is worse than no help at all. Bonny Thompson, for example, sent air fare to her mother. Bonny wanted her mother to see the baby, to love her; she wanted some sort of family base. She also wanted help. "But it turned out that all my mother wanted to do was hold the baby. So I was cooking for my mother, cleaning for my mother, taking my mother sightseeing. And my mother was holding *my* newborn baby. I'll never forgive her for that."

Another woman didn't feel "in charge" as long as her own mother was around. "I've always felt incompetent in the presence of my mother," said Cheryl Valin. "And although Mom helped me out a lot while she was with us, I just felt incompetent the whole time. I started to think, Maybe she's right—I can't take care of this baby by myself. My parents wanted me to come live with them. My father, who had been raised without a father himself, wanted to be father as well as grandfather to my child. But I think it's funny that they didn't see why I couldn't go live with them. I'd start feeling like I was ten years old again. So I encouraged them to leave, and once they left, everything was fine.''

Some women did not have the kind of relationship with their mothers that permitted the latter's presence to be helpful. The new mother has to feel comfortable, which she cannot possibly do if she has to pretend to be supermom or if grandma wants to be impressed.

Sometimes it's a relief when well-intentioned folks go home, leaving new mother and baby to get used to each other. Critical relatives can generate tension (felt by both mother and child), and undermine confidence. Micki, whose parents were somewhat elderly, found their presence a burden and a damper on her own enthusiasm. "They fussed and exchanged looks whenever the baby cried. She was constipated for the first six weeks so she cried a lot. And they muttered under their breath about the newfangled ideas of this modern generation. They seemed to think I was doing it wrong—and *I* thought I was doing things wrong—but they wouldn't come out and say it. And they couldn't get the baby to quiet down either. But actually, once they left things settled down.''

The mother of a newborn can survive without twenty-four-hour help; in view of the awesome responsibility of caring for that helpless but mysterious baby, however, especially when one is tired, it *is* nice to have help and support. A friend or relative who stops in daily to take a turn with the rocking and holding, to cook a meal or two, to answer the phone, or to fold the laundry is a welcome visitor. Precious are the minutes for a new mother to take a nap, shower, change clothes, or read a letter (forget about writing one). If grandmothers are too old, too far away, or too domineering, sisters, roommates, or close friends can take their place. One mother we know went through her address book and lined up friends to come and stay with her for a day and a night. "I had no pride. Each day it was someone different. But I was determined that I wasn't going to be alone for those first couple of weeks.''

Only one woman we talked to had the baby's father move in to take care of her. It was a disaster. "After Brian was born, John moved in. I was totally consumed with the baby and wasn't that conscious of other issues, like my relationship with John. But he was feeling trapped, resentful, jealous—all negative to the point that he couldn't even enjoy the baby.

"Shortly after I got home from the hospital, I started to get sick, although I didn't know I was sick. I just thought it was the emotions of being a new mother. I was feeling weak and terribly tired, and John just kept dishing out shit. He expected me to clean and do laundry and take care of the baby and everything else. He'd yell at me how terrible I was. I'd tell him to shut up, but for some reason I couldn't tell him to leave.

"I was feeling real dependent. I couldn't get my act together. I was getting sicker and sicker. I couldn't understand then why I wasn't able to kiss him off. Every ounce of strength I had went to the baby. The whole thing was a nightmare.

"Then the doctor put me into the hospital. I was there for two weeks—John took care of the baby. But all he did the whole time was bitch.

"When I got out of the hospital and I was feeling stronger, everything started shaping up. When I wasn't dependent on John, he was nicer to me, more willing to help out. But he was still miserable. And I knew he'd make me miserable. It was good for him to be with the baby for bonding, but it wasn't good for me to have him living here. His presence made things worse, not better, for me. So I told him it was probably time for him to leave. We were both relieved.''

The lesson, then, is that the mother who is just home from the hospital with a newborn may need a lot of help. She should admit that need and accept help, but the helper must be willing to do assigned tasks graciously and quietly. While sisters, close friends, or in the right circumstances the baby's father could supply that assistance, our study indicates that one's own mother is the most popular and most dependable source of support.

COPING IN THE HERE
AND THEREAFTER

Just because the baby is over three months old and no longer qualifies as "newborn" does not mean that the mother should refuse further help. Child rearing can remain exhausting! The question becomes not if but whom and when the single mother can ask or count on for moral support, consultation, and relief. Over and over again, we heard emphatic references to support systems. Again, as reassuring as the reference books and baby magazines are, rearing children is not an absolute science, and one is bound to have all sorts of questions. Furthermore, every mother needs time to herself away from the baby.

One's parents can continue to be a considerable source of aid and support. Sara Destry's mother helped her "115 percent." When the baby was demanding and she needed rest, she'd call her mother. " 'Come and get him. If you want him, you're welcome to him,' And my mother came at the drop of a hat, staying for days, for weeks. And she did my laundry for a year. I felt I was blessed."

Judith Lawrence fell sick one night and had to call her mother at four in the morning. "There was no one else I could consider calling to come over to take care of the baby while I was in the bathroom vomiting. Who else would I call but my mother? And she came, just like that." And indeed, single mothers found that being sick or injured made for an extraordinarily difficult and problematic time.

While some women used their mothers only in emergencies—when they were sick, when the baby was sick, when the regular baby-sitter called in sick—others had a regular schedule with grandparents. One seventy-two-year-old grandfather, for example, baby-sits once a week. Familial bonding appears to thrive on such arrangements.

Nearly all the single mothers we interviewed found themselves developing close relationships with at least one other mother to whom they could turn with questions at any time, day or night. Admitting the absence of absolutes, it is still comforting to be able to discuss the relative merits of various kinds of pacifiers, diapers, powders, and feeding techniques. It is particularly helpful to compare notes on various behaviors, functional or dysfunctional. Given the remarkable regularity of babies' development, the friend whose child is only a few months older is bound to have experienced many of the problems a new mother confronts.

Some mothers sought out pediatricians or family practitioners who seemed nonjudgmental, if not supportive, and who were accessible. Several mothers chose doctors who sat by the phone for an hour or so each morning to take calls and/or who encouraged emergency calls at any hour. Others, anticipating that they wouldn't always trust their own judgment, resigned themselves to frequent visits to the doctor, taking into consideration the location and the price of an office visit; or they sought out a nurse practitioner. Some joined a prepaid medical group or a health maintenance organization. "What would I do without Kaiser's advice nurse?" remarked one California mother.

For many women a support group proved crucial and highly successful. Self-help groups are not for everyone, but the women we talked to who did join (some of our interviewees had themselves organized such groups) found their membership tremendously satisfying. Carolyn Norton said, "Parent support groups are helpful places to be overwhelmed and let it show." Groups specifically organized for single mothers or mothers of biracial or adoptive children were particularly helpful. One woman even signed up for a group for single women who had adopted "problem kids."

A West Coast woman who helped found a single mothers' group that meets weekly can't say enough about it: what it means to her, how it has eased her sense of isolation and loneliness. Indeed she believes that the very fact the group exists at all helps women—by rendering the experience normal and legitimate. Members of this group—part of the resource center at a local YWCA—find that the group both gives them the courage to say, "This is what I'm doing," and introduces them to others who accept it.

The group co-founder says, "Just knowing other single mothers helps. If the baby is sick or if I'm sick and can't go to a meeting, I really miss it. It's just a really encouraging experience. I don't feel so overwhelmed or depressed then. The things some other women might discuss with husbands or boyfriends we discuss in the group—and we get incredible feedback and support."

She adds that helping others in a similar situation has been as satisfying as the support she's received. "It's rewarding to help other people who are going through the same things. I get a real kick out of making it easier—even a little bit—for someone else."

Not all women found it necessary to join a group restricted to single mothers. Sara Destry, for example, joined a group of married mothers when her baby was eight weeks old. "Someone dragged me out of the house saying I was suffering from postpartum." Sara doesn't think she was depressed as much as harried and isolated, but she found that it was good for her to get out, to have other mothers to talk to and listen. "At first I just thought it was a hassle to get up and get out, but I guess I needed someone to tell me how to do it. And now I'm thankful to have met those other women. It didn't matter that they were married and I was single. In fact, it was kind of a plus because I found out that the feelings I was having had little to do with being single—they were merely part of being a new mother."

Just as single mothers often liked talking to married mothers as a way of checking that their problems were not unique to them, single adoptive mothers frequently found solace when they joined groups that included birth mothers. For example, Laurie Black, who adopted two children after having been a foster parent, said, "I find it very supportive to talk to birth mothers with kids the same age to find out that some of the feelings I feel, they feel— to find that some problem results from a stage that all kids go through rather than only adopted ones. My kids act up for weeks on end and I get sick of it, but I was putting a lot down to 'Oh, these kids are adopted and I'm not properly committed.' So it was a revelation when I found out that other ten-year-olds are like that, and birth mothers also would like to strangle their kids. Talking to these women makes me feel a lot better. Then they are my children, not my adopted children. You can lose your perspective very easily if you don't come into contact with birth parents as well.''

DECISION MAKING

Nevertheless, best friends and support groups did not always compensate for the absence of another adult with whom to discuss the minor and major issues of child rearing, or even to share the joys of seeing the children mature. Many women still complained that they lacked a "sounding board." Said Carolyn Norton, "I don't know what I'm doing right; I don't know what I'm doing wrong. I think one of the hardest parts of being a single parent is not having another person on whom to bounce off ideas and experiences."

A woman who adopted a child with a learning disability confided, "Sometimes I wish I had somebody to sit up with at night and talk about the things that happen, choices that aren't clear, difficult decisions. It would be nice to have someone who's just as invested to discuss this with."

Other women were fairly confident of their ability to make reasonable decisions; when those decisions were controversial or went against others' advice, however, they admitted they would have liked someone else's support. Then, too, it's nice to get a sympathetic pat on the back during a crisis. As one mother stressed, "It's not hard to diagnose whether he's got a temp of one hundred and five. I'm perfectly capable of doing that. But when he does have a temp, it's the reassurance and the hug that I miss."

Yet another woman denies the importance of someone to lean on in time of crisis. The first time Pam Wood's daughter had a seizure, a close friend who was visiting called an ambulance while Pam did mouth-to-mouth resuscitation. The next time Pam was alone. Was it harder to handle the crisis then? "It wasn't any different when he was there than when I was on my own. If you're going to lose a kid, it doesn't make any difference how many people you have around you. It's scary as hell either way.''

GETTING HELP

The mothers are nearly unanimous in telling us of their need for moments of peace and quiet. Even if they have nothing in particular to do, nowhere to go, they require breaks. One, for example, claims that not sending the children away once in a while for a night would be ''suicidal.''

Apparently the trick is to accustom the child to being away from Mom right from the beginning, to accustom oneself to asking for (or accepting) help, and arranging it so that child and the care giver enjoy it as much as Mother does.

Many women rely on friends, since good baby-sitters may be expensive and difficult to find. Naturally it is imperative that one be considerate of friends' time, energy, and patience—or risk losing such friends. But if it is not an imposition, why not let a friend take the kids to the park or zoo on a Saturday afternoon? Marsha claims, ''You can get time for yourself if you're smart enough to take it when it's available. And some people without kids of their own genuinely enjoy a child's company for a few hours.''

The problem lies in getting rest when the mother needs it, not simply when a friend offers it. Scheduled breaks are preferred to spontaneous ones, but mothers are again reluctant to impose.

A woman who lives on a small farm outside Seattle supplies a neighbor with rabbits for the privilege of dropping off her two children a few hours every Saturday morning. She admits that at first she was too caught up in being ''machisma'' and refused to admit she needed people. ''I had a friend with a couple of kids and she just assumed that everyone would help her out. I really resented that attitude. I was glad to help her out, but not when she just expected to be able always to shuffle her kids off. So I swore I'd never do that to anybody. But I was too careful.

That hurt everybody. The kids suffered because I was getting so burned out. Now I see that it's OK to need people. And I've found a balance that works.''

Now she is glad she has learned to accept help from friends and neighbors, as well as father and brothers. ''They are happy to share. And by being able to accept from people I've become more giving. If somebody were needy and asked me for help, I'd feel honored. I'd feel glad that I could share part of myself with them, because asking for help opens doors. Confessing a need makes for intimacy, makes it easier for the other person. In the end there's reciprocity.''

It's worth noting, however, that some women call only on other single mothers. They believe that only single mothers know what their needs are, and that married women either do not approve of their R & R or don't understand. In any event, even mothers who cannot afford sitters can work out an exchange of services.

Either way, single mothers agree that ''You cannot do it alone. You must not be too proud and think you can do it alone. You'd better realize that up front.''

The unhealthiness of refusing help (and not getting help) from friends is illustrated by the case of Kate Farley, who would be the first to admit that spending all her time either at work or alone with her daughter is driving her crazy. She's tense, frustrated, bitter, chronically irritable. Sometimes she puts the toddler to bed at six P.M., afraid that otherwise she would become abusive.

Sometimes Kate tries to rationalize her martyrdom, and it's worth recalling one such attempt. A friend from work offered to take the baby for a weekend, having noticed that Kate was on the verge of losing control. Kate refused, saying she would feel guilty. That Friday mother and child stayed up the entire night, yelling and screaming. ''I would hit her and she would hit right back. I'd stomp out and she'd follow me and holler some more. But that's what we needed. We needed to get a whole lot of that out. Eventually she crawled into bed with me, exhausted—but she patted me, and the next day it was better. Being separated would have taken us out of the situation, but we would have come back to the same thing. We needed to work it out.''

But if Kate did not see the problem there, she is only too well aware now of the problems of being too private and too proud. (She attributes this, rightly or wrongly, to her Catholic upbringing.) "I'm so much into the martyr role that I can't break the habit. But I know this is not healthy. It's pitiful to have your whole life wrapped up in being a martyr.''

If Kate was extraordinarily isolated, she certainly was not unique in giving in to anger—the kind of anger that could have pushed her to become violent. She was not the only one to fantasize about not picking the child up from the baby-sitter. If single mothers agree that emotional strength and stability are crucial to the woman embarking on this course, they all find that single-handedly meeting the demands and needs of a baby is emotionally and physically draining. Many of them admitted to running out of patience, loss of control, and venting their frustration.

And again, well-intentioned as they might have been, several women were plagued by the incongruity of expectation and reality. Dianne Judson put it most poignantly. She thought having a baby would be fun and instead found: "What having a baby really was was, I was still one hundred fifty pounds and endlessly tired, endlessly upset about something, not able to get a job, not having any energy to do anything but take Valium, lonely as hell, crying all the time and saved by those occasional times this baby would look into my eyes. That was the only joy of my life. It was a lot different than I expected. There is no way someone who hasn't done it could know what it's like. A woman who hasn't gone through this could go home now and purposely deprive herself of sleep for a week and take Valium and wake up every two hours—and still she wouldn't know what it was like.''

In fact, Dianne compares the experience to that of a political prisoner being tortured. She says she can understand child abuse—how women feel "alone, helpless, frustrated, and angry, they can't stand it anymore, they think it will never end."

SURVIVAL TECHNIQUES

There appears to be a direct relationship between loss of control and patience and lack of help and support. But many mothers believe that this extreme frustration can be kept in check by a variety of commonsense and fairly obvious techniques, if they cannot pass the child off to a nanny or other care giver.

Having someone to talk to helps a great deal. Sally Kohn admits that one afternoon, after the baby had fussed all day, she felt like dumping him in the garbage can. So she wrapped the baby in a blanket and ran down the street to a neighbor who, at the sound of crying, came to the door offering tea and sympathy. As soon as Sally calmed down, the baby did too. Sally adds, "So when I get drained, we have to get out and talk to somebody. It's incredible how much help it is just to talk to somebody for a little while."

Another time Sally dealt with stress by talking to herself. She was trapped on a downtown bus with a screaming baby. "I really felt like screaming back and shaking him. But I realized that if I did, he'd just scream more. That kept me from doing it. I stayed calm on the outside. I soothed him and continued to try to quiet him down. I kept doing what I had to do. I thought, Well, I've got to keep going somehow. And that calmed him—and finally me."

Another survival technique is learning to discard the image of the ideal mother. Certainly the single mother cannot expect to work full time, have a spotless house, cook gourmet meals, and also spend all waking hours at home reading Golden Books to the just-bathed toddler. Quite a few mothers simply let the housework go, or they accepted whatever standard of cleanliness could be produced by the children. Eleanor Gates decided that her personal growth is more important than housework. "There are long periods when we won't have clean dishes, because it's more important that I do what I want to do. Sometimes it's more important that I take time out and do nothing rather than run out to do laundry. And I don't cook.''

Absolute emotional stability can be elusive. The mother of two says, ''It's OK to be tired and even irritable. People don't say that, but it is OK. Sometimes I yell at the kids and sometimes I put them in their room and admit that I need time out. Nobody's perfect all the time.'' And returning to the issue of support systems, another mother says that when she is sick and the baby is uncontrollable, ''I'm not afraid or ashamed to ask for help. I don't have to be a supermom just because I'm single. I can be an ordinary mom.''

And while few of the mothers we interviewed required professional services for the problem, many were aware that private and governmental agencies offer help to the potentially explosive parent. For some, simply knowing the telephone number of the local hotline for parents was a safety valve. Nearly all of the foster and adoptive mothers, moreover, did avail themselves of the advice and support of professional counselors (therapists and social workers).

Women shared other techniques for managing their bursts of anger and frustration, which they largely attribute to the experience of being alone. Singing loudly to drown out the baby's cries helped Eleanor. Lamaze techniques for relaxation were good for Sally, who reminded herself to hold out for just one more minute—and then another and another; in taking the situation a minute at a time, like the contractions, the day passed. A prominently posted sign in the bedroom promises Kate that ''This, too, shall pass,'' though she sometimes wonders. Martha recommends calmly and deliberately chanting, ''She's only a baby, she's only a baby. She doesn't understand. She can't help it.'' Finally, going out with the child can do wonders, be it for a drive, a walk, a carriage ride or whatever.

Ironically, one way that these untraditional mothers often console themselves is by comparing themselves to what turns out to be a radically stereotyped version of the traditional two-parent household where the father/husband has no child-rearing interests or responsibilities. That is, single mothers assume first that the traditional father won't change a diaper and that he snores through the two A.M. bottle. Then they reason that they at least don't have anyone to resent. They can't complain because, of course, they knew nobody would be there to rock and feed the baby at two A.M. As Gail Jordan says, "I don't have any resentment because I didn't have any expectations. Since I had no expectations, it's not a drag." In amazingly similar language, Kara Lavel states, "I had no expectation of help or experience of help, so I had no sense of burden." Whether or not this reasoning is fair to contemporary fathers, many mothers found comfort in the presumption that husbands call for beer and popcorn while wives must simultaneously cook dinner and discipline the children.

It's worth noting that for several single mothers the situation was easier than anticipated. With her child one year old, Phyllis Fields was able to say, "I thought it was going to be more difficult. I had anticipated no sleep for the first few months, going through a couple of months of a colicky, crying baby, feeling really dragged out and tired, feeling frustrated, and wanting to get away, none of which I've felt."

Margaret Richards admits to often being tired and occasionally overwhelmed, but then she remembers being tired and overwhelmed by her job or her involvement in community organizations. In fact, she claims to be less "stressed" by motherhood than by work. Margaret explains that motherhood keeps her from burning out in one direction or another. She's learned not to overload. "I realize that I not only want to be physically with my son but I want to be accessible and responsive. I just can't let myself get too tired or emotionally stretched out."

FINANCES

Being emotionally stretched out is one thing. Being financially stretched out is quite another. Child rearing is expensive—indeed, increasingly so. In addition to the inevitable costs, it may entail loss of income. For example, we talked to one business executive who had generally considered herself well-off. But with the baby came all sorts of new expenses, and she received no money from the child's father. Further, she could no longer derive income from the extra bedroom she had formerly rented out, since it had been turned into the nursery. And she was paying a salary (plus round-trip air fare) and providing room and board for her Swedish au pair girl. Finally, she chose to reduce her hours at work, despite the 20 percent pay cut. All in all, she says it was like having one-third less money to spend. No wonder she described herself as feeling "fiscally vulnerable."

Nearly every one of the mothers we interviewed regarded finances as one of the most problematic aspects of single parenthood. If there was any advantage to the two-parent family, they agreed, it was the additional source of income. "The money thing can be very, very worrisome," said a nurse earning $20,000—which she considers the bare minimum. "The money can get you down quicker than anything because it confronts you every day."

Single mothers almost unanimously warn women considering this option to consider carefully the monetary question. "Make sure your financial house is in order," they recommend. "Only women who are sure they can handle the money should do this," says one. "If you cannot deny yourself that dress or cocktails after work or other non-necessities, you're going to be hurting for money pretty quickly. Because you don't realize all the unexpected things that come with having a child," says another. Nonetheless, one cheerful optimist, a real estate broker, claims that women shouldn't marry just for economics. "That price is too high. If you really want to have a baby, then have the baby and the economics will work out."

In terms of their financial status, single mothers fall into three basic categories: fairly well-off, working hard and scrimping, and welfare. We'll start at the top if for no other reason than these were the women who as a group were the most unquestionably happy and the most satisfied with their lives and their decision to have children.

We met some women who were quite comfortable, either

because of family money and well-placed investments or because of their professions as doctors, attorneys, corporate managers, and executives. These women still feel the money squeeze (we met no one who was actually "rich"), but they continued to live the good life. They can afford a lot of baby-sitting time and support services, so they can get away for relaxation and socializing. Several have housekeepers. They can even afford a few luxuries and indulgences. One woman described the freedom that earning $35,000 brings her: "When you make a decent salary you can hire child care, you can hire cleaning ladies, you can buy a new dress when you're in the dumps, you can take a short trip when you're worn out. Money means a lot. Money helps a lot."

These women are relieved to know that they can indulge themselves once in a while (though certainly not as often as before) and that they can buy what they want for their children. We found no one who admitted to buying designer diapers, but they did want the "name" strollers, bikes, memberships at the zoo, music, and ice-skating lessons—partly because they believed any child deserves this and partly out of guilt and a sense of compensating for other "lacks." Although they were not explicit about buying only the best, they do not want to look back years later and think that their children had been deprived. Said one, "I don't want my daughter to think that all we can ever have is secondhand. I feel sorry for women who have to buy stained things for their babies."

A clinical psychologist who adopted two children said she waited until her practice was well established before embarking on motherhood. She wanted to make sure her children would not be materially deprived. "I wanted to be able to provide reasonably for them. I didn't just want to do some poor kid a favor—quite the other way around." Similarly, others emphasized that they were not trying to make themselves out to be martyrs; they did not want their children to feel guilty about having forced their mothers to sacrifice on their behalf.

The second group of women manage to get by financially by working full or part time, but they live extremely close to the bone. One freelance secretary described herself as having taken a "vow of poverty." Not a few found themselves having spent their entire savings within the first year of having the baby—and still paying off bills. (It is not uncommon for doctor and hospital bills to top $3,000 or $4,000, even without serious complications; medical insurance, therefore, is a must.)

For these women, life is more of a struggle. They feel forced to keep working. Especially when they were not altogether thrilled with their jobs, they resented having to work so hard and so long simply to pay for baby-sitters and diapers. A number of women described that moment of horror when they realized how single mothering limited their options; that is, they felt "trapped." Said one social worker from a well-to-do upper-middle-class suburb, "The icky part is when I think of having to work full time for the rest of my life to support him. When I think about it, I get depressed—because I hadn't necessarily planned to work at this job the rest of my life. For example, if I didn't have a child— or if I had a husband around—I might have just quit and gone to law school. Or if money were not an issue, I would stay home with my children and volunteer my time. I would sit on boards of directors of organizations, so that I could do the work I love to do and also be home with my children."

And since it is hard enough to save for braces and college for one, the financial bind impels many of these women to rule out having more children.

In several cases the mothers found some other adult to move in, someone who might baby-sit as well as share rent or mortgage payments. These arrangements usually worked out nicely, despite the clearly felt loss of privacy and the difficulty of finding someone acceptable. (More complex communal arrangements involving several adults seemed to succeed less often, however.)

Bonny Thompson roomed with a woman who also had a toddler, so they shared such things as baby-sitting costs, car pooling, and cooking. More important, Bonny liked the feeling that the whole responsibility was not on her shoulders. "If I come up against any problem or I stub my toe or whatever, someone else is around. There's somebody to share with and somebody to step in and take the pressure off, and another single mother is really the only one who understands what it feels like.''

Bonny misses her privacy, however, and she misses the time alone with her daughter. She adds wistfully, ''It used to be that it would be a special time for me when I'd come home from work. We'd cuddle. We'd play. And now all of a sudden there's this rival. There's a kid to play with. That's been hard for me.''

Finally, a dozen or so women chose to go on welfare for a time (one stayed on welfare four years). Some of them intended to return to work soon after having the baby but decided they just did not want to leave home during the child's formative years. Others had planned all along to seek some kind of government aid.

For these college-educated professional women (one described herself in this context as Miss Middle Class, USA), accepting welfare was surprisingly easy. A black junior college instructor explained, ''It didn't bother me to be on welfare because I knew I didn't have to be. The effects are greater on people who have to be on welfare the rest of their lives; it affects their self-image. But for professional women whom I know, who have been on welfare while they have their babies alone, it's no big deal. People who hear I'm on welfare say, 'What's your problem?' I say, 'Hey, I don't have a sugar daddy. I don't want to take money from my parents. The baby's daddy doesn't give me a thing. And why not? This is what Aid to Families with Dependent Children is there for.' ''

On the other hand, not all women were comfortable with accepting AFDC. One woman who grew up in a university community and now heads an adult education program confessed, ''The AFDC people put you through a real mill. Your self-image goes down to almost nothing.'' And the process itself of applying is time-consuming and even tedious. One California woman told us, ''Being on welfare is like a half-time job.''

As we explain in an appendix on the legal issues of single parenthood, another disincentive to applying for welfare is the federal legislation requiring welfare mothers to identify the biological fathers of their children. The states can reduce their welfare costs by going after a father for support payments, and now they can require mothers to cooperate in determining paternity. (Our appendix also explains the exceptions to the rule that women applying for AFDC must identify the father.)

Furthermore, the recipients agree on the difficulty of making do with welfare. A woman who was in graduate school while she was trying to scrape by on welfare stressed, "Lack of money puts a real emotional burden on you. It's an extra strain."

In any case, with savings, welfare, and cutting back—eating tuna fish and shopping for bargains (they found secondhand shops and garage sales to be excellent suppliers of children's clothes and equipment)—the single mothers get by. And by trading baby-sitting time (or relying on friends and family) they even manage to get out once in a while.

Indeed, not only do the children not suffer, according to their mothers, they may even learn to be more responsible. They learn about money and the value of things. One mother complains, for example, that her five-year-old sees television mothers doing everything and buying everything. But she has taught her daughter a more realistic view, and the child knows now that she must make choices; she can't have everything.

The lesson here, then, is know thyself and thy budget. Women must figure out how much money they have or can get, how much money they need and how much they are willing to give up. In estimating the costs, err on the high side—things may cost more. And there *will* be more costs. But it can be done.

One of the most solidly comfortable and happy mothers we met offered sage words relevant to this chapter. "First of all, if you have financial resources, God knows it's easier. And second, if in general you're a good manager, you'll manage. It sounds a little cold, but look at your life experiences and you'll probably parent the same way you've done everything else—your career, your personal life, your emotional life. You sort of divide up the cake between work and baby and house and expenses—all those little balls going all the time. If you're good at juggling, you'll come out OK."

CHAPTER
7
BEING THE CHILD OF A SINGLE PARENT

Single mothers are stung when family and friends claim that choosing to bring up a child alone is "selfish" or "unfair." Women believe not only that their decision brings them joy and enriches their lives but also that their children do not and will not suffer serious ill effects as a result of their mothers' singlehood. They believe that the implications are more worrisome for themselves than for the children. Presumably they would be much less apt to pursue this course if they thought it would leave psychological scars on the children.

On the other hand, single mothers admit that they are concerned whether, or in what ways, their singleness affects their children. Passive-choice mothers are particularly susceptible to feelings of guilt and insecurity, but even active-choice mothers are always alert to the problems the child may have because he or she doesn't have a father.

Bonny Thompson knows she is not unique. "I'm always looking for potential deficiencies. I dissect everything. I think she's not talking when other kids are and it's because I'm not stimulating her enough. Or she's not making friends or she's not sharing. I always feel that I'm not giving her enough. But actually I'm finally becoming convinced that she's just a normal kid, which is nice, because it takes pressure off both her and me.''

This chapter is about potential or actual effects on the children of single mothers, as perceived by those mothers. We talked to a few of the children, and we'll introduce you to one of them at the end of this chapter. For the most part, however, the children were too young to be interviewed. And possibly it is simply too early for anyone to assess the impact. Quite probably the most serious and dramatic problems aren't realized until the child reaches teen years. So, while this chapter is not definitive, potential hazards—and solutions—can be identified.

SOCIAL STIGMA

When asked whether their children had been or might be stigmatized as born ''out of wedlock,'' almost all mothers gave us a firm no. Some of them rejected out of hand that such a social stigma was even relevant; others had thought about it but had long ago discounted the possibility.

Those who had been most concerned agreed that the children adopted by or born to single mothers were not stigmatized as such. As described earlier, the mothers may feel that they themselves bear the brunt of critical reaction, but they see no evidence of this with their children. Mothers of older children agreed it had not been an issue (although a daughter, now twenty, told us she had been called ''bastard'' and it hurt). And mothers of younger children did not anticipate major problems for their children.

A couple of mothers were concerned that when their children reached adolescence there might be ''talk.'' One said, ''There may be some people who will never understand us, who will take it out on the kid, but she and I can cope with that.'' These women suggested that if the children were bothered by this and wanted to fabricate stories, they would be willing to go along with them. But another guessed that, if asked, her daughter would tell people, "My mom had me because she wanted me."

Mostly we found consensus that two shifts in our social environment have eliminated any stigma. First, women note that the high divorce rate and the large number of single-parent households prevent their children from standing out. Second, biological mothers cite changes that are making unmarried motherhood more common. Non-marital sex, they say, has become a non-issue and pregnancy outside of marriage has ceased to be either an object of ridicule or a source of shame. As such, being the child of a single parent is losing its onus. As the mother of a one-year-old put it, "Look, this isn't a 'Father Knows Best' world anymore. If you live in the city, there are a lot of single parents. Granted, most kids have a father they see on occasion, but a hell of a lot of kids get by with Mom only. And five years from now there will be more kids who have unmarried mothers. There are many things a kid has to deal with, but I think that social stigma about my marital status will be the least of my son's problems."

If mothers summarily dismiss the possibility of children being stigmatized, single mothers, as well as would-be mothers and curious onlookers, do wonder about the behavioral and psychological implications for the child. There appear to be two issues: the effect of not having a male role model and the effect of not having a daddy.

MALE ROLE MODELS

Not surprisingly, the mothers most concerned with the absence of a male role model were those with sons, especially women whose work and social lives seldom brought them in contact with men.

Dorothy Wold now laughs at how she confronted this issue. When she first planned on having a child, she was "absolutely convinced" that she would have a girl; she even tried to time her artificial insemination to maximize the likelihood of having a girl, precisely because she figured that growing up without an "in-house male model" was less important for a girl. Then she had Bobby.

"For the first day or so after Bobby was born," Dorothy recalls, "I really had trouble dealing with that. I worried that he'd find out I wanted a girl and feel bad. Or that he'd turn into a homosexual. Or . . . I had all these fears of how terribly wrong it was going to be. Then a friend with three grown sons came over and gave me a marvelous pep talk on how much easier it was to raise boys than girls. And even though I don't have time to date anyone seriously at this point, I've been very aware of the importance of men like my brother, my dad, my baby-sitter's husband, the pediatrician—just to make sure there are men around."

Dorothy adds that she treated Bobby differently from the time he was a baby. (A lot of research demonstrates that in general parents—especially fathers—treat their children differently, even as newborns, depending on their sex. But of the single mothers we interviewed, only Dorothy admitted to this.) "I played rougher with him. I did more wrestling and more physically active stuff with him than I would have with a girl. And I think part of that had to do with his being a boy, and part of that had to do with my feeling I had to be both mother and father. I had to cover a wider range of things. Fortunately, I love camping and fishing."

Dorothy was not alone in her wish for a girl because she thought a girl has less need for a father. Most of the women we spoke to wanted girls for the same reason. A very thoughtful and articulate feminist, Martha Stevens, describes herself as "overjoyed" to bear a daughter: "I had convinced myself that I was going to have a boy but that this would be OK because society needs 'good' boys to be raised. But when she came out a girl, I couldn't believe it. How could I be so lucky?" Conversely, Eleanor Gates says, "The ultimate challenge was when I found out he was a boy. It was like, 'OK, this is *really* it.' I had just assumed I would have a girl."

It should be noted that a few women who raised the role model issue concluded that although it might be healthier to have decent male role models around, finding a good one was nearly impossible. And they didn't want a bad one—so they didn't worry about it and saw no ill effects on their sons. Carolyn Norton, for example, says she was initially nervous about raising a son on her own. "That's why I lived communally," she explains, "until I realized that the male input was all negative and negative male input was worse than no male input at all." And thinking back on her own childhood and how domineering her father had been, she believes she would have been better off if her father had not been around.

Sometimes this "no father is better than a crummy father" theory rests on a stereotyped version of the traditional, uncaring father. One mother explains, "At the beginning I thought I needed a man, some man. I thought my child would be deprived without a father. But that isn't true. There is no such rule. I don't want a man. Because along with the man might come unpleasant things that I can do without. Who needs a father who doesn't spend time parenting and doesn't want to?"

One highly politicized feminist is actually glad that no men are around, because men are raised to be aggressive, she says, and she doesn't want that role model. "I think raising my children alone without the influence of a man means that I can at least try to teach my children to be strong but not aggressive, to be gentle and compassionate."

Irene Sullivan, a single mother who teaches anthropology, echoes these sentiments. "I think the mythology of the need for male role models is just that—mythology. If you think there is some advantage to perpetuating existing sex roles with their stereotypes of female passivity and nurturance and male aggression and insensitivity, then, yes, it's important for little boys to have a strong male model to identify with. But personally, I reject this line of thinking. I'd just as soon my son did not grow up to model himself in the traditional male role."

The total absence of a male does concern her, though. "I still believe my son needs to see displays of affection between adults. I do want him to develop a healthy view of his own sexuality. I want him to be able to relate well to men and women."

One concerned mother consulted the physician who heads the child psychiatry department at a reputable medical school. He assured her that growing up in a home without a father need not have any ill effects. According to the doctor, "The important thing is that the child be loved by *some* male family members or friends. A boy needs a good masculine image so he can identify with his own sex and develop male sexuality. But it doesn't have to be the father!"

Intuitively following this line of reasoning, many women made a self-conscious effort to find role models for their sons. They appoint a godfather. They seek out a male pediatrician. They hire a male music teacher. Several chose as baby-sitters women whose husbands are home part of the day and involved with the children. Others hire male sitters. One woman estimates that her child is with men more than children in the more traditional two-parent family!

Anita Lewis watched her son very carefully over the years, because of her concern about the lack of a father. She concluded: "A boy needs men in two ways. He needs men as models. He needs to be around men, to learn what their mannerisms are, what their ways are, what men act like, how decent men act toward women. That's all easy to provide if you've got married couples, male friends, or some relatives of your own that children can be around, or if there are good coaches or camp counselors. You can set him up for a lot of good models.

"But a boy also needs to be very significant to one man. It has to do with his self-image—being of value to another man. Seeing his value reflected in a man helps him to identify his own manhood. About two years ago, when Danny was six, I decided he needed more than all those casual contacts with men. The friendly uncle or brother who came to dinner once a month wasn't enough. Since I didn't have anyone who really cared a whole lot about Danny, I went to the Big Brothers organization. I was really impressed with them. I got Danny matched up with a man who's sixty-three years old and kind of grandfatherly, and he loves Danny to death. They spend a lot of time together, and he gets as much out of it as Danny. He's kind of lonely, too. That's why men go into it—to meet a need of their own. Well, this meets Danny's needs, and they just have the most wonderful relationship. He doesn't baby Danny, but they spend tons of time together. They spend weekends in the mountains, and Danny's gone to a thousand ball games this year. It's made that crucial difference.

"Before, I noticed a kind of wistful way that Danny would act when he was around men. Not a very comfortable way. It was as if he wanted something. And in school he was underachieving—just not trying very hard, not setting high standards. This is all changed. He got matched up with this man, and the change came gradually; but all through the school year his work has started to improve more and more. He brightened up. And his relationships with other men lost that wistful quality that used to worry me so much. It's all gone. I used to say maybe men are not necessary for kids growing up, but I do think that, at least for a boy, a relationship with a man is necessary. But I don't think you have to be married to one to provide it."

MISSING DADDY

Some people predict that children of single mothers will grow up with a built-in longing, that they will always miss that (usually) unknown father. A few of the mothers we met confirmed this. Said the mother of two adolescents, "I think I've done well by my girls, but I look at them and I think they are missing something. They think they're missing something, too, but they don't know what it is."

More often, however, single mothers refuted this suggestion, especially those with younger children. Perhaps it is too early to detect a pattern of inchoate but deep longing—and perhaps the children will never suffer this.

Several women cited examples of their children's apparent healthy adjustment to the lack of a father. One mother told us that her six-year-old disabuses his friends of the idea that every child has a daddy by asserting, "I don't have a daddy, and if I don't have one that means you don't have to have one. There's no rule that says you have to have a daddy."

Another woman told us that when her son's playmate mentioned his father, her son remarked quite coolly that he did not have a father. According to the mother, "His tone was not regretful and it was not questioning. It was matter-of-fact. He knows some families have a mother and a father. Some have a mother and a grandmother or a mother and an aunt. His family has a mother only. So there are different kinds of families and he's worked it out."

The mother of a five-year-old told us, "She'd talk about not having a father every now and then, and I'd discuss it with her. And one day she said, 'It's OK, Mom, I don't mind.' " Similarly, a seven-year-old told his mother, "It would be nice to have a dad, but it's OK to have just you."

It's not OK with all children. Many single mothers report specific instances when their children seemed to want to have daddies, ask or demand to have daddies, or fantasize about having daddies. These mothers feel they can deal with the abstract concept of a daddy as well as the reality of a lack of a daddy. (We discuss how mothers answers questions about paternity and the biological father in the next chapter).

For example, Sara Destry's son wanted a daddy to "play ball and take me to the park and roughhouse with me." She promised to find "someone" who would care for him and love him and roughhouse with him, though it wouldn't be his real daddy. "That seemed to satisfy him."

An adoptive mother of two told us, "There have been times when they've had a fantasy father who would rescue them when I'm upset with them. There was a point when my youngest would call for her make-believe daddy to save her from her witchy mom. When my oldest daughter needed a rescuer, she called for her grandfather—but she did that before she really had a close relationship with him, so it was more of a fantasy, too."

Other mothers also sense a peculiar quality in the relationships that their children develop with men. One boy, his mother notes, always searches out other men. "It's as if he's saying, 'Could you be?' . . . 'Would you be?' " And a three-year-old girl called every man she saw "Daddy." "She'd get on the bus and call the bus driver 'Daddy'," her mother told us. "It was kind of weird."

There are children who worry about their lack of a father without saying anything. A woman in San Francisco whose son sees his biological father two or three times a year told us, "He's a very quiet child and he never asked about his father. Then when he was about four he came in from playing one day and he said, 'If I'm a good boy, can I have a daddy?' And I told him he did have a daddy, and his daddy was Ron. And he was delighted— not so much that it was Ron but that he was like everybody else. He had one." But, rarely, as we'll see in Chapter 8, do biological fathers take a continuing interest in their children, so we must caution women that biological fathers typically do not suffice as symbolic—let alone real—daddies.

Another woman anticipates potential problems but doubts they will be overwhelming. "When she's sixteen, she'll probably get mad at me and scream, 'Why did you do this to me?' That will be her object of adolescent rebellion. If not that, it would be something else she'd hate me for."

The importance of daddies is made clear by the changes noted when daddies are supplied. For example, Judith Lawrence noticed a dramatic shift—for the better—in her son after she got married. "He seemed happier, more secure. But who wouldn't be with two people to love you instead of one?" Ironically, she adds that it was difficult for her to give up the closeness with her son and even to give up her identity as a single mother. As pleased as she is that her son and her husband have a very close and loving relationship, she's just a bit jealous that she no longer has her son all to herself. "But it's better for him."

Kara Lavel supplied a "daddy" in a different way. Kara had been married and divorced. After her marriage ended, she had a daughter by a man with whom she had had a brief fling. When

Tammy was three years old, Kara and her ex-husband tried to get back together. It didn't work. But her ex-husband developed a wonderful relationship with Tammy. Even after he and Kara split again, Tammy continued to call him "Daddy" and to see him once a week as well as on weekends. So Tammy, while she's never seen her biological father, has her "daddy." And it's made her happy. As Kara tells it, "From the time she was about two, she'd ask about her father and cry and say she wanted him to live with us. I'd explain that he lived far away and couldn't be here, but that didn't satisfy her at all. When my ex-husband came back into my life, that stopped. She knows that my ex is not her real father, that her real father lives far away. But she hasn't asked about her real father, let alone cried about him, since my ex became her 'daddy.' "

Yet another woman's story suggests that supplying another father does not necessarily eliminate the child's concerns about the first, though this need not mean pain for the child. Doris Barns married when her son was one year old. "When we got married, my husband knew he was marrying both of us. If he wanted me, he wanted the baby; and if he wanted the baby, he wanted me." He and the boy, now fourteen years old, are very close. He is the boy's "father." But Doris has explained to him that "Father" is not his biological father. "Sometimes I think it concerns him. When they're developing, when they're growing up, they wonder, Whom do I do things like? He knows he's not exactly like me and not exactly like my husband. And that makes him aware that he must be like somebody else. Once he said to me, 'I wish that man were dead.' I think when they're going through adolescence, when the situation is far from perfect, it's difficult. I don't think it's bad, though. I think maybe it gives him a little more to work for. There's a person out there that he doesn't know but who is a part of him. He wants to prove himself. He has a drive you wouldn't believe, and he's very independent. Because of this I think he has a desire to be a famous writer. I don't think it's bad that he has something extra to think about. It might give a child more depth."

NORMALIZING SINGLE-PARENT FAMILIES

Whether or not mothers identified problems with role models and/or lack of daddies, many were sensitive to the possible effects of being different or isolated. Mothers concerned with these issues tried to normalize them, rationalize them, and minimize the potential effects.

One way to normalize the experience for the children was to bring them into contact with other children of single mothers, a consideration that may influence a mother's decision on where to live, where to send the child to day care or school, and what extracurricular activities to join.

Socializing with children from similar situations becomes particularly significant for minority or biracial children with white mothers. A woman who adopted a boy whose parentage is black and Puerto Rican notes that he was far happier after they moved from Kentucky, where they knew no children adopted by single parents, to Denver, where they have become close friends with a group of thirty or so, many of whom are biracial, Oriental, or Hispanic. Her son often refers to the fact that he became more comfortable when he saw the other "mixed" children in Denver. "You know, in Kentucky everyone is either black or white. But here there are lots of people like me. I'm not so different; I'm just accepted."

Another adoptive mother who is part of that same Denver support group emphasizes the normalizing aspect of their "ready-made extended family," saying, "The kids get used to seeing all kinds of people. So instead of seeing themselves as unusual, they take the variety of races and the presence of only one parent for granted."

Mothers who gave birth to racially mixed children may seek out biracial single-parent support groups. They worry that they are unable to help develop the cultural perspective of the father's race and that this will further complicate their child's identity question. The support groups provide resources for mother and child and opportunities for cultural and social events they may not be comfortable seeking out on their own.

While some women want interactions with families like their own, there are those women who are concerned that their children see "normal" two-parent families. Many women, even those who had not been particularly close to their parents, encouraged the grandparents to become involved as a sort of second family. And one California woman essentially cut her ties with her gay male friends and sought out friendships with married couples as part of her campaign to provide her daughter with some modicum of "normalcy."

Baby-sitter's families often become the good examples of "normal" families. One woman who had wanted to hire a sitter to come into her home regretted that she had to "compromise" with a day-care home, but subsequently she concluded that her daughter was better off. "I found a day-care mother who's really great, and I changed my view of sitting outside my home. There are aspects of my home life that are skewed. There's this heavy-duty career woman raising this little girl and she doesn't see any other family styles. At the sitter's house she sees a mommy who stays home and a daddy who comes home from work in the evening—it's a whole scene she doesn't get from me. So I decided that instead of being a compromise, it's actually an advantage."

Another woman notes that her son has gone to the same sitter for five years. "They've been like an extended family to him. And since her husband's a pilot and home a whole bunch, and he's very supportive of her taking care of kids, my son gets to see a nice normal family."

Women also take steps to bring people into their own homes so that the children will have other sources of influence, will learn to respond and adjust to other people, and will develop other emotional ties instead of depending quite so much or so exclusively on Mommy. Frequently they find another adult to live in the house or apartment, not simply to share costs but to provide another contact—a healthy measure for child and parent. One New York stockbroker noted the difficulty of finding a housemate with compatible goals and ideology. But the adjustment and the compromise were just plain necessary for her son's well-being—and not that different from the bending she'd have to do in marriage. A Chicago teacher bought a two-family home next door to her closest friend and rented the upstairs to good friends with a baby of their own, to insure friendly contact for her child and herself.

Eleanor Gates notes that she has always had a housemate to provide a buffer. Her son not only forms close, loving relationships with these adults but can go to them with problems. "Sometimes it's a real drag for the child to be around Mother— especially when she's getting down on him for something. I think it's useful to have another adult there to whom the child can go and ask what's wrong."

The value of having another person around is confirmed by those women who lack such arrangements. Several mothers who live alone with their children expressed their regret that their children had no one else to go to when Mother was grouchy or angry. When there is no one else to talk to, to explain the situation to the child, the frustration may escalate.

Most often, women counted on a close and accessible friend to provide balance and perspective. As one mother who encourages a nearby neighbor to discipline her two children whenever necessary put it, "It's a problem when the mother is 'it'—the only good guy and the only bad guy, the playmate and the disciplinarian. I've had to, in a sense, manufacture other input so that my kids lead a relatively normal life. Otherwise they'll have a very narrow, distorted perception of what life is all about."

Several women mentioned the role of friends in caring for the child. In addition to providing alternative perspectives and breaks from mother (necessary for both child and mother), they offer love and affection too. These women believe that the emotional well-being of mother and child depends on a good "support network." One woman, for example, is entirely willing to allow her son to spend a few hours with any of a dozen friends. From birth her child was held and loved by others, and she criticizes women who are afraid to be away from their children. Her advice is explicit. "Let your child be loved by other people.

That's the most important thing. Share the baby from the beginning. First, invite people over to your house and help them become familiar with the baby and the baby become familiar with them. Let them change diapers. Don't think you're the only one who can do it. And then, and always, let the child spend time with others. It really works in the long run. That way the child knows he or she is loved by others and grows up with a sense of confidence.''

SIBLINGS

Of the women we spoke to, those who bore or, more likely, adopted a second child did so in part to give the first child someone else to relate to and so that the child would learn to share Mother's attention and energy. Many women take seriously the notion that having siblings is more important than having a father, even though another child may compound the physical, emotional, and financial strains on the mother.

One woman adopted a second child specifically because she was concerned about the intensity of her relationship with her two-year-old. ''I was concerned that she only had one other person in the family. I'm not sure that my second daughter has diluted the intensity particularly, but it does give my first someone else to relate to besides me.'' And morbid as it is, she adds, ''And certainly if something happened to me, they would have each other.''

Another woman unofficially adopted an older child when her son developed into a rather demanding and active preschooler. She says, ''They can bounce off each other instead of bouncing off only me. Having done it both ways, I think it's better with two kids.''

The mothers who have two or three children agree, in fact, that sibling relationships are good for the children and that the presence of the sibling produces certain positive changes for the older child. Anita Lewis, an adoptive mother whose second son has severe emotional problems, says that once she understood how disturbed Jeffrey really was, she worried a great deal about the effect on Danny. "But it's ended up that Danny has grown up a lot. If anything he's become an even better person. He's become very sensitive to Jeffrey's needs and he's become stronger. He certainly hasn't been hurt by it. Of course I don't know what the implications will be in the long run for Danny. He could be in for a rough time because children like Jeffrey often grow up to be sociopaths. The boys are too involved for them to not affect each other after they're grown."

Of the women we talked to, most birth mothers and some adoptive mothers had only one child. A few saw problems in their children that they attributed to an overly intense and dependent relationship with mother and an inability to share. Others said they had avoided such problems by putting the child in a playgroup or other child-care arrangement. Says one, "There are the other children in our building, and they all love Elizabeth. They have all been real playful with her, and she has gotten a lot of attention and stimulation. I think, in part because of this, she's grown up to be a very giving, sociable sort of kid." Says another, "If my daughter can't go to day care for a couple of days, she gets twitchy. After two days with only Mother she's bored out of her mind, and she's running to the door to get back to her day-care friends. It's been a thoroughly positive experience for her. She's learned to share and to respect other people and to relate to kids instead of just me."

Still others simply do not see the intensity of the one-to-one mother-child relationship as problematic. These women enjoy and defend the closeness and intimacy they share with their children.

ADVANTAGES OF THE
ONE-PARENT FAMILY

Although few mothers rationalize that single parenting is superior to two-parent parenting, many cite certain potential advantages for the child. Most often they argue that theories of child rearing, disciplining, and instilling values can be applied consistently. "The buck stops here," they say. "There's only one person to ask." A child cannot play one parent against the other, doesn't have to mediate in arguments, doesn't have to judge the merits of one parent's style or philosophy against that of the other.

Moreover, these mothers claim that they have more energy and attention to devote to their children because they don't have to divide their time between children and mate, don't have to cook and clean for a mate, don't have to "entertain" a mate. Some say the child of a single parent gets more than the usual amount of stimulation and that this leads to better performance in school and elsewhere. Others cite greater emotional adjustment and maturity as outcomes of more of Mother's attention.

Yet these advantages are not offered as reasons to *prefer* single parenting. Most often we were told that two "good" parents, two committed, caring, involved, and emotionally healthy parents are better than one; but one "good" parent is better than two "bad" parents or one "good" parent and a dissatisfied mate. One mother expresses it this way: "I'd vote any day for one good, strong, healthy parent as opposed to two half-assed parents who are locked in marital problems and who are so busy dealing with each other that the kid gets nothing." Another mother offers: "I've always thought that there are three levels. Number one, the best, would be being with a man whom you really love and you really get along with, one who really wants to be a daddy, and there's no resentment at all. Number two, the next best, is doing it this way—as a single woman. Number three, the worst, is being with someone you don't love or who doesn't love the kid, someone you resent because he isn't there enough or because you don't like the way he is with the kid. The first is better than the second, but the second is certainly far superior to the third."

In the end, the mothers whom we interviewed regard their children as happy, healthy, well-adjusted, and not at all traumatized or disoriented. They don't think that having only one parent is ideal, but they don't think their children are being cheated either. The problems that have arisen for their children seem manageable. The kids are okay. Cheryl Valin speaks for many when she says, "My son is happy and healthy. And there's no reason that he shouldn't continue to be happy and healthy as long as I continue to do what I'm doing. He's perfectly normal.''

ONE DAUGHTER'S RESPONSE

As we noted at the outset of this chapter, most of the children of the mothers we interviewed were fairly young—under seven years of age—and thus too young to be interviewed.

However, we met one twenty-year-old daughter of a single woman, and she was willing—indeed eager—to share her feelings on this subject. Hers is an instructive view.

Ellen hasn't turned out badly. A business major at a California university, she's attractive, articulate, earnest, energetic, and smart. She dates frequently but not very seriously, and she plans to be fully settled in a career before she gets married, which she does expect to do someday.

Ellen describes her mother as ''great.'' ''She's level-headed and loving, independent and giving.'' Ellen's mother became pregnant by a married man she was in love with and chose to have the child because she wanted to ''have a part of him.'' Although he provided no financial or emotional support, Ellen never lacked for anything—except a father.

Ellen says she was unhappy as a child. She was raised by two aunts so that her mother could work. But her aunts and her mother constantly fought about child rearing. ''My mom had her ideas, and the aunts had theirs, and they were always pulling and tugging me between them.'' She was a projectile vomiter until she was four years old, and she suffered a chronic cough. Both were without discernible physiological roots but in apparent response to her situation at home. They disappeared when one aunt died and the other moved away.

And she was lonely. For several years she went to a neighbor's house after school, an experience she remembers fondly as ''full of children and pets.'' But Ellen was an outsider, wishing she could enjoy that ''normal'' life too. To this day Ellen regrets not having had siblings. In fact, when we asked her if it was more of a loss to have no siblings or no father or a working mother, she answered firmly, "no siblings." Ironically, when she was eighteen years old, she met the daughter of her biological father and is now quite close to her "half-sister."

Ellen is both hurt and resentful when she thinks of her biological father not wanting to see her and not having anything to say to her the two times they did meet, once when she was nine and again when she was eighteen. She says she is still jealous of children who are close to their fathers. "Every so often I see a father paying a lot of attention to a kid and I think, I'll never know what that's like. It hurts me that there's this guy who has a kid walking around somewhere and it doesn't bother him." And she still carries with her the painful memory of coming home and destroying the Father's Day cards she made at school every year—"I just felt so stupid."

Ellen is not ashamed of herself or of her mother. She does not criticize her mother's decision. She explains her situation quite truthfully to anyone who asks. "I don't think there's anything to be ashamed of. I think nothing of telling people my mom's single, that she was never married. When I was young and people would ask, I'd explain that I don't have a dad, but that never bothered me. It doesn't bother me now." The word "bastard" does bother her, though. "To this day, I hate that word. I've only been called it a couple of times, but that hurt more than anything."

Did Ellen experience any social stigma? "No. Not at all. Periodically I would get tired of explaining to people about my mother's boyfriend, or explaining to the people at financial aid or the driver's license place that I had no father, but I don't think it's anything major." And as she's gotten older, she finds she gets positive responses when she tells people her mother never married. "Girls in the dorm think it's wonderful. They say, 'Your mom must be a hell of a woman.' "

Ellen adds that she was not disadvantaged. Her mother saw to it that she had a "perfectly normal childhood." She thinks she's better adjusted than some of her friends whose parents are divorced. She has no bitterness toward her mother and now feels that given the type of person she's found her father to be, "I think I was better off without him."

Yet next to these displays of emotional health are other issues that confirm some of the worst fears of single mothers. Working mothers worry about their children being alone much of the time. Ellen says she was painfully lonely and felt like an outsider. Mothers worry about causing their children to feel guilty about the sacrifices they've made for them. Ellen feels guilty about the emotional and financial stress that child rearing entailed for her mother.

Some mothers worry about their children being too close to them. Ellen admits to feeling jealous when her mother first began to date after twelve years of abstinence. Mothers worry about their children growing up with unhealthy attitudes about men. Ellen distrusts all men, she says, and is consistently cynical about human nature, but at the same time she harbors wistful fantasies about nuclear families.

Still, it is difficult to know what conclusions to draw from this. It is only the story of one girl, born twenty years ago. And causality is tricky to determine even in the best of circumstances, however easily Ellen assigns cause. Ellen herself thinks intentionally becoming a single parent is inherently wrong. "The kid is behind from day one. No matter how much you want the child, you're depriving it of a father." While she says she has been neither disadvantaged nor damaged, she adds that not many women could have done as well as her mother, whom she regards as uniquely capable. But in fact, our interviews have demonstrated that many women could do as well—and many would be happy to have a daughter as responsible, charming, and commonsensical as Ellen.

CHAPTER
8
THE BIOLOGICAL FATHER

For those single women who became birth mothers there is a third principal in the story—the biological father. How he reacts to the pregnancy, how (or if) he relates to the child, and how the mother explains his status to the child have important implications for all three of them.

RESPONSE TO THE PREGNANCY

The results of our survey are unswerving: the biological fathers were at best nonsupportive during the pregnancy and at worst outright rejecting. Although some relationships continued rockily throughout the pregnancy, most ended—sometimes at her initiation, usually at his—all too often leaving the women disappointed, angry, or hurt.

THE RELATIONSHIP ENDS
The majority of the men did not volunteer to father a child. They were enjoying a sexual relationship with a woman who either (a) had consciously made an active choice to get pregnant and

did not tell them, (b) had unconsciously made a passive choice to not prevent a pregnancy, or (c) had accidentally become pregnant and after the fact made a choice not to abort.

Regardless of the women's intentions, the response of the men who did not agree in advance was overwhelmingly negative. This is the story we heard most often: she told him she was pregnant; he insisted on an abortion; she refused; he got angry; she assured him she would accept responsibility; he disappeared.

Cheryl Valin had always wanted children, but the man she married in her twenties did not. Several years after her divorce, as she was planning to move across the country to start a new life, she began an affair with Robert, a married man. She got pregnant and is not entirely certain she didn't do it on purpose. When her test proved positive, she knew she wanted to have the baby. Robert had other ideas.

"He was very worried and very concerned, and he thought I should have an abortion. I told him it was just out of the question. Then he suggested I let the child be adopted, and that just stunned me. I hadn't even thought of that, it was so outrageous. I told him I was going to have the baby—and keep it—and I knew I could handle it alone. I saw him once or twice after that to talk to him about it. He was very upset. I told him I would be leaving town as scheduled and that I'd write to tell him when the baby was born. He said he might write, but I didn't think I'd hear from him. He felt guilty about seeing me in the first place. Then he felt guilty about having to stop seeing me and was very worried that his wife would find out. He was afraid she would leave him and take the children away from him."

Cheryl wrote to Robert after she moved, but he never responded. Even though she knew he wouldn't keep in touch, at some level his lack of contact made her sadder and lonelier than she might otherwise have been in a new city. While she clearly wanted the baby even if he wasn't involved, she admits that throughout her pregnancy she kept hoping he would appear at the door announcing that he had left his wife. Eventually she stopped hoping and resigned herself to never seeing him again.

There is more than a touch of sadness to her admission that "I shouldn't have expected anything more from him. He's not a very strong person."

A feisty twenty-nine-year-old lawyer, accidentally pregnant, responded to her lover's hostile rejection not with disappointment but with anger. "He thought I was trying to 'trap' him into marrying me," she told us briskly, "but that wasn't the case at all. Actually I wasn't interested in getting married—not to him or to anyone else at the time. He wanted me to have an abortion, and I was very upset because he didn't ask me what I thought or what I wanted. He just announced that that's what I had to do. He was freaked out. I said, 'Fine, I will accept full responsibility. All I ask is that if you don't carry your weight, you do not interfere with our lives. You stay completely out. If you want to play, you have to pay.'

"Then he started screaming that he wasn't going to have anything to do with the child because it wasn't even his. That's when I got really angry. It was absolutely humiliating. What was he saying about my character? I screamed back, 'You must think I'm some trashy slut.' I didn't mind his not wanting to be a father. That I could deal with. But I was not going to let anyone make me feel like a tramp."

A woman who was told by her doctor that she couldn't conceive and was therefore delighted when she did, received a stunningly negative response from her long-time boyfriend. "He was very much against it. He said, 'Don't go through with it. Get an abortion.' He just went wild. And when I told him I was going to have the baby, he said, 'You do it and I'm not going to see you.' I told him he wasn't going to be responsible for supporting it. We continued seeing each other for a while, but when I started showing, he was embarrassed to be with me. Then our relationship changed. We started fighting a lot and he started calling less and less. In about my seventh month we stopped seeing each other."

Was she disappointed? Angry? "I guess mostly I was sad. I never had considered marrying him before, but once I was pregnant I started picturing this future photograph on a mantel of the three of us. I fantasized about our walking through the park pushing the baby in a stroller. For the time we did see each other, I tried everything I could to put the relationship back together, but he had shut down and closed me out. No way was that fantasy ever going to become a reality.''

And now that her baby is two, does she still have fantasies of his being involved? ''Not actively,'' she said, and then added with a laugh, ''but if you give me a minute I'll work one up for you.''

The women who got pregnant by passive choice or made the choice to continue an accidental pregnancy were more likely to be disappointed, angry, or hurt. Pregnancy made them want to have a closer, more stable relationship with the biological father. While these women tried to keep in touch, patch things up, and work things out, they either suffered throughout the pregnancy or realized that for their own sanity they had to let him go.

Women who actively chose to get pregnant and decided to not tell the man were more likely to meet his rejection with an attitude of ''I'm sorry he felt that way, but I didn't have any expectations.'' Yet even if these women were not upset by the man's rejection, they found dealing with it less than pleasant. Says one, ''It would have been better for both of us if I hadn't told him.'' And another, who conceived two children by different men, says, ''Based on what happened when I told the first one, I didn't tell the second one. I wanted it to be as clean as possible.''

The biological fathers who did volunteer were not much more supportive; most of them just faded away during the pregnancy.

Martha Stevens asked a friend to father her child. After she conceived, however, their friendship floundered. When she first told him she was pregnant, he was very happy. ''But the more pregnant I got, the less friendly he got. He's not a very communicative person, so he never really talked about how he felt. To this day, I don't really know whether he has any conflicts about it or what it ended up meaning to him that he could never take his kid home even though she was his. I think in his mind we're still friends, but we never see each other. Neither knows anything about the other's life in any way at all.''

Was she depressed by his withdrawing? "I didn't let myself get depressed,'' she told us. "I just never let myself think 'If only things had been like this' or 'If only things had been like that,' because that's not the way it was. Everything was proceeding according to plan, and the most important thing was having a healthy baby. I did care about this guy who was her father, but I never had any illusions that it was anything significant or long-term. So I never had any expectations. Maybe it's just well-developed defense mechanisms. I did not dwell on being alone. I did not let myself think, Oh, wouldn't it be wonderful to share this moment with someone.''

Margaret Richards had a similar response. A man with whom she had been having an intermittent, long-distance affair agreed to father her child. Margaret says he was pleased when she wrote that she was pregnant; but their affair ended. She hasn't seen him in the four years since she had her son. "He's never been a source of distress,'' she told us. "He never suggested I have an abortion or threatened to deny paternity.'' Nor did he return for a visit.

Margaret did not allow herself to indulge in fantasies or create false hopes. Yet while she kept in mind that things were going as she wanted, she did feel a twinge of desire for more involvement. "I always understood it to be *my* pregnancy and *my* motherhood. When I first came home from the hospital I began to wish that he was here with us, but I just told myself: '*Stop that!* That was never the deal. That was never what you said to him. That was never what you yourself planned. Now don't start throwing this in now, making him unhappy, making yourself unhappy. Because that isn't what the deal was.' I just told myself quite fiercely, 'Quit this fantasizing.' I never started raising expectations in my own mind for him to meet. I told myself that I was thankful that I had somebody who wanted to father a child, thankful that I was able to have a baby, and thankful that he was not displeased.''

Lucy Kramer's story points up the confusion the voluntary

father might experience. Lucy had asked her boyfriend to "get her pregnant." He agreed eagerly. After she conceived, Lucy began to distance herself from Jeff. She told him she didn't want to have sex while she was pregnant, didn't want to go out a lot. "I did it purposely so Jeff wouldn't get attached to me," Lucy says.

Lucy succeeded in limiting Jeff's attachment. He saw her little during her pregnancy. After the baby was born, she called him. "He came the next day and he brought us a dozen roses and he just stared at her. He didn't know what to think. He kind of counted her fingers and her toes. Maybe he wasn't sure she was his. I didn't see him for two months, and then I called him to thank him for this beautiful baby I had just fallen in love with. He said that he was confused. He knew what our agreement was from the beginning—that he would just be a biological father and I would have full responsibility for raising her—but he still felt confused. When the whole thing was to get pregnant, he thought it was a great idea. But he never considered the outcome: that there is a real live person born."

Jeff was so confused, Lucy told us, that when he filled out an application for a credit card that asked if he had any children, he didn't know what to put down, and so left it blank. "He doesn't know what to think, the poor thing. He's afraid that if he admits he's a father, he'll be attached. And I'm afraid of his being attached, too. I told him that. I said, 'You know, Jeff, I'm afraid that you'll get too fond of her and you'll want to have her.' And he said, 'Are you nuts? I can't even face being a father.'

"I think he feels sort of foolish wondering if he was just a stupid kid from Cleveland that did this crazy thing with a sophisticated New York lady. It's more complicated than I ever thought it would be."

It may be that the complications and confusion so dissuade the men who did not choose to be "real" fathers that they don't remain involved during the pregnancy. But complications and confusion are not the province of the men only; the women have their share, even those who are the most self-assured, independent, and highly motivated.

THE RELATIONSHIP
CONTINUES

Not all biological fathers faded away or were pushed away. A few of the couples continued to have a relationship throughout the pregnancy, but those relationships tended to be marked by tension and ambivalence.

Christina Lash, for example, who juggled the dates on her rhythm chart without the knowledge of her boyfriend, describes their relationship as "terribly traumatic." "God, did we fight the first four months. He'd call up and say, 'It's OK, we won't discuss it; let's go out for dinner.' Then at dinner he'd just berate me for hours. I started taking my own car and meeting him because I knew I might want to get out and drive myself home. He was really pressuring me to have an abortion. He said I would have to make a choice between him and the baby, and he was even more upset when I said I had made the choice of having the baby. I assured him time and time again that he could be as much or as little involved with the baby as he wanted to be. Then in about the fifth month, he accepted it. He wasn't happy, and he kept saying that he might leave town, but at least he stopped screaming at me. But he didn't go away. He stayed around. We had no commitment to each other. Our relationship had always been pretty day-to-day. I didn't know what would happen after I had the baby. I didn't know how he'd react after we got home."

Rose White, having unconsciously permitted an accident, said of her child's father, "He wasn't happy. We continued to see each other, but the relationship had its ups and downs. During the whole pregnancy he never adjusted to the fact that I was going to have a baby. I think he thought if he ignored it, it would go away. And I gained forty pounds, so it wasn't an easy thing to ignore. He was always upset. He wasn't supportive, period." But they kept seeing each other.

Christina and Rose were both quick to clarify that they were not counting on the relationship continuing.

"There really wasn't any question in my mind of a choice between him and the baby," recalled Christina. "I wanted the baby. And it was clearly, absolutely *my* baby. I had fantasies about the things the child and I would do together, but it was always the two of us, not the three of us. I sincerely meant it when I told him he didn't have to take any responsibility, and I was quite prepared for him to leave."

Said Rose, "I didn't know how he was going to react. I wasn't counting on anything. Once I made the decision, that was it; whatever he did was beside the point. I would have preferred for him to be involved, but if he wasn't, I was still going to continue the pregnancy. It was my decision."

Neither couple married, and apparently this in itself presented no problem. Christina went on to say, "He said we could get married, but he didn't push it that hard. I don't believe in marriage. I've always said that women don't need to get married, and I strongly believe that. Most marriages don't work. Fifty percent wind up in divorce, and of the fifty percent that remain intact, how many are miserable? I think women ought to consider that when they get to a certain point in their lives and they haven't married, maybe it's because they don't want to."

Rose's lover did not suggest marriage, but even if he had, she would have said no. "I'm not interested in marriage. I was married long ago. My husband was delightful. It wasn't that I didn't like him; I didn't like being married. I'm me. I'm not part of anyone. I might consider a partnership with someone, but it would never be a legal marriage. That doesn't interest me. And I would never even contemplate it with this man—we're just too different. It would have been a disaster."

Another woman who saw her baby's father throughout her pregnancy—a relationship colored by tension and fighting—succumbed to his pressure for a token marriage and immediate divorce. Norma told us she didn't want to get married, but John persisted and persisted until finally she gave in. They got married the day before she was due to have the baby. She describes it as the most awkward, most depressing thing she had ever done. "I hated it. Here I am with my big tummy waiting for my water to break, agreeing to take as my lawful wedded husband someone I don't love and don't want to marry, and knowing I'm going to get a divorce in a week. So I'm getting married, but I'm not getting married. And we don't know if we should go out for dinner afterward to celebrate, because there's nothing to celebrate, but we think we should do something. And then after I had the baby, I got sick and couldn't get it all together to see a lawyer, and when I did I found that divorce—even no-fault divorce—is complicated when you have a kid. So we had to deal with custody and visitation and support, and oh, it was awful.''

The women who maintain relationships with their baby's father—whether they rejected marriage, weren't offered it, or gave in to marriage and divorce—are unusual. For most of the women we spoke to, this was simply not the case; the fathers of their children ran away, faded away, or were pushed away.

RELATIONSHIP
WITH THE CHILD

It follows that if most men did not maintain a relationship with the woman while she was pregnant, most men also did not subsequently have a relationship with the child. There were the exceptions, of course: the man who stayed around through the pregnancy and then became involved with his child; and the man who had little or nothing to do with his lover while she was pregnant but wanted to be an active part of the child's life. But these were very definitely exceptions. The norm appears to be no relationship with the child (though mothers vary in their interpretations of father absence).

NO RELATIONSHIP
WITH THE CHILD

Some mothers held out the possibility of some future relationship between the father and the child, even though such relationships had yet to develop.

For example, the mother of a four-year-old who has never seen his father says, "I hope they'll meet, but my son's too young to benefit now. His father will never be an active part of the scene. I'm hopeful that there can be some sort of a little relationship between them, but it's not too practical to think there could be a strong involvement."

A woman whose daughter has never seen her father stated, "I have left it open for him to have a relationship with her—whatever way he and she want it to work out. I don't know how it will end up. It's between them."

Other women quietly resign themselves to the permanence of the man's lack of involvement. Laura had not seen her baby's father since three days after the birth, when he came over and announced that he was leaving town and would never see them again. It wasn't until her daughter was two that she resolved her doubts. "I kept thinking, Maybe he'll change his mind. Maybe he'll want to contact us. Maybe he'll want to keep in touch. So I called his sister and asked if he had ever said he was trying to contact us—just to see if that was a possibility. And no, it wasn't. She told me he had left the country and she didn't know where he was. That was a bit of a disappointment, but it was also a big relief. At least I knew exactly where we stood. There would no longer be a doubt. He's not going to contact us. OK."

Cheryl Valin reached a similar conclusion when her son was a year old. Cheryl had moved from the town in which her baby's father lived during her pregnancy. She wrote to Robert during the pregnancy and sent him pictures after the child was born, but he never responded. When the baby was one year old, she returned to visit friends. "I called him when I was in town. I felt I had a responsibility to. When I called, his wife was there, so he was constrained and couldn't really talk. I asked if he wanted to see the baby. And he said he didn't know. So I said, 'OK, good-bye,' and he said "Good-bye.' And that was that. I felt really bad for the baby, but if he didn't know after a year whether he wanted to see him or not, there was nothing I could do about it."

Other mothers whose children have no relationship with their fathers find the topic so emotionally charged they won't even discuss it. One said, "His relationship with the child became a very bitter scene, but I don't want to go into it beyond that." Another told us angrily, "Look, there were no ties between us. I never expected a permanent relationship. It was going to be me and my baby. If you want to talk about why he has no relationship with the kid, go talk to him."

Optimism, resignation, and resentment were the most common reactions we encountered. However, three of the mothers responded to the father's lack of involvement with a lawsuit. Each of these women would have liked the man to act paternally, although they recognized that the court could not force him to love or want to be with the child. Therefore, each reasoned that if the father wouldn't have an emotional relationship with the child, he should at least contribute financially.

One of the women who got pregnant accidentally decided to sue her baby's father only after he started to show some interest and then withdrew again. He had stepped out of the picture when she said she was going to have the child, but he reappeared when her daughter was four-and-a-half months old. "He said he wanted to see her, and when he did, he was obviously completely smitten with her. He started coming over once or twice a week to sit with her. It was really fantastic. He wanted to be on her birth certificate, so we got a special form and amended it so he would be listed as her father. Then expenses started piling up—doctors' bills and clothes and the sitter for when I was working—and I called him and said I was having financial trouble and I really needed some help. He got very snippy and that was the last I heard of him. I called him back again, but he refused to talk to me.

"I decided to pursue child support. There had been all of this interest on his part and suddenly nothing. He owed us something. If not emotional support, then financial support."

A second woman, who was very much in love with her baby's father and was crushed when he said he wouldn't marry her, filed a paternity suit. "I wanted both recognition of the baby and child support. I thought that for my son's sake there should be an admission of paternity, and I knew it was going to take a lot of money to raise a child. So I filed. It was a two-year battle.

He couldn't deny that he was the father because the blood test is ninety-nine percent reliable, and he couldn't deny that we had a relationship because I got depositions from all of his friends saying they had seen me in church with him and at parties with him. So his attorney's tactic was to try to make me out to be promiscuous. It's as if a prostitute has a child—the man who is the father isn't held responsible. But it was obvious that that wouldn't work. I mean, could a jury ever believe that a widower who's on the schoolboard and a member of the church and an upstanding member of the community is going to bring a woman into his house who is a slut? Come on. So in the end we settled out of court for thirty thousand dollars. I accepted a lump-sum settlement with a denial of paternity because I didn't want to continue any contact with him—even if only a check every month. Initially I was after proof of paternity, but I grew up. I realized it was more for my pride than anything else. I could never have forced him to have a relationship with my son, so this way I avoided a great deal of hassle, and now we have some financial security.''

A third woman is considering a paternity suit. The man has never seen the child. "I feel that he does have some responsibility. I've written him letters and told him, 'Look, I don't want any money from you. I just want you to make some effort, like call her, send her a card, something acknowledging that you're her father. But if you don't, I may file a paternity suit, because she deserves something—if not acknowledgment, then money.' ''

It's worth noting that in two cases in which the biological father did not maintain a relationship with the child, his parents did—a sense of family appreciated by the mother. In one, the paternal grandparents visit once or twice a year when they're in town on business and send gifts at Christmas and Easter. In the other, the paternal grandparents have been sending gifts, and the grandmother calls often to check up on mother and baby.

AN ONGOING RELATIONSHIP
WITH THE CHILD

A few biological fathers did establish relationships with their children, though these relationships fell short of the responsibility and reliability of true co-parenting. The mothers of these children agree unanimously that a relationship with the father is good for the child, but it does add confusion to the mother's life.

Sandra Franklin had a baby with her former lover, Ron. Ron not only gives her child support but comes over once a week to visit Sandra, the baby, and Sandra's son by her previous marriage. But while the children adore him, Sandra has found that his presence makes it difficult for her to break off her attachment to him in order to get on with her social life. For her children he's like a father in a divorce. He plays with them, brings them toys, and gives them a great deal of love; for her it's "like getting a weekly fix so I can't get over loving him, and I can't have him." She can't tell him to leave her life, because the children would miss him; but with him in her life she can't break the attachment.

Helen, a nurse in Seattle, encountered the same problem but finally came to a satisfactory resolution. Her lover stopped seeing her after she decided not to have an abortion. He reappeared in her life when the baby was a month old.

"He called and said he wanted to see his daughter, and he came over and fell in love with her. It was something he said he had not expected, but now he wanted to be a part of her life."

And he did become an active part of her life. He came to see her three days a week. He changed diapers, mixed formula, and went to the pediatrician appointments. He set up a trust fund into which he makes regular payments. He built a fence around Helen's yard so their daughter would have a safe place to play.

His establishing a relationship with his daughter led to re-establishing a relationship with Helen. "He started seeing her in June, and in October we started our relationship again. That lasted until February or so, and then we stopped seeing each other again, though he continued to see the baby. Then we got reinvolved again in the spring, but it was very brief. I can't have the kind of relationship he wants. He wants us to sleep together but not to have any commitment. But I can't do that with him because there's too much emotional involvement. Then we went back to just being platonic friends when he came to visit her, but that didn't work either. So I finally told him, 'This is nuts. We're just friends, and that goes on for a few weeks, and as we get friendlier and everything, it leads to being involved again; but you don't want any commitment and I can't do that.' So I decided that we'd have to arrange his seeing her at a time when I'm working. So we only see each other passing at the doorway. It's working fine.''

In addition to emotional confusion for the mother, a steady and close relationship between the father and the child can create the same resentments divorced mothers experience. "I want my son to have a relationship with him, but there's a real temptation to be vindictive when he's being a shmuck," says one single mother forcefully. "When he wants to go off hiking instead of spending time with his kid, he has that choice. I do not. When he's playing tennis instead of accepting responsibility as the goddamned parent he is, then you bet there's resentment. But it doesn't work if I get vindictive. If I start laying a guilt trip or getting angry, all that happens is I get upset and he gets upset and my son feels it.''

Norma experiences the same resentment in her joint-custody situation. "I think joint custody should mean you both participate fifty percent in the economics and fifty percent in the caretaking. And while he pays fifty percent of the baby's expenses, I have to do a hundred and fifty percent of the caretaking, and he only does what he wants to. Like right now, he's on the ocean—enjoying himself, getting sun, and tanning and playing—and he'll come back when he feels like it. And I have to be here or find a sitter twenty-four hours a day. If the baby gets sick, I have to get up at six the next morning to go to work. And he's not experiencing that. He goes to bed when he wants to go to bed and he gets up when he wants to get up.

"I think hands down, as far as the child is concerned, the father should be involved. But there's no question it's a problem for the mother.''

But there exists a more germane question: If these women chose to have children while they were single—whether choosing to get pregnant or choosing not to abort or not to permit adoption—why do they hope for or want to pursue a relationship between the man and their child?

The answers are several. If a woman had a child because she counted on the man participating in child rearing, she has reason to be sad or resentful if that expectation is not fulfilled. Second, women who became pregnant accidentally and for whom abortion was not an option might well conclude that since it took two to create a child, two should be responsible for it.

Two further reasons for desiring a relationship in the absence of formal ties are less expected and, it turns out, more universal. Many women find that they are so in love with their child that they don't understand how the father cannot be. "If I enjoy the baby so much," they reason, "he would too."

Lastly, these single mothers are products of their culture. Almost all assume they have escaped or eschewed that segment of our socialization that holds as an absolute the need for a traditional nuclear family. Yet once pregnant, many find that they long for a closer relationship with the father. It is part of the cultural vocabulary: pregnancy is "supposed to be" shared. Then, when they have the child, they discover they want him or her to have a relationship with the biological father. Again, parenting is "supposed to be" shared. So even if they accepted the man's lack of involvement philosophically, at some level they think he should care for the child. And even if they were convinced their child does not need a daddy, they begin to think there would be a benefit to having one.

EXPLANATION

Whether or not they expect a relationship, every single mother who bears a child must deal with the issue of explaining to the child why she has no husband and her child has no father.

Mothers of infants invariably affirm: "I'll just be honest." Witness Eleanor Gates. "I'll simply tell him that Mommy and Daddy aren't married. We decided not to."

Martha Stevens announced, "I plan to tell her the truth: that I really wanted to have her, that I wasn't married, that this man

I really liked had her with me, and that's how I got her. And I'll tell her that her father had another family besides having her and that he lives with them, and that's why she doesn't know him. I don't know how she'll explain it to her friends. If contradictions arise, we'll have to deal with them then, but I don't think it will be a big problem."

And from Gail Jordan we heard: "My mother wanted to tell her I had had artifical insemination, but I don't want to do that. I think that would be harder to take. I found out as much information as I could about him so if he left town and we couldn't find him, I would have some facts to tell her. I've pretty much decided that I'll tell her that it was somebody I liked a whole lot. It just didn't happen to work out. I don't know if I'll get carried away about how deliberate it was. I'll say that I didn't want to get married and he had other plans. It was just a decision that we made between ourselves. I'm not worried about it. I don't feel guilty about what I did."

The experience of women with older children confirms the value of honesty in explaning their single status and the absence of a father.

Doris Barns, now the mother of a fourteen-year-old boy, married when her son was one year old. Her husband, Alan, adopted the boy. She explained her son's parentage to him in stages. "From the day I married Alan, I talked about him as 'your father', because he is. When Nick was about two, when he started to talk and could understand words, I explained, 'Your father has chosen you.' I didn't actually tell him that Alan wasn't his biological father until he got a bit older."

Doris volunteered information long before her son asked. She thought it was better to start early and talk naturally about it. "He would understand maybe one word of the whole thing, and the next time I brought it up he would understand two words. It would be easier that way. He would have always known." She feared that if she waited until he was ten or twelve to tell him, it would have been a shock and "might have pushed him away from us. He would have thought, How could this be? It couldn't be, because no one told me. So I always told him.

"When he was about three, I started telling him, 'You didn't come from Father; you came from another seed.' I told him that the man whose seed he came from was a wonderful person, and he would have loved him because he's very much like Father. Alan would tell him too, 'You know, you didn't come from my seed, but it doesn't matter since I love you and you are really mine.' So when he was young, I kept it very, very simple. Sophisticated questions came later.

"As he got older, we talked about it in greater depth. I'm sure he thinks about it. But I've always tried to treat the topic with the utmost respect. I've always told him that he didn't come from some strange seed, that he was loved from the moment he was born, that if he had known this person—I never say 'father,' because Alan *is* his father—he would like him.

"When he needs to talk about it, I seem to know. He says something like 'I wish I knew who I looked like.' He's never asked to meet him. He knows his name and he knows where he lives. I said, 'One day you might like to meet him.' And he said, 'No, I wouldn't.' And I said, 'You would like him. Daddy would, too.' So one day, maybe they'll both meet him.''

Dorothy Wold pursued a similarly simple, honest explanation of her son's conception by artificial insemination. Dorothy's talks about her son's origins began indirectly with a book she created for him. The book documents with photographs and hand-printed text her decision, her pregnancy, and his birth. It tells the story of how she talked to her friends about having a child and shows those friends smiling. Then it shows who the doctor was, what she looked like during the pregnancy, what the hospital looked like, and how happy she was walking into the house carrying a little baby.

As Dorothy describes the book, "It doesn't exactly talk about artificial insemination. But it does show that there wasn't a man around. It talks about a mom wanting to have a baby and it talks about people asking, 'Will your baby be sorry he doesn't have a daddy?' So that's in there. Children like looking at pictures and we looked through the book long before I got around to any actual explanations.''

The questions came later. "The first one that came up was the old business of 'Can I marry you?' And in my case there was no using the old line, 'You can't; I'm married to your daddy.' So for that one I said, 'You can't; I'm busy being your mom and will go on being your mom for ever and ever and ever. You will be fifty years old and I will still be your mom, and that's a full time job, so I can't marry you.' That was at some nice oedipal time, like three.

"Then he called me 'Daddy' a few times. Most of the time it was said jokingly, and I returned it jokingly: 'Come on, I'm not your daddy.'

"About a year ago, when he was four, he got into wanting to know where babies come from—or rather how they got there, since he'd known from talking about pregnant women that he'd grown inside of Mommy. We already had the book *Where Did I Come From,* so we read that. And that answered some questions. The book explains very nicely about sperm and eggs, but he didn't personalize it. I figured that he was still getting information, and I wasn't going to go beyond that.

"After that he hinted that he wanted to talk about it more. Then I told him that because I wanted a baby, I had gone to the doctor and talked to the doctor about having a baby, and the doctor had found a man who was willing to share his sperm. So the doctor asked that man to give him some sperm and he did, and the doctor gave it to me. And that was how I got pregnant. There was a man somewhere who was willing to share.

"It took a while, but he finally asked who that man was. I said, in all honesty, 'I don't know. That was somebody that the doctor found. Other women have babies that way also, and when it's done that way, who the man is stays a secret, and nobody knows.' "

Too much honesty may prove a burden to the child. Women who resent the biological father for his lack of involvement are very cautious not to communicate their negative feelings, wishing to spare the children concern about their origins. "No one wants to think they were sired by a good-for-nothing," advised one.

A relationship that was only fleeting or purely functional might need to be shrouded in some romantic imagery, suggested a mother who pursued "complete and total honesty" and now says she agonizes over whether that was right.

Judith Lawrence intentionally got pregnant by a man with whom she was ending a not very intense relationship. She asked him, as a favor, to "get her pregnant" but not be involved with her or the child. He agreed, she got pregnant, and he has not been heard from since.

Her son received the following explanation. "I talked to him about it as soon as he started verbalizing a little bit, which was around two. I told him that I had wanted to have a child very much and that I loved him very much and that the man—I called him his biological father—who was responsible for him being here was somebody I did not care for a whole lot but who did me a favor. My feeling was that I would always be totally honest with him from the start, but I was never totally comfortable with what I was saying.

"I made it clear to Ethan that his father was someone who was not part of my life. We had chosen it to be that way. Ethan had a hard time with that. He would draw pictures of me and him and this very foggy other person in the corner. And when you asked who this faint person was, he'd say, 'That's my biological father.'

"I don't think I handled it very well, but for some reason I had this real need to make it clear to Ethan that I intentionally had him on my own. It was like I valued my single-mother status."

Judith has learned that the mind of a child does not work like the mind of an adult. What makes sense to one does not necessarily make sense to the other. It would appear that the safest approach is the one that is sensitively wrought—the one that screens facts too harsh for the child to absorb, that tempers the explanation to the child's ability to receive it.

A CHILD SPEAKS

As in Chapter 7, it is instructive to look at the response of a twenty-year-old child of a single mother.

Ellen's relationship with her father has been virtually non-existent. She has seen him only twice: when she was nine and when she was eighteen. Both visits were at her initiation. When she was nine and was asking about her father, her mother arranged a visit, but Ellen recalls little more about their meeting than the Santa Claus in the middle of the restaurant he took her to. Nine years later, when she graduated from high school, she again asked to see him—perhaps as some rite of passage. Of this meeting she says, "It was kind of sad. He really had nothing to say. He told me he wanted to buy me a dress but he didn't know what color my eyes were. Imagine having a child and not knowing what color her eyes are! I felt bad for him."

Does she feel any attachment for him? "No. But I think about what could have been . . . the potential."

Apparently Ellen's mother employed the approach of an honest and early explanation with a romantic theme that undoubtedly had its basis in truth. Ellen says, "She was always very honest, very open. I don't remember when she first told me. I always knew. She answered questions whenever I asked. She'd always said, 'This is the way it is.' She told me she really loved him a lot."

Consequently, Ellen feels she has "nothing to hide," and she also feels the explanation helped fit her into the cultural myth of being "conceived in love." She reflects, "If she had gotten pregnant intentionally, I think I might have resented her. If she hadn't loved him, it would make a big difference. It seems to me it should be something beautiful."

While Ellen harbors no resentment toward her mother, she is unquestionably bitter toward her father. "He doesn't call to ask if I'm all right. He doesn't even make a token show of emotion. I know I have a father in a biological way, but I really don't have a father. That man isn't my father. I have no feelings toward him except anger for never helping my mom out, and I think he's a real jerk for having a kid and not caring about her."

Ellen believes this resentment of her father has made her cynical about men. "I really don't trust men. I think they're usually just after sex. And I know that comes from my feelings about him."

Ellen's is only one story. While it verifies the importance of what a mother says by way of explaining the situation, it also illuminates the effects of the biological father's contribution—or lack thereof. Perhaps in addition to an honest, sensitive explanation there have to be some supplementary experiences that undercut negative generalizations. Indeed, this brings us back to the issue of male role models. Our interviews indicate that only mothers of boys worry about the need for a consistent, strong male attachment for the child. Ellen's response appears proof positive that mothers of girls ought to consider this, too. The complex of thoughts and feelings about fathers may be more labyrinthine than mothers expect and may well need to be countered with positive experiences.

CHAPTER

9

IT WILL CHANGE YOUR LIFE

Clearly, motherhood changes women's lives. In what ways and to what extent? For most women, having children profoundly changes *all* aspects of their lives.

The changes are resounding, and the impact resonates through their personal, social, and professional lives, their personality and sense of self.

LEARNING ABOUT ONESELF

Women who are not afraid of sounding corny emphasize that motherhood enriched their lives: the sharing, the giving, and the loving, they contend, made them wiser and better people. The particular challenges of single motherhood matured them, made them more responsible and independent. "Kids force you to go through a process that's definitely very growth-producing," they claim. "Being a mother—and this goes for all kinds of mothers—forces you to grow up in a new way, a way that's been really valuable for me. There's a commitment and a certain something that makes you a richer person, a deeper person, a fuller person. Somehow you are 'more.' There's more to me now. I've learned a lot about myself.''

Carolyn, who sometimes misses the hiking, climbing, and foreign travel she used to do, adds that even the self-denial and sacrifices have been good for her. ''The child has needs and you have needs. But you're the adult so you have to be understanding of them. You've got to step back and say, 'My needs are important, but I'm big enough to listen to this little guy's needs.' That giving up, that surrendering your own way makes you wiser, deeper.''

Carolyn speaks for many in turning this description into prescription. ''Some of my friends who have decided not to have children now seem to me to be still kids themselves. They haven't had to be responsible. And they can squander themselves away. I think women who don't have children ought to find another way to learn self-denial and responsibility. They owe it to themselves. They have to get out of having their own way all the time. Motherhood is a kind of discipline—like music or art—that's hard to do, that you have to dedicate yourself to.''

Other mothers, while they certainly won't casually recommend single motherhood and while they believe that not all women can ''handle'' it, agree that the giving one does as a parent is a humanizing and maturing practice. ''I suppose there are other ways of growing up, and some of those ways might even be easier—but I doubt any would have been as rewarding.''

And at the same time, at least for some women, motherhood has brought out in them a more relaxed attitude and sense of playfulness. ''It's a chance to relive one's childhood and, along with the child, experience simple pleasures anew—to rediscover the world,'' says a satisfied mother who's a great fan of zoos and miniature golf. Ellen Sawyer observes, ''I don't know if it's a change or just a chance to let loose with what was there before, but now it's really enjoyable to be able to play with kids. I don't have to borrow other people's kids for an excuse to go to puppet shows or Walt Disney films. And I can spend hours with them drawing or baking cookies or playing 'Let's Pretend.' Gosh, they're fun!''

Occasionally the fact that their lives are no longer their own frustrates them. Some women envy their childless friends who come and go as they please, who sleep and wake and eat and leave when they want. The mother of two active, bright little boys explains that in her "single" days, when she had a bad day at work, she could come home and cuddle up with a juicy novel and a glass of wine. "That was it. I didn't have to cope with it, with anything. I could just hide from it. I could come home and go to bed at six o'clock. You can't do that with kids. And unless you want to allow your kids to become cartoon addicts, there's no more sleeping until ten on Saturday mornings."

But while constant and unending responsibilities may be irritating or even frightening, more often the women felt better for having become mothers. They enjoy knowing that their own lives have new values and purposes and that their children depend on them—and them only. Judith Lawrence, who got pregnant at twenty-eight, says, "I think I was forced to examine who I was as a person sooner than I would have otherwise. And I realized that I had taken on a huge responsibility. I couldn't wake up one morning and decide I didn't want to change diapers any more. I couldn't quit a kid like I could quit a job."

In fact, that knowledge leads them to value their own lives differently. Several women explained that they consciously redefined or limited their activities in deference to their child rearing obligations. No more all-nighters. No more whitewater rafting when one is accountable to and for a child. As one former sportswoman revealed, "I have a very different attitude about myself. Before I had two kids, I thought that what I did with my life was pretty much my own business. If I wanted to go skiing and break my leg, well, it was my life. But now I have to think of my life as important to someone else. It just isn't mine anymore."

Another woman who is self-employed explains that she is now fanatical about taking care of herself, and about staying away from people who may be sick. "Before, if I got sick one day, I was just out one day's pay. But now if I get sick, it's double jeopardy. Not only do I lose a day's pay—and I need the money more—but what if the baby catches it from me? Then I have to stay home twice as much.''

Sometimes the lessons were unexpected. For every woman who learned to be patient, steady, calm (or discovered that she already was that way), there was another who found out that she was emotional and volatile. A thirty-eight-year-old foster mother who adopted two children suggests, ''Be prepared for the possibility you will discover you're not the person you thought you were. I thought I was placid and easygoing. But I find I'm very authoritarian, dictatorial. And I can yell. And I don't always like the thoughts going on inside me—unexpected emotions like anger, guilt, frustration, resentment, and fury. But then I also hadn't known I could be so loving and caring, that I could form such emotional bonds. You may not necessarily like who you turn out to be, but it's worthwhile.''

And for these women—again, many of whom were so independent and self-reliant—finding out that they are capable of commitment, of giving and loving, was itself a delightful bonus.

It's worth noting here that some of the women we talked to while they were pregnant anticipated few changes in their lives. They didn't expect a baby to change them or their relationships with others. At the same time, we listened to other mothers tell us how undone they were by the enormity of unpredicted, unanticipated changes. If they had thought a baby would only slow them down for a couple of months before they resumed active, busy professional and social lives, they encountered a lot of shocks.

Yet it may be possible to overstate the changes a child brings to one's life. A baby certainly doesn't solve one's problems. Sara Destry commented, ''If you were lonely before, you're going to be lonely afterward. And if you didn't like yourself before, you're going to hate yourself afterward. Then that baby's going to be just another entity that you can stab yourself in the heart with.'' Other single mothers concur. Motherhood is not a cure-all for problems at work, with others, in oneself. Indeed, it will more than likely exacerbate them.

DATING

Nearly all single mothers find that their choice of life-style affects their pattern of dating—their ability to make time for dating, their interest in dating, their image of the appropriate date. Certainly their socializing loses several degrees of spontaneity. "Has my social life been affected?" asks one mother rhetorically. "What social life?" she answers with a laugh.

The fact that they are single mothers, however, does not limit their attractiveness to men, does not affect their ability to "get" dates. Several tell us that their status is advantageous. One woman claims, "My daughter has been an asset to dating—she's very cute and men are drawn to her."

Some women mentioned that divorced fathers may be particularly attracted to women with children, although Kara Maver twice ended relationships with divorced men because they complained that she didn't spend enough time with them. "You'd think men who have had children would understand what it's like to have children, but it apparently doesn't make any difference at all."

When we talked to them, a few women were dating men whom they had met through their children. One woman was living with a man whose child attended the same day-care center as hers; the children loved having "siblings," and Mother and Father enjoyed the arrangement!

Only one woman told us that being a single mother was injurious in this sense—not because the man held it against her but because his "hoity-toity" parents and friends disapproved of her and thought something was wrong with her. Another woman implied that men would be put off by her toddler. "No more free dinners for me, because no one wants to take me out with that baby hollering and screaming," she said. And indeed she had not dated in several years. But this probably has less to do with the presence of her child than it has to do with her general negativism or, at best, ambivalence about her status as a single mother.

If there is a problem in dating for single mothers, it's the relationships that the children forge (or attempt to forge) with the dates. Some mothers are uncomfortable with the fact that their children so easily "take" to a male who is not the biological father. Those women who continue to long for more active involvement by the biological father especially resent the easy banter and play their children direct to their mother's lovers. Even some of the single mothers who eventually married found themselves at first ambivalent when their husbands acted like—and were regarded as—fathers. But they concede that this is precisely what's good for the children. One mother didn't want her boyfriends to meet her daughter, she says, because she thought *they* might resent not being her biological father.

On the other hand, single mothers also worry about the consequences—especially for older children—of breaking up with a man. This can be especially traumatic for children, who may be disappointed for their mother's sake (perhaps they hope she will get married after all) or for their own sakes (they enjoy having that adult friend and become attached). Judith Lawrence reflects: "I think it was hard for Ethan because some of the men who came into my life also liked him and spent time with him. When they were out of my life, they were also out of his. I think that was sad for him, and I don't like that. But that's the way it went."

So while some mothers do not take great pains to protect their children from this trauma (one woman lived with four different men in six years, with no apparent detrimental effect on her daughter), others, like many divorced and widowed mothers, are reluctant to introduce their children to a date or a lover until it is "very serious."

And, of course, some women eventually married. One single mother married her five-year-old son's biological father; the wedding announcement read, "Adam Handel is proud to announce the marriage of his parents."

More often, however, those who married did not marry the child's biological father. Doris Barns, for example, met her husband during a European vacation. Her one-year-old son, Nicky, was not along, but immediately after meeting Alan, Doris showed him pictures of her son. She now claims, "Even Alan says he probably wouldn't have married me if I hadn't had Nicky, because I would have been a different kind of person. To Alan I was different. Motherhood made me more responsible, more of a challenge, made me look for better things. I was less flighty. And I don't think I would have appealed to him as much during that trip otherwise. He really loves children. He liked it that I showed him Nicky's picture and told him how much I missed Nicky.''

Motherhood also changed women's standards and expectations for men and dating. Victoria stated a preference for casual, brief relationships with men after her baby was born. She says she did not want to be touched emotionally by anyone but the baby, partly because she was so wholly invested in the baby and partly because of lingering bitterness and resentment toward her daughter's father. But she is the exception rather than the rule. Most women who dated found that they were quite choosy about what they did and with whom; they became ''very picky.'' They broke off with men when they didn't like the way these men behaved with their children or they didn't like the way their relationship with the man was affecting them. One woman, for example, lived with an alcoholic for six months before she realized that she was becoming abusive to her child because of the troubled relationship with the man. Once she and her son moved out, she never hit the boy again.

And women who at least considered the possibility of eventually marrying stressed that they would never get involved with a man who didn't relate well to children, who wasn't supportive, who wouldn't share equally in domestic and child rearing obligations, and so forth. If nothing else, they learned some of what they needed and wanted in and from a man.

AND NOT DATING

For many women, the shift to qualitatively different dating also led to quantitatively less dating. A psychologist and adoptive mother of two explains that ''In the first place, time took on a different meaning to me. When I was 'single,' I would go out a lot. If it didn't turn out to be a nice evening, it didn't matter; it was just one night. But now if I'm going to leave the kids, I must be going someplace where I know I'm going to have a good time. I'm not going to be away from something precious in order to do something that may not be really enjoyable. So I have a different attitude about time and how to fill it.''

Anita Lewis echoed this, noting that ''some boring date seems so much less important and less satisfying when you have a child at home.'' An adoptive working mother, Anita had been warned by her social worker that she should get outside stimulation and relaxation, that she should get relief from the home and baby on a regular basis. That sounds logical, but it's not, according to Anita. ''Instinct won't let you turn around and leave the baby at night when you've been away at work all day. It's not good for the baby, and it's not good for you.''

Carol Mead, seven months pregnant, agreed, predicting, ''This kid is very important in my life and she's going to know that she comes first with me. Everything else is second. I can't see dumping her every weekend to go out. I can't see bringing guys home and telling her to get out.''

Other women had different reasons for not dating for a while. For some it was not so much that they were self-consciously building in a period for bonding but that they found that their sexual interests and energies had been transformed into maternal energy. Carolyn Norton explains, ''I stopped missing men. A mother is touching all the time—the whole thing is full of affection. I don't think I'd feel anything sexual for a man. I bet married new mothers have a hard time with that, too.''

Others preferred to be alone when they were not with the children. Pam Wood is emphatic on this point. ''One night when a friend took the baby, I did a jigsaw puzzle, and afterward I realized that this was the first time I had been alone with myself. And that was more important than having someone hug me or touch me. Having those moments to be by myself was far more important than going out. I couldn't have cared less about dating. Whenever my mother watched the baby, I would rather do laundry and be entirely alone than go out on some stupid date and have to socialize.''

Of course, many women went through a period when they would have liked to date but couldn't because they were ''too damn tired,'' had no money, or couldn't find a baby sitter. Some harbored more resentment about incursions into their previously active social lives than others. The pattern is consistent: women who chose to have children at a point when they had done the things they wanted to do—travel, adventure, dating—either did not particularly want to date a lot, or they wanted to and managed to do so.

But women who were less prepared, who made a premature decision, were less pleased about closeting themselves with a screaming baby. They missed dating, weekends away, theater and ballet, discotheques, and after-work socializing. They also perceived themselves as less able (or perhaps wholly unable) to enjoy these activities. Some of the women who weren't ''ready'' for motherhood found themselves financially strapped, so they really couldn't afford to go out. Alternatively, their general ambivalence and self-pity pushed them into a downward spiral of feeling resentful, overwhelmed, lonely, tired, trapped. They felt flabby and dowdy. They felt it was too much trouble to find a friend to babysit, to carry the baby and diaper bag and infant seat to the car, get a parking space, drop off the baby and paraphernalia, and then go out for the evening; so instead they decided to stay home and feel sorry for themselves. Their resentment grew to include their single friends and the father.

Yet these women who perceived themselves as ''stranded'' usually could cheer themselves with the notion that the situation was a temporary, if necessary, stage. And meanwhile, they do try to remind themselves that it is not the child's fault.

The only people we met who did not foresee some relief were two lesbian mothers. One lives in fear that if someone finds out she is gay, her child will be snatched away. Thus, she finds it difficult to enjoy a social life, but she also feels constrained when she does socialize. ''I can't hug or hold hands in public. I can't discuss my social life with anyone. It's too dangerous. What if the court removes my children?'' And another gay woman fears that if the biological father—a man with whom she had a one-night stand—ever finds out that she is having an affair with a woman, he will try to get custody of the child.

GENERAL SOCIAL LIFE

Outside of dating, nearly all single mothers note that relationships with old friends change perceptibly. They find themselves in altogether different circles, in different networks, as do married mothers. That relationships with women friends should change (*deteriorate* is more to the point), more than their ability to date men, only seems ironic; a closer look reveals just how unsurprising a development it is.

First, the single mothers we talked to expected their women friends to stick by them, while they did *not* expect to be able to meet men. Their expectations dashed, the mothers are more conscious of and more bitter about the "desertion" by women friends.

Second, mothers—perhaps anticipating more support, interest, and empathy from women friends—often took their children along when they were going out with women friends or attending a meeting. (For a date they might hire a baby-sitter.) But friends—that is, single, childless friends—were not necessarily enamored of sticky-fingered toddlers or crying babies and apparently did not welcome their presence. Or as one single mother sighed, "You find out who your friends really are."

Some mothers made the choice to withdraw from former social circles. A few didn't want their friends to see them as mothers, wrapped up in diapering and playing dress-up. A graduate student reports that she dropped out of school for one semester when her child was two; she simply didn't want her professional peers to see her involved in potty training and fingerpainting. Others didn't see themselves as having much in common with single friends who were still involved in the "dating scene." Still others didn't have much time; spare moments were reserved for sleeping or being alone. "A lot of friends wanted to come by for a visit, after work, or on weekends. But either little Ben was awake, and I wanted to play with him; or he was asleep, in which case I would rather be dozing off myself, or reading, or doing just nothing at all," said one.

More often, however, the mothers blamed the friends. Judith Lawrence recalled, "Some of my friends disappeared. I got criticized because when friends came over I would ask them to hold the baby while I took a shower or fixed lunch. So they felt like they were baby-sitting whenever they came over for a visit. There were a lot of women who didn't want to have anything to do with children and felt that that was their option. And there was this attitude that my life should be the same, that nothing should change because of this child, that I shouldn't change the amount of time and energy I put into my friendships."

It is hardly surprising, then, that single mothers develop new interests and find new friends—usually other mothers, married or single—whom they meet at such places as support groups and day-care centers. (Again, this parallels the experience of married mothers.) As their priorities and values shift, so do their friends. They feel more comfortable in these new circles, feel their needs are more effectively met. They feel understood and liked.

Even single mothers who are very involved in the women's movement and in other political-social causes found themselves in less than empathetic company. One active feminist dragged her baby to meetings while she was still nursing. "And people tolerated me at first," she says. "But it was very hard to participate in meetings. Nobody could understand why. People would get angry with me and I would think, Well, what am I doing here? What I really need is a rap group because I'm going crazy with this baby."

Another feminist adds that part of the problem can be traced to the unrealistic theories about children circulating through the feminist movement. Her own political group tried to encourage mothers to stay involved by organizing rotating child care. Everyone signed up for fifteen minutes; every fifteen minutes the children would get another adult supervisor! Says Irene, "That's just crazy. I would never put my kid in a situation like that."

Of course, not all mothers experienced the same degree of deterioration in their friendships. One woman told us that she has dozens of childless friends who baby-sit for her and visit her and her child. "They feel they were part of the process. They were all so excited for me, and they all baby-sit for me when I need them. They all vicariously had this child with me."

Another woman notes that although some friends disappeared after her baby was born (including a very close friend who had had several abortions), she saw much more of other people. "I don't entirely understand why, but although I didn't want to continue certain close relationships, I saw other people in a completely different light. Things shifted. Some people that I had known for a long time and who had faded out of my life came back with a lot of strength. There was one couple whom I had seen only in their work role. But they see themselves very strongly in their parenting role. So when I became a mother, they were so interested in the baby. They invited me to their house and gave us gifts. Our friendship was sort of rejuvenated."

And one politically active woman told us that her baby had not diminished her political involvement but enhanced it. "There's a lot of good work to do right in this neighborhood: work with the schools and church, work against the gangs. If you're not a parent, you don't make sense to people. Like 'Why should you care about this school?' or 'What does this community mean to you?' But a parent, whether she's married, divorced, or never married, has a stake. You can get involved in real grass-roots projects that make a difference."

PROFESSIONAL LIFE

Child rearing responsibilities affect mothers' work lives in various ways, as we would expect. It can be a worrisome issue, for women for whom a job is necessary (what if they get sick? what if they lose their jobs?) and for highly professional women accustomed to defining themselves in terms of their work. Said one government administrator, "I am a very capable professional woman, and a lot of my identity and self-esteem is wrapped up in my accomplishments and success in work. So now I have some anxiety that whereas my son is a great bonus personally, he's a handicap professionally. Can I still produce? Am I still going to be successful? Can I still be the best?"

They all agree, however, that "you can't be married to your job—you can't be a workaholic—when you have kids on your own." Ironically, perhaps, some of the women who were most "professionally oriented" found this to be a godsend. They were relieved that motherhood helped them put their work into perspective. As one school psychologist put it, "If it hadn't been for my son, I would have continued being a very single-minded, career-oriented woman. I'm still concerned about my career, but it's no longer *all* my life. It's nowhere near the percentage of my life that it was before." Another woman, a teacher, explains, "You find that you have to let your career take a back seat and you find that you want to. You find a whole new side to yourself."

The flip side is represented by Laura Burton, who owned her own bar and restaurant before getting into personnel work at a large corporation. Laura agrees that she would have been more "driven" if not for her son Michael. She would have worked longer hours, traveled more. On the other hand, she says, "Work would have less meaning if it weren't for Michael. His existence has a lot to do with how good I feel about work. Having him gives all my life another level of meaning."

One bank administrator was perhaps less pleased with the shift in priorities; but she saw it as temporarily necessary, after years of putting her job before all else, of making sacrifices for her career. "So now these things are taking a back seat," she said, using the same metaphor as women who were more appreciative of this. "I think I've got enough points at work that I can afford to rest on my laurels, or coast, or even slighty abuse my employment. As soon as he's older, I think I'll have available more personal energy and focus to go back to that, but for the time being I feel OK about the change."

This thirty-six-year-old banker adds that ten years ago, when she was still struggling up the ladder, she would not have felt so secure. "When I was still establishing myself, it would have been too painful for me, too difficult to trade off the blood and guts of career advancement for personal goals. But now I feel I owe it to myself. I've paid my dues."

Several other women also felt that motherhood inevitably demanded a more relaxed attitude about work, such that they were no longer the "best" stockbroker or the "best" C.P.A. Something had to give, and very often what gave was the job, although some employers specifically cautioned single mothers not to expect to slough off responsibilities or to expect apologies to be made on their behalf. Perhaps it is not surprising that the women most comfortable with this changed attitude were the ones most comfortable with their jobs in the first place. Frequently, the whole arrangement worked because the women were well established in their careers.

Yet, depending on the job, for some women it was not so much a more relaxed attitude about work as an adjustment in the kind of work they did. A few women found they couldn't manage the inflexibility or long hours or aggressive competitiveness of their old jobs. But they could do something else. Dorothy Wold returned to graduate school so she could get into school psychology and out of social work. It also put her on the same schedule as her son. "I wanted a job where emotionally I didn't have to put out so much and where physically I'd be available more. Down the road I didn't want to have to look at my son and say, 'Because I've been working my buns off, I don't even know you.' "

Others found, as have some married working mothers, that they couldn't do the same sort of "thinking." One poet told us she could no longer write after her baby was born. But she could do readings—and that was something. "I thought I'd have to give up my professional life for a long while, until Kala was in first grade or so. But as it turned out, I discovered adjustments can be made. It can be worked out—I can have Kala and she can be well on her way, and I can also make progress in my career. This summer she's going to her grandmother's for a visit, and I think that while she's gone I'll be able to do a lot of writing again. And I just got a tremendous lift: somebody asked me to do a reading. I said to myself, 'See, I have a baby and people still want me to come and read my poems.' "

For another category of single mothers, motherhood offered a sort of solace, a haven from a job they disliked. While some women felt trapped in their jobs, felt they *had* to stick with a miserable job because they needed the income, others *could* stick with the job because it was no longer their whole life. One adoptive mother remarked, "Having the child enabled me to stay with a job that was becoming progressively more miserable. I was able to tolerate it because when I came home, I had something else to think about, and I could forget about the job. That helped me last longer—while I was shopping around for alternatives." These women agree that having children doesn't solve the problem of a bad job any more than it solves other problems, but it may ease the pain until Mother comes up with something better.

Clearly, the fact that children are at home—or at the sitter's—constrains mothers in particular ways, especially since no other parent is there to provide parenting. The single mother cannot travel or work overtime very much—at least not easily. But the working mothers we interviewed worked it out. Several were in a position to refuse overtime or out-of-town travel. A doctor, for example, had the responsibility for making out the call schedule, so she arranged it for her convenience and for that of her sitter. Others situated themselves near helpful relatives or with helpful housemates who were available evenings and weekends. Still others found work where this was not an issue.

Even in the best of circumstances, constraints aside, managing work and motherhood can be difficult. There is the nagging guilt about leaving the child with a sitter (if a reliable one can be found), which may compound lingering doubt about the rightness of one's decision to parent alone. And even those working mothers who manage to throw off the sense of guilt must still contend with the problem of finding time to be with the child. Working mothers who commute (particularly those with toddlers) are especially upset about the few hours they can spend with their children during the week.

We found that most women managed to continue working after the arrival of their children. No one—neither stockbroker nor machinist nor doctor nor bus driver—*had* to quit. The motivations varied, of course. Some worked because they depended on the income and were unwilling to go on welfare; others, because they were just plain committed to their professions. The only thing that few of them managed to do was work at home (although some tried this for the first couple of months or so) or bring the baby to work. A college administrator tried unsuccessfully to avoid the high costs of day care by bringing her daughter to work. Her colleagues were supportive and tolerant, but all Ann could do (indeed, all she wanted to do then) was play with the baby.

Many women were glad to have the escape hatch of work. They would have "gone nuts" if they had stayed home all day with a child. Laura Burton says simply, "Work kept me sane. During those three months when I was home twenty-four hours a day with the baby, I thought I was going crazy." One woman who returned to her hospital job when her baby was six weeks old doesn't mind admitting that she grew antsy after four weeks. "The last two weeks I almost went out of my gourd. I really loved breast-feeding, but those tiny babies can be boring." Other women argue that working provided an opportunity to think and talk about matters and things outside motherhood; otherwise they were "totally engulfed." Said Judith Lawrence, "It was like the baby swallowed me up. Working rejuvenated me, gave me back my sense of self. I could function better at the emotional level when I started back to work."

Several women reasoned that working was good for mother *and* child: they were less isolated, less exclusively dependent on one another. Dorothy Wold suggests: "It would be a terrible trap for both of us if I were around all day long, all evening, and had minimal outside interests. As it is, he likes having me to himself. I can watch his nose get out of joint already when I go out on a casual date, so I know we would have been in trouble if he hadn't gotten used to my going out to work.''

And as we noted in Chapter 8, there are day-care centers to provide children with wider social contact and experience than they find at home. A woman who has left her daughter in a day-care home for forty hours a week since the child was six weeks old says, "At home she has only me, and that's fine because we're very close. But at day care she has other children to play with and a second adult, Madge, who she knows loves and takes care of her and whom she can depend on.''

THE QUESTION OF SACRIFICES

Many mothers don't want their children to feel that they made great sacrifices for them. Nor do they want their children to feel guilty about altering their mothers' personal, social, and professional lives.

A few mothers don't believe that they made such great sacrifices. Predictably, they are the older, financially stable mothers, such as the East Coast doctor who said, "I think what is important here is that I did all that I wanted to do. I got all that adolescent business that I needed to do out of the way. I dated around and all that; I even was married—and divorced—a long time ago. I am totally settled now in my career. I will never feel like there are still some things I haven't done and think, You ungrateful little wretch, look what I'm sacrificing for you. That would be an awfully heavy thing for a child to carry. But I don't feel that way and that's why I love it.''

It's not always that easy. Many single mothers are only too well aware of the costs of their courses of action. They've compromised, adapted, reoriented, changed—often more than they anticipated. And because they are the lone parent, it stands to reason that they give up more than most traditional mothers.

We believe that it's worth pointing out the way single motherhood changes women's self-definition and self-concept, their ability to (or interest in) work and play, to dramatize the enormity of these changes.

But we also point this out to demonstrate that these mothers—whatever their motivation for having children, whatever the circumstances of motherhood—don't treat their children as playthings to be cast aside when something better comes along. They put their children first, before and above all else.

Of course, sometimes they are frustrated, impatient, disgusted, overwhelmed. They want time away from their children; they need time away. A mother who had always enjoyed hiking in the woods alone recalled, "Once my mother took care of Timmy, and I went camping for a couple of days. It was like heaven; it really was. I didn't miss him. I was happy I wasn't with him. I didn't want to go back. It was so wonderful. And I remembered how nice it was not having any responsibilities." But she quickly adds that while no Timmy for a few days was heaven, no Timmy at all would leave her life hollow. "I love him more than anything, but I'm no different from a married parent. I needed a break."

Single mothers get burned out and need time alone, as do married mothers. And like married mothers, single mothers love their children, want the best for their children, and put their children's needs ahead of their own.

CHAPTER
10
AN
EVALUATION

In the preceding chapters we've described the various stages and effects of single parenting. Now we turn to an evaluation of single parenting as a family style—for whom and under what circumstances single parenting works best; when conceiving a child with the intention of remaining single is fair to the biological father; and whether having a child by birth or adoption as a single person is fair to the child.

Overall, the mothers' personal evaluations were positive. Few of the women we talked to would dissuade others from becoming single parents. Nearly a third said they would neither encourage nor discourage other women from following their path, claiming that the decision is a very individual and personal one.

Roughly a half dozen, who also refrained from offering advice, thought they might have made the wrong decision for themselves at the time or under the circumstances.

Almost two-thirds of the women said they would recommend single parenting. A few gave a blanket recommendation: "If you want to have a baby, have a baby." Most gave conditional recommendations: "If you are a certain kind of person, and you are in the right position, and you can't or don't want to wait for marriage, then do it on your own.''

Only two women had unwaveringly negative advice: "Don't do it. No matter who you are or what you think, don't do it.''

Generally speaking, many were extremely happy, many experienced some combination of joy and burden, and very few were overwhelmed and miserable. Our observations lead us to conclude that for most of these women single parenting is a viable option. But based on our analysis and the women's comments, we've identified a series of characteristics that help determine whether single parenting will be wonderful or woeful.

DO IT IF . . .
OR DON'T DO IT UNLESS . . .

The responses to this question varied, no doubt reflecting the women's particular needs and circumstances. Our analysis suggests, however, that the vital ingredients for successful single parenting are financial security and social supports.

FINANCIAL AND
SOCIAL RESOURCES

Financial security has several components: a reasonable and rising income from a steady job with potential for advancement, solid health insurance benefits, and enough savings to extend a maternity leave and cover other emergencies.

Woman after woman commented on how expensive raising children is. A good deal of strain is removed when one can afford sitters or housekeepers and when one has enough of an economic cushion to not worry about sickness, emergencies, or "little extras.'' Several birth mothers were shocked by $4,000 hospital bills or surprised that they wanted to stay home with their new baby for months instead of weeks. Mothers with older children thought about paying for camps and lessons and sports equipment and college.

Many women see economics as *the* key to parenting alone. The mother of a three-year-old told us, ''If I hadn't had financial circumstances in my favor, I would have been more inclined to have an abortion.'' And the mother of a five-year-old said, "For the sake of the kid and the sake of the mother, don't consider doing this if you're not in an excellent economic situation.''

Even those who do not feel financial security is the key, acknowledge that it is highly desirable. Says one business executive, "You can probably manage on less than I make, but God knows it helps to have enough money.'' And one woman who had been on welfare when her son was an infant offers: "It's been much more fun and much easier since we've had some money.''

Also essential to a satisfying single-parent life is support from close friends and family. One aspect of support systems is physical help. Comments one woman, "I would only recommend single parenting to a woman who has a lot of really caring friends who are actually willing to commit time to help her out. And I don't mean coming over and playing aunty. I mean shit work— taking care of the child so the woman can take a shower, go grocery shopping, do something besides be a mother. You need a lot of people to fall back on if you get sick, if you want to go away for a weekend, if you're going crazy and can't take it for another minute.''

For these needs, support systems are interchangeable with financial resources: money can buy the help that friends and family offer for free. Indeed, the need for support systems was most heavily emphasized by women with limited finances and least emphasized by women with more discretionary income. As a doctor put it, "Money has made it easier, but I realize I could do it with less money and more leaning on my friends.''

Support systems offer more than physical relief. An adoptive mother of two told us, "You need a support system—friends who will listen to you when you're pulling your hair out and crying, friends who won't mind your calling at ten o'clock and talking nonstop for two hours about what this child's done that's made you think you're insane.''

Support systems are beneficial to the child too. As one mother claimed, "You cannot do it alone. You need either family or friends or preferably both who can help you and can love your child. You need breaks, and the child needs other adults to relate to and to depend on." Other pluses for the child are the alternative viewpoints and attachments. Says one woman, "No matter how much you have to give, a child needs other important people around. Children need consistency, yes, but they also need variety and they need to know their world has more than one adult who loves them."

MOTIVATION

Of the personal characteristics, motivation is probably most important. The desire to have a child must spring from healthy sources—healthy not in a physical sense but in a psychological sense. A woman must feel good about herself, satisfied with her life and her relationships, loved and valued and happy. She should not want a child in order to make her happy or keep her company or bring her love or give her life instant meaning or purpose. These basic emotional needs should have been met. She should be ready to share herself with a child and should really want to be a mother because she wants to bring a child into the world to care for and nurture and raise to be a responsible adult.

Several of the women raised this issue. Dorothy Wold told us, "The parent has to be emotionally healthy and not be having a child for crazy wrong reasons like looking for something that's going to fill a life that's otherwise empty, or wanting to be loved and needed. You have to be your own person first. You have to be happy with your life and want to make an addition to it rather than looking for something to make your life worthwhile."

Having a child doesn't change how a woman feels about herself; it amplifies it. If she is happy before she has a child, she will be happy after she has one, possibly more so. If she is depressed before, she'll be depressed afterward and possibly downright miserable. And then the child will suffer.

Women who enter motherhood with unmet personal needs for love, companionship, worth, and accomplishment find child rearing a sacrifice. They feel they give and give and don't get enough in return, and some resent the fact that the child's needs always come first. In contrast, mothers who feel they have done what they want to do, whose friends and career give them a sense of worth in an adult world, say motherhood does not require sacrificing. It is not draining but enriching.

While many women add that looking for fulfillment would be the wrong reason for a married person to have a child, too, one mother notes that having a child as a "substitute for other things in your life" is more detrimental for single than for married parenting. "Of course, you can find married people who try to fill their lives by having a child. But with two parents, if one is emotionally needy, they might balance each other or dilute the messages they give the kid. With a single parent, you are all of it. No one is going to dilute or counter what you do. So it's especially important that single parents have met their basic needs in normal adult ways and not lay any inappropriate expectations or needs or guilts on a kid."

The second element of motivation is one of degree. One should not only want a child for the "right" reasons, one should also want a child intensely. This issue is often raised by adoptive mothers; adoption takes so long and is so frustrating that a woman must be highly motivated to stick it out. She has to "really, really" want a child. This may be one reason why there were no adoptive mothers of the women we interviewed who thought that they had made the wrong decision, compared to about one in eight of the birth mothers. The adoption process weeds out all but the most strongly motivated women; the birth process does not. Unlike adoption, in the birth process there is no connection between degree of motivation and the end result. Women can decide to get pregnant or they can decide not to abort when they are uncertain about wanting a child but fear missing out on the chance or when they want a child but are not realistic about what that means. Women who are not strongly motivated or who do not approach realistically the question of having a child are more likely to be surprised by the amount of time, energy, and commitment child rearing requires and to find the demands and stresses of motherhood overwhelming.

One woman who had been uncertain about whether she was ready to get pregnant and who had had little notion of what motherhood would involve told us, "Before, I used to think that it was better to do it this way than to miss the chance of having a child, but now I think women should only do it if they're certain having a child is worth giving up everything else. If you have the least bit of question about whether you want to devote your life to a kid, the least bit of worry about cutting back on your independence or your travel or your career or your dating, don't do it. I've always been antiabortion at a gut level, but it's definitely worth giving a lot of consideration to if you're not absolutely positively certain that you want to be a single mother."

ATTITUDE TOWARD
PARENTING ALONE

In order to be a good single parent, one must feel positive about doing it alone. That doesn't necessarily mean being philosophically opposed to marriage or anti-male, but instead satisfied with being single and prepared to raise a child alone, and not really wishing for marriage. One woman put it this way: "There are some women who shouldn't have a child alone. Women who need to have a man around, who are happiest when they feel appreciated by a man, who feel more complete, more whole, happier in a partnership, who always wanted to be married—these women should not do it." Another said, "If your definition of what you want is a nuclear family and a partner, then know that in yourself. There's a lot to be said for husbands and fathers, and if that's what you want, hold out for marriage. You'll be happier and so will your child."

For biological mothers, parenting alone means not counting on the father to be involved. Women who long for the father's participation are not only very lonely during pregnancy, they are prone to sadness or bitterness about that person's absence, about not having someone with whom to share the joys and pains of child rearing. They are also the most likely to feel deserted. And these feelings do not ebb with the birth of the child but may linger for years.

Our observations move us to conclude that if a woman wants a man to co-parent, she should get married (or at least be entrenched in a long-term, living-together relationship). While husbands may not always be as active as mothers in parenting, at least they are *there*. As such they are more likely to be involved with their child and more likely to contribute emotional and financial support than biological fathers in non-married situations.

Surely the idea of sharing a child is pleasing. It is not, however, a given, especially in the situations under consideration here. As a single mother pushes toward this goal, the biological father may pull away. Such a situation may yield nothing, then, but a well of disappointment and bitterness for the mother.

Finally, being satisfied with parenting alone means genuinely feeling that bearing a child or adopting a child as a single woman is both socially and morally acceptable. Other people's views of whether single parenting is moral or immoral, or whether it's reason for pride or shame, are not relevant. The woman's own feelings are what count. Her moral evaluation will influence that of the people around her and will largely determine whether she receives support or ostracism.

If a woman feels confident in and pleased with her choice, she is bound to receive positive responses. On the other hand, if she feels her single status will injure a child, if she feels guilty, if she questions the rightness of her choice, she will undoubtedly communicate this, and the responses may not be favorable.

Says a woman who received a great deal of support from her friends and colleagues, "If you're positive and you're happy and you're thrilled to death, that's how people feed it back to you." A woman who thought having a child outside marriage was immoral—as was abortion—confided, "You're so isolated. The social stigma of an unwed pregnancy cuts you off from supports among friends and family." It would seem a self-fulfilling prophecy.

Along with communicating her positive or negative feelings to her peers, it is likely the mother would communicate these feelings to her child (although we've no hard evidence of this).

The child who senses that Mother is happy and pleased with her status would be more likely to have a strong self-image, whereas the child who senses that Mother is ashamed would be more likely to feel stigmatized and deprived.

YOU'D BETTER HAVE . . .

Self-confidence, self-acceptance, and flexibility, all in good measure, figure prominently in the makeup of the successful single mother.

The most frequently mentioned was self-confidence. As a single parent, a woman must be able to make decisions on her own and know that she can meet both her needs and her child's. Someone who is insecure, who agonizes over whether she's doing the right thing, who doesn't trust her own judgment, will have a difficult time of it.

Yet as women point to the need for independence and self-reliance, they note that one also must be able to recognize those times when help is needed and be able to ask for it. Mothers need breaks and sounding boards, and children need other adult influences. Isolation is dangerous for both.

With self-confidence must come self-acceptance and realistic expectations for self and child. As the mother of two small girls put it, "It's OK to be tired and irritable. People don't say that, but it's OK. Sometimes I yell and sometimes I put them in their room and admit that I need time out. Nobody's perfect all the time. There's no such thing as the perfect parent, and there's no such thing as the perfect child. You have to learn to read the signs that you need time away, that you need time alone, or that you need someone else to intervene."

A third trait is suggested by a psychologist who, within a year of adopting her daughter, collected the telephone numbers of one hundred baby-sitters—most of whom couldn't come. "You darn well better be flexible. You can't be the kind of person who has to have everything in place, who has to depend on her schedule, who would get angry or frustrated if the sitter quit or if the kid got sick, or something totally unexpected happens. It doesn't mean you have to know in advance how you're going to cope; you simply have to know that you can. And if you're pretty set, you probably shouldn't have kids. Kids are a disruption—but that's true whether you're married or single. You have to be able to flow with it.''

WHEN IT WORKED AND
WHEN IT DIDN'T

The presence or absence of these characteristics affects the mother's experience and the type of home environment she offers the child. The following cases are instructive.

Raya Moss was thirty-nine when she began the adoption process. A clinical psychologist and university teacher, Raya couldn't have been in a better situation to have a child on her own. She had recently gotten tenure at her university, and her part-time clinical practice was steady, so she had additional income. The combination of university teaching and private practice gave her financial security and more time flexibility than most jobs. In addition, Raya had several very close friends who had children, and her father lived nearby—a real plus. "He's too old to baby-sit, but I knew he'd be delighted to play with a grandchild.''

Raya had always wanted to have a child but waited until she not only had the external resources but had met her own needs. "I had a period in my life where I could do anything I wanted— take off a year to write, pick up and go on vacations, date lots of men. I wasn't ready to be committed to other responsibilities and other relationships until I had that for myself. I realized that in having children I was choosing to give that up for more important things. I was ready for children. It was going to be an enrichment for me. In some sense it was selfish, but I think in an acceptable way. I was ready, I wanted a child, and I knew I had a great deal of love to give.''

Raya says she thought marriage would be nice, but she enjoyed her life as a single person and felt no great drive to find a husband. She liked dating, but her emotional mainstays were her friends and family. "The right man would be great, but life was fine as is."

Raya's choice of adoption was based more on age than on social or moral reasons. She did not want to take the risk of a first pregnancy at forty. She wanted at least two children. She did, however, weigh the rightness of taking a child who would otherwise be placed in a two-parent home. "I recognized that if I didn't take the child, it could have been in a two-parent family. I had to feel that I could at least provide that child with some of the equivalencies, so the child wouldn't suffer as a result of having been placed with me. I knew if I got a child, it would not be economically deprived, and I knew there would be a close relationship with my father. So I thought I could offer as good a home as a two-parent family."

Raya's confidence and realistic attitude were noticeable. "I'm used to making decisions. It's interesting, I had much more concern about handling a house than I did about handling a child—and I still do. I still have fantasies that someday the house will fall down around me, but I never really had any serious questions about a child. I had experience with my friends' kids. I knew I wasn't going to be a perfect parent; I didn't expect to be. I figured everybody makes their own set of mistakes with kids and I was much more mature than the average parent. I just figured I could cope with situations as they came up."

How would Raya evaluate single parenting? "I don't think I could ever have imagined the joy. I thought I did, but it exceeded anything in my imagination. I was almost drunk that first year. I wouldn't stop smiling, and I'm sure people thought I was nuts."

Has she ever thought it might have been more enjoyable or easier with a man? "It's hard to say. I don't know if it would be any more satisfying to do it with somebody else. I must say that my level of satisfaction is so high in general that it's hard for me to imagine that I would be more satisfied.

"I've thought sometimes that it would be easier if there was someone else around. There are lots of times when I think it would be convenient, like when I have to pick one child up in one place and the other in another. And there are a lot of times when I'm paying my bills that I think it would be awfully nice to have a second income. There are times when things break down and I think it would be nice to have a handyman in the house, and sometimes when I come home and I'm tired, I think it would be nice to have dinner waiting for me. All those things would be nice, but I don't think of them as major lacks in my life.

"I made choices that I'm pleased with and I'm doing what I want to. I feel like I had options. Not only was this not something I had to do, quite the contrary; I had a lot of trouble doing it. It wasn't thrust upon me; I sought it out. That's the main difference between intentional single parents and divorced ones who are single by default. If you get married, have a child, and get divorced, it's harder. You didn't ask to be a single parent—you were stuck with it. You didn't think you were going to do it alone. You thought you would have help. And you're resentful that you don't. But that wasn't the case for me. I knew from the beginning that I would be the one to do everything and I never questioned doing it and never resented doing it. That was part of the deal. I don't feel I'm missing anything."

And are her daughters missing anything? "Yes, they're missing something, but they're very happy. We all are."

Marie Field got pregnant intentionally at age thirty-five. Like Raya, she had all the requisites. Marie had known she was going to have a baby for five years. She was "sort of setting myself up, getting myself ready." Part of her preparation was buying a condominium: two bedrooms, nice neighbors, nearby pre-schools. Her neighbors, she claims, are her main support. "It's like having two sets of grandparents, several aunts and uncles, and three cousins in the building."

As a pediatric nurse in a private clinic, Marie had both a stable job and a good salary. She felt good about her career, her home, her friends, her life. It was time to add a child.

Marie describes herself as "content to be single." She had been married in her twenties and had no need to do it again. Of her ex-husband she says, "He's a lovely man and we're still friends. Our interests and values are just too different for us to live together." But while she couldn't be married to him, he would be the perfect person to have a child with. "In fact, he volunteered. I told him I'd been thinking about having a child and he offered. He hadn't remarried either, and he didn't think he ever would. He has no desire to be a real father but is pleased to have pictures and a call now and then."

He even offered to remarry Marie, but she said no. "If we got married, it would just complicate our lives. People don't look askance at single mothers anymore, and I don't think my daughter will ever suffer because her father and I didn't marry. I'm doing fine on my own. I can handle the decisions and the scheduling and the expenses. I think one good strong loving parent is basically what a kid needs. She'll know who her father is and perhaps visit him when she's older. He even said he'd like that."

Marie's confidence extends to her feelings about child rearing. "Ever since I've been working with children, I haven't had any doubts about my ability to cope with a kid. I've occasionally had a fear of my temper, but there's help available. I have baby-sitters and I have the people in the building. If I'm by myself and I have the flu and this kid hasn't shut up for three nights in a row, I'm not afraid to ask for help. I don't have to be a supermom just because I'm single. I can be an ordinary mom. It's not a shame for me to say, 'Look, I can't handle her anymore; would you take her?' And there are folks who will."

Marie's response to single parenting? "I love it. It's unbelievable. I thought I really wanted a child and this was going to be so wonderful, and what happened was it was even *more* wonderful than I had anticipated."

Does she wish she had a husband to help? "I don't think it's that hard. If I got married, that would be a bonus. That would be neat and nice. But if I continue to raise her alone, then that is exactly what I bargained for. I went into it with my eyes open, so there's no sort of resentment. I think the fact that it was a conscious, firm decision is an advantage to me and an advantage to her. She'll never feel that she shouldn't be here.

"She's added so much to my life, and I think she's gotten a lot too. I don't see it as a hazard for her. But a lot goes into making it a good life for her, and I think it's easier when you've got things like good support systems and a job that pays well and a clear-cut relationship with the man.''

And what of the women who embarked on single parenting with fewer external and internal resources? They do get pleasure from their children and cannot imagine what life would be like without them, but some acknowledge that it was the wrong decision.

Eleanor Gates got pregnant when she was thirty-two. She was neither firm nor positive about why she wanted a child. She had not considered having a child in her twenties, but as she approached thirty she began wondering if she could get pregnant. She had her IUD removed and got pregnant. Uncertain, she had an abortion, then two years later got pregnant again.

In fact, it seems that Eleanor was more interested in getting pregnant than in having a child—an important distinction. She had "no idea what it was like to raise a child." And although she had not discussed her desire to get pregnant with her baby's father, she hoped the pregnancy would "tie us together forever."

If Eleanor's motivations were shaky, so too was her career. She describes herself as "fairly adrift in terms of my direction." She was working part time as a temporary secretary so she could devote her emotional energy to a community orchestra. She had no financial security, no savings, and when the community orchestra folded, no external source of adult contacts.

Contrary to her hopes that pregnancy would bind her lover to her, it was the impetus for their breaking up. She took it hard. "I felt abandoned and lonely and unbelievably needy. It would have been easier if I hadn't been so attached to him. It took me years to work out the anger and the hurt feelings that were involved in the pregnancy." Today she feels she was saved by "a skilled psychiatrist and friends who listened and helped."

Of single parenting Eleanor says, "It's much more work than I ever imagined. The emotional responsibility of raising a child alone is mind-boggling. It's much more of a commitment than

I ever thought possible. I somehow thought, 'Oh, children can always go to baby-sitters.' But it doesn't work out that way.''

Would it have been easier if she had been married? "I don't know if I want to be married, but I know if I had it all to do over again, I wouldn't want to do it by myself. I don't get enough for myself. Everything is focused on the child. Perhaps if I was back in the orchestra and feeling that I was doing something important, or perhaps if I had a man who made me feel beautiful and exciting—I don't know. But I do know that I need more.''

What advice would she give a single woman considering having a child? "Don't think that it's going to be easy. It's going to be your grand challenge. Know that you're never going to have another day alone. Maybe he'll go away for a night, but he'll come back home and be your responsibility. Know that for the next eighteen years you're stuck. You have all that weight on you. Know that it's just so much harder. . . .''

Dianne Judson also got pregnant intentionally. She was thirty-three. "The most pressing thing was my age. I figured if I was going to do it, I better do it now.'' She asked the man with whom she was having an affair and he agreed. Sometime after she conceived, he left. She did not want to discuss him. She would only say that the issue of his relationship with the child became "a very bitter scene.''

Dianne had been working as a waitress but went on public assistance after she gave birth in order to stay home and take care of her baby.

Like Eleanor, Dianne had little idea of what having a child entailed. She thought she would return to work immediately and bring the baby along. Life would be as it was before except that she would have a baby. She found instead that her new life was isolating, exhausting—endless devotion to "a demanding little animal.'' She couldn't get out to visit friends, let alone find a job. She "just couldn't get up the energy to do things that would make life more satisfying.''

And life *has* been unsatisfying for Dianne. She admits that, in part, her isolation is of her own making. "I know my houseboundness is probably my own fault. I tend to do things in a rigid pattern and don't search out friends to help me or to bounce ideas off of.''

Her needs are not being met. Of single parenting she says, ''You never get to do anything for yourself. The child is always saying, 'Me, me, me. I want to be played with. I want to eat. I want more attention. *I* want. *I* want. *I* want.' It's your child above everything else. And it will never end. You're never going to be able to do what you want—ever. I had no idea it would be this difficult, this time-consuming, this psychologically binding.''

Would she offer words of wisdom? "Don't do it.''

WHEN IS IT FAIR TO THE BIOLOGICAL FATHER?

His is a difficult path. His life may be enhanced, disrupted, or possibly destroyed. He may feel pleasure, confusion, or anger. To fully explore the situation for the biological father we would have to research and write another book. Therefore, we can only offer here conclusions based on the women's experiences. There are three: (1) It is better if the woman has the resources to parent alone; (2) It is better if the man agrees in advance rather than find himself an unknowing participant to conception; and (3) It is better if the woman is not in love with him and does not want him involved with her and her child's lives.

First, if the woman does not have financial security, emotional security, strong motivation, and self-confidence, the results could be as disastrous for him as they are for her. The father may face an onslaught of bitterness, resentment, unhappiness, and maybe even a paternity suit. Her actions and reactions may well surprise them both.

Second, the father should know in advance. We suggest this for both ethical and practical reasons. On the ethical side, it seems to us that in not telling a man that one is trying to get pregnant—either actively or passively (by not using birth control)—a woman denies him the right to decide for himself whether he wants to participate in conception. We assume that a woman has an absolute right to have control over her reproductive system, and we also assume a man has an absolute right to have control over *his* reproductive system. He should be able to choose to contribute to conception or to prevent it.

There is also a practical reason for the father's knowing in advance. Men who offer to participate, while not necessarily more supportive than men who do not, are less likely to get angry, to try to pressure the woman into having an abortion, and to surround the event with hostility. Pregnancy is an emotionally charged time during which a woman is very vulnerable. It's not a time for encountering rejection.

And third, because pregnancy brings with it such bared emotions, we think both man and woman are better off if, as long as she's doing it on her own, she is not intensely attached to him. Because our culture defines pregnancy as something shared, many women find they become more attached to the man after they conceive. Even the most independent woman finds she has to consciously stop herself from fantasizing about the man being part of her life. Our study has shown that most of the biological fathers do not become involved. Instead they disappear. The situation is ripe for resentment and feelings of desertion.

Considering the loneliness and unhappiness endured by those women who let themselves fantasize, who did love the father and hope for a relationship, we conclude that women are better off keeping themselves emotionally aloof from the man.

But at the same time he can't be someone she wants *nothing* to do with. By law the father can have visitation or joint custody, and by right the child should have the possibility of a relationship with the man. So his presence should not be painful to her. The balance needs to be delicate.

And where does a woman find a man who agrees to father a child but with whom there will be minimal emotional attachment? Someone she cares for but doesn't love? Former lovers who remain friends or intermittent lovers are probably best. And artificial insemination should be considered a reasonable alternative because it eliminates emotional and legal ties. Adoption sidesteps not only practical concerns about who should be the father but social concerns about bringing a child into the world without a father.

IS IT FAIR TO THE CHILD?

An adequate answer to the question of fairness to the child would require researching yet a third book. For the present book we interviewed few children, since most were under seven and therefore have yet to experience or deal with conflicts deriving from their status. Again, our opinions and conclusions are based on what the mothers told us.

Even the strongest proponent of single parenting agrees that a child is better off with *two* good, loving, caring parents. Yet having a single parent does not mean that a child will have a bad life. A bad life, the mothers feel, comes less from the absence of a second loving person than from the presence of an unloving person. Indeed, it is possible that the child of a single parent has advantages over the child of parents who are either unhappily married or unhappily divorced. A child in an unhappy home witnesses more conflict. A child in a broken home experiences more disruption and probably more guilt. And because the parents' state of mind determines how much they have to give to the child, an unhappy parent or a divorced one who is preoccupied with her own problems may offer less affection and consistency to a child.

It does not necessarily follow, however, that motherhood without marriage is as good as having a child in a happy marriage. Perhaps we could tease out how comparable the two family styles are if we look at which of the child's needs are met by a father and whether these can be met without one.

A child does need people other than the mother for love, influence, discipline, and attachment. But such needs can in large measure be supplied by adults other than a father: aunts, uncles, grandparents, friends, sitters. These important adults must, however, be consistently available, willing to make a commitment to the child, and able to demonstrate love, affection, and concern.

A child—boy or girl—needs consistent positive male figures, but again, this could be met by an uncle, grandfather, family friend, or Big Brother.

A child needs a healthy, happy, loving home environment. A single person—woman or man—can provide this if she or he is already personally fulfilled, has satisfying adult relationships and a satisfying career, is not resentful, and has access to physical and emotional supports.

A child needs to feel that he or she came from loving origins. Single parents can supply this with early, simple, satisfying explanations phrased to make the child feel loved and lovable, respected and respectable.

But even if the child of a single parent suffers no lack of love or positive male images, even if the child is not put into a position of meeting the mother's needs, even if the child feels no discomfort about its origins, something comes from a father that cannot be supplied by anyone else: the symbolic value of having a daddy like everyone else.

Ours is, after all, a two-parent culture, in spite of the rising divorce rate. All things being equal, a child is better off having a daddy, even a daddy who isn't home often, as long as he's not an abusive daddy. A minimally active daddy or a minimally present daddy is still someone to talk about and to feel part of, and therefore better than no daddy at all.

The symbolic value of a daddy is important, but we're not sure how important. We don't know enough about the children's later development to say whether the longing for a father will prevent their lives from being happy and productive. Our best guess is that if all other needs are met, including those tangible ones traditionally supplied by fathers, a child could make it and make it well with only one parent. It's not ideal, but few situations are.

If a single person can offer a child a good life—a life with lots of love and lots of stimulation, a life without material or emotional deprivation, a happy, full, challenging life, a life that makes the child feel good about him or herself and feel good about men and women in general—then we think it's fair. Some of the women we met gave their children all of this. They are great mothers. Their children are lucky to have them as parents. Some of the women we met did not give their children all of these benefits. They were not ready for motherhood, let alone single motherhood. Their children were less lucky. Their children's lives might have been improved by having a father because the mother was not prepared to meet the child's needs. But even married, the mother would have been immature and so might the father have been. The child's needs might still have gone unmet—except that symbolic need for a daddy, but that's not enough.

There are single people who should not become parents just as there are married couples who should not become parents. But some single women and some single men have a great deal to offer a child. If they become parents, their children will endure some costs but enjoy many benefits.

If single people doubt that they possess the requisites we've discussed, we think they should either (a) get their lives in order and then reassess, even if that means missing the biological time to bear a child; (b) find a mate who will help meet a child's needs; or (c) borrow their friends' children and be aunts (or uncles) instead of parents—a joy for them, the friends, and the children. We are, after all, talking about alternative family styles. And just as single parenting is a viable option, so too is remaining childless. It's a tough decision.

Since it is technically possible to prevent pregnancy and socially possible to parent while single, the decision to become a parent or not is one that is bound to confront more and more people. It is a decision to be made consciously and deliberately, not just allowed to happen. We hope we've helped some people make that decision and helped others understand how and why that decision is made.

APPENDIX
LEGAL ASPECTS OF SINGLE PARENTING

If you are interested in becoming a single parent yourself, or if you know someone who is planning to do this, a number of legal questions may have occurred to you. Can the biological father get custody or visitation rights against the wishes of the mother? Can the child inherit or collect social security benefits after the death of the biological father? Are there legal entanglements with the donor of sperm in cases of artificial insemination? Is it legal to adopt a child through the black market?

We cannot advise you specifically on these matters because we are not lawyers and because laws vary significantly from state to state and often change. Indeed, this variance in state law means not only is it hard for us to say what "the law" is, but that a person must be especially careful about the possibility of conflicts in state law—which may occur, for example, when the child is conceived or born in one state, now lives with the mother in a second, while the father lives in a third.

Our best advice: when you have particular questions, consult a lawyer. If you don't have or know of a lawyer, the local bar association or women's resource center may be able to refer you to an attorney specializing in family law. We *can* provide a general outline of some of the relevant legal issues and of the line of reasoning the courts typically seem to take.[1]

THE UNIFORM PARENTAGE ACT

Having said that these legal issues are complicated and variable, we can now add that the answers to certain legal questions are somewhat easier for people living in states which have enacted the relevant "Uniform Acts." In order to promote uniformity in state laws on various subjects, the National Conference of Commissioners on Uniform State Laws has drafted several uniform acts which, when finally approved, are recommended for general adoption throughout the United States. Each state may choose to enact this set of laws, modify it, or to reject it entirely.

The Uniform Parentage Act, which deals with paternity, was approved by the National Conference of Commissioners in 1973 and since then has been substantially adopted by California, Colorado, Hawaii, Montana, North Dakota, Washington, Wyoming, Minnesota and Nevada. Some of its provisions have been adopted by Indiana.

The Uniform Parentage Act (UPA) was written at a time when the Supreme Court was rendering a series of decisions which essentially mandated equal legal treatment of legitimate and illegitimate children. Many states, however, continued to differentiate significantly in the legal treatment of illegitimate children. These states' laws on the subject were either "unconstitutional, or subject to grave constitutional doubt."[2] The UPA, then, was

---

[1] One of the best statements and summaries of the laws which concern us here is in *Unmarried Couples and the Law*, by Graham Douthwaite (Indianapolis: The Allen Smith Co., 1979). After detailed explanations of various legal issues generally, the book has a state-by-state analysis. Both parts are filled with references to cases, as well as Law Review articles. An appendix listing specific citations to all state statutes on child support enforcement and paternity is found in Harry D. Krause, *Child Support in America* (Charlottesville, Va.: The Michie Co., 1981).

[2] Quoting Commissioners' Prefatory Note to *Uniform Parentage Act* in *Uniform Laws Annotated, Vol. 9A* (St. Paul Minn.: West Publishing Co., c. 1979), 580.

a response—an attempt to modernize law and end legal discrimination against illegitimate children. From the beginning, moreover, the UPA emphatically stated its principle: "The parent and child relationship extends equally to every child and every parent, regardless of the marital status of the parents."[3] That is, regardless of the marital status of the parents, all children and all parents have equal rights with respect to each other.

An analysis of the UPA, from a feminist perspective, may lead to criticism of the Act for ignoring the possibility that single mothers might want to have and rear children on their own. For the UPA and other relevant laws are not really designed to address specific issues raised by electively-single mothers; these laws simply assume that the best interests of a child demand establishment of a relationship with his or her father. At the very least, these laws will be appreciated more by the single mother seeking to establish paternity than by the mother seeking to distance herself and her child from the biological father. Writing for the *Review of Law and Social Change,* Boston attorney Carol Donovan says the UPA "ignores the potential conflict between the rights of nonmarital children and the rights of unmarried women to procreative and family autonomy."[4]

Again, not many states have formally adopted the Uniform Parentage Act (although some states may have rewritten their laws on these subjects). But we will refer to the Act as a statement of what the law is in some states, and what it may be, if more states adopt the Act.

PATERNITY

Single mothers may wish to sue for paternity for symbolic reasons, as the basis for suing for child support, or in anticipation of other monetary claims against the biological father. As we discuss further in the section on child support, women must co-

---

[3] *Ibid.,* 588.

[4] Carol A. Donovan, "The Uniform Parentage Act and Nonmarital Motherhood-by-Choice," *Review of Law and Social Change* (New York University, Summer, 1983) XI: 2:194.

operate in paternity hearings in order to receive Aid For Dependent Children (AFDC) benefits; and acknowledgment of paternity becomes particularly important in litigation over inheritance and social security death benefits. According to the Uniform Parentage Act, the court's decision about paternity can be used for all purposes. A paternity judgment may contain provisions dealing with support payment, custody and visitation, and guardianship. It may even order the father to pay "reasonable" expenses incurred by the mother during pregnancy and birthing.

In cases of unwed parents, the Uniform Parentage Act stipulates that a man is *presumed* to be the natural father if "he receives the child into his home and openly holds out the child as his natural child" or if "he acknowledges his paternity in a writing filed with the 'appropriate court or bureau' which shall promptly inform the mother of the filing of the acknowledgment and she does not dispute the acknowledgment within a reasonable time."[5] The Act adds that any interested party may bring an action at any time for the purpose of determining whether a father-child relationship presumed in one of those two ways exists.

If there is no "presumed" father, legal action to determine paternity may be brought by the child, the mother, an appropriate state agency, the man alleging himself to be the father, or by somebody representing the mother or father, if the mother or father has died. For our purposes, the Act stipulates that since the principle interest is that of the child, the mother and father cannot agree to bar a paternity suit. Establishing a parent-child relationship is seen as a basic and crucial right of a child—and one not to be signed away by a parent.

Until recently, serologists and blood-typing experts could only show with certainty that a particular man was not the father. Now, however, genetic tests allow experts *practically* to prove paternity. That is, they can identify, with a high degree of accuracy, who the father is with a test known as HLA (human leukocyte antigen) tissue typing. This test involves analyzing genetic markers called antigens, which are found in white blood cells and other

[5] *Uniform Laws,* 589.

body tissues. Once the antigen markers of the child and mother are matched, the child's remaining genetic markers, which can only be inherited from the father, identify the father with a high degree of certainty (at a 95 percent level and sometimes higher).

In the late 1970s, a California appellate court ruled that the positive findings of the HLA test to establish paternity was relevant and admissible. Since then the test has been admitted in cases in New Jersey, Massachusetts, Illinois, New York, Washington, Florida and elsewhere.[6] North Carolina and New York laws provide for the test statutorily. One New York court said the right to HLA in a paternity hearing is "fundamental" and cannot be made dependent on financial resources; in some states, when a social service or welfare bureau is initiating a paternity case and the parents are indigent, the government pays for the test, which is expensive. On the other hand, some judges do not use (or believe) blood typing evidence.

The Uniform Parentage Act says that courts may (and if requested, must) require the child, mother and alleged father to submit to blood tests, performed by a court-appointed expert. But medical evidence, evidence of intercourse at the probable time of conception and so forth are, of course, also allowed.

Paternity actions are civil rather than criminal and are governed by the rules of civil procedure (where the standard of proof is "preponderance of the evidence," rather than the stricter standard used in criminal procedures).[7] In some states, the father can request a jury trial. A paternity action accompanied by allegations of nonsupport is typically a criminal action.

According to a 1974–78 study, a contested paternity trial without a jury takes about two hours, while one with a jury takes about five to eight hours. In 75 to 90 percent of contested paternity cases, the defendant is judged to be the father.[8] To help

[6] Paula S. Seider, *Family Advocate*, 3:2 (Fall, 1980): 13-15.

[7] Harry D. Krause, *Family Law in a Nutshell* (St. Paul, Minn.: West Publishing, 1977), 141.

[8] Harry D. Krause, *Child Support in America* (Charlottesville, Va.: Michie Company, 1981), 164, 166.

explain the procedures for bringing a paternity action, a University of Southern California research center has published a booklet which provides a detailed explanation for bringing a paternity action and includes forms and checklists. It is available through the Department of Health, Education and Welfare.

Paternity suits can be costly, not to mention emotionally painful. But such suits can be avoided when the father voluntarily acknowledges the child as his. Says Leonore Weitzman, "It would be wise for all unmarried couples with children to prepare a formal acknowledgment of paternity as protection for their children's rights in all possible contingencies."[9] The document need not be elaborate. It simply has to state clearly that X and Y are the parents of Z. She adds that consulting a lawyer is wise, but the acknowledgment of paternity can be drafted by a non-lawyer, signed by both, and notarized. In some states, voluntary acknowledgment results in full or partial legitimation of the child.

Incidentally, it is worth noting that at least one court has ruled that a woman's "misrepresentaion" of her contraceptive precautions is not enough to let the "putative father" (legalese referring to the alleged biological father) out of a declaration of his paternity. During a New York paternity hearing, the putative father argued that the woman told him she was taking adequate contraceptive precautions because motherhood was incompatible with her career plans (she was a cosmetics executive). The court held that Nathan failed to establish Inez' fraud and deceit by clear and convincing evidence; and that, in any case, the public policy against fraud must be subordinated in view of society's "profound commitment" to family and children. So, the court entered an "order of filiation."[10]

STATUTE OF LIMITATIONS

The time limit applicable to paternity suits varies widely. Some states impose no statute of limitation for paternity actions, the thinking being, apparently, that since the obligation of the father

[9] Leonore Weitzman, *The Marriage Contract* (N.Y.: The Free Press, 1981), 373.

[10] *Inez M. vs. Nathan G.*, 114 Misc. 2d 282, 451 N.Y.S. 2d 607 (1982).

to provide support is ongoing, there should always be the possibility for bringing suit to enforce that obligation.

Other states apply statutes of limitation to the institution of paternity hearings, even by the child, but the courts differ on whether such statutes deny illegitimate children equal protection of the law. Some courts uphold the statutes because of the state's strong interest in preventing "stale" and fraudulent claims.

In a 1983 case, the Supreme Court, in unanimously striking down a two-year statute of limitations, noted that the relationship between a statute of limitations and the state's interest in preventing the litigation of stale or fraudulent paternity claims has become more attenuated as scientific advances in blood testing have alleviated the problems of proof surrounding paternity actions.[11] The Court did not say, however, that progress in blood testing eliminated the concern.

Other state courts have invalidated the statutes because it is felt that they set up "impenetrable barriers" to the illegitimate child's right to support—barriers that have been condemned and forbidden by the Supreme Court. For example, the one-year statute of limitations in Texas and the two-year limit in Tennessee were found to be unconstitutional because no similar barrier confronts a legitimate child seeking support, and one or two years is too short a time to provide bona fide opportunities to obtain parental support. In upholding a two-year statute of limitations, the Tennessee Supreme Court concluded that "two years is long enough for most women to have recovered physically and emotionally, and to be able to assess their and their children's situations logically, and realistically."[12] But the United States Supreme Court disagreed, its decision repeating the language used by Justice Sandra O'Connor in a concurrance issued the previous year. The Court noted that not only in the first, but also in the second year, a mother may be inhibited from filing a paternity suit because of financial difficulties caused by the child's birth, loss of income attributable to the need to care for the child, continuing affection for the biological father, a desire to avoid

[11] *Pickett vs. Brown,* —U.S.—, 76 L Ed 2d 372 (1983).

[12] *Pickett vs. Brown,* 638 S.W. 2d 369, 371 Tenn. (1982).

family or community disapproval, and the emotional strain and confusion that often attend the birth of an illegitimate child.[13]

The Uniform Parentage Act says that an action to determine the existence of a father-child relationship must be brought within three years of birth, if brought by the parent or a party other than the child. Nevertheless, an action brought by a child or on behalf of a child whose paternity has never been established, is permissible until three years after the child reaches the age of majority (generally twenty-one years). That is, the Uniform Act encourages promptness, since extending the time limit causes problems of proof; on the other hand, it does not prohibit later action. (An earlier draft of the Act stipulated that if a child had no presumed father, and no action to determine paternity or adoption was brought within one year of birth, a state agency must promptly bring action. This provision was not included in the final version of the Act.)

In any case, the first response of a putative father against whom a paternity action has been filed seems to be to claim that the statute of limitations has run out. (Ironically, some states allow the natural father more time than the mother in which to bring a paternity suit, presumably because the mother can conceal the pregnancy.[14])

On the other hand, the single mother or child of a single mother need not abandon the attempt to establish paternity simply because the statute has expired. These time limits may be pushed still further—or eventually be eliminated altogether—in response to legal challenges. Attorneys from the Women's Bar Association or the American Civil Liberties Union might be able to provide assistance in this matter.

CUSTODY

According to very early English law, the custody of an illegitimate child was the responsibility of the parish in which it was

---

[13] *Mills vs. Habluetzel,* 102 S. Ct. 1549, 456 U.S. 91 (1982); *Pickett vs. Brown,* ——U.S.——76 L Ed 2d 372 (1983).

[14] See, for example, *Joye vs. Schechter,* 112 Misc. 2d 172, 446 N.Y.S. 2d 884 (Fam Ct. 1982).

born. In the United States, nearly all current statutes on custody of children—legitimate or out-of-wedlock—are based on the legal precedent set in 1881 by a Kansas Supreme Court chief justice. The judge wrote that a parent's right to custody of a child "will depend mainly upon the question of whether such custody will promote the welfare and interest of such child. . . . Above all things, (this is) the paramount consideration."[15] That is, the award of custody, when adjudicated by either marital or non-marital parents, is based on the "best interests of the child."

And if until recently, all else being equal, it was assumed that a young child belonged with its mother, in recent years, the unwed father is seen as having a claim to custody equal to the mother's. Since the primacy of the mother's claim had been predicated on a concept of traditional sex roles, courts applying concepts of equality cannot presume the superiority of the woman. At the least, the biological father cannot be presumed to be "unfit."

For example, a recent Ohio court awarded custody to the (unwed) father. When the mother appealed, saying that she must be specifically deemed "unsuitable" before he could get custody, the appellate court responded that when the father of an illegitimate child participates in nurturing and demonstrates his concern by filing for custody, and when the mother admits he is the father, the biological father has equality in standing with the mother regarding custody. And here, it was judged to be the best interests of the child to live with the father.[16]

Indeed, although case law suggests a pattern of preference for the mother, especially in disputes over out-of-wedlock children, one writer dismisses the notion that men have been unfairly disadvantaged in custody litigation. Her analysis of recent court decisions suggests the contrary is true—mothers are losing custody as a result of inappropriate criteria, insufficiently related

[15] *Chapsky vs. Wood*, 26 Kan. 650, 40 Am. Rep. 321 (1881), quoted in *New Trends in Child Custody Determination*, by the Committee on the Family of the Group for the Advancement of Psychiatry (New York: Harcourt Brace Jovanovich, 1980).

[16] *In re: Byrd*, 66 Ohio St. 2d 334, 421 N.E. 2d 1284 (1981).

to the best interests of the children, and of sex discriminatory judicial reasoning.[17]

That "best interest" doctrine has been incorporated into the Uniform Child Custody Jurisdiction Act of 1978 and the Uniform Marriage and Divorce Act of 1970. Michigan, for example, which basically follows the Uniform Child Custody Jurisdiction Act, spells out the criteria by which a determination of best interests can be made. Michigan looks for evidence of: the love and affection of parent and child; emotional ties of parent and child; and the capacity of the parent to give guidance, raise the child in its religion or creed, and to provide food, education, clothing, medical care, and so forth. It also examines evidence of the moral, mental and physical health of the parent, the environment of the proposed custodial home, the length of time the child has already lived in an emotionally stable environment, and the home, school and community record of the child. Finally, it considers the child's preference.[18]

What this means is that each custody case is decided on its own facts. Judges act as substitute parents, or, in the words of one, as a "wise, affectionate and careful parent."[19] Judges presumably try to be objective and rational, but clearly the subjective nature of such decisions and the imprecision of the "best interest" notion give judges a great deal of latitude.

Again, the attorney cited above says that courts hearing custody disputes among divorced couples regularly emphasize the criterion of economic support and devalue the nurturing caregiving role. She criticizes courts for ignoring the question of which parent has been the primary caretaker.[20] In fact, mothers interviewed for this book typically were trying to involve the biological father, not fight custody battles. But to the extent that cus-

---

[17] Nancy Polikoff, "Why Are Mothers Losing: A Brief Analysis of Criteria Used in Child Custody Determinations." *Women's Rights Law Reporter* (Rutgers Law School, Spring 1982): 236.

[18] *New Trends, op. cit.*

[19] *Sovereign vs. Sovereign*, 354 Mich. 65, 92 N.W. 2d 585 (1958).

[20] Polikoff, *op. cit.*

tody becomes a matter of litigation, an extension of the pattern of preference spells legal trouble for the woman who works little, sporadically, or at low pay—or, ironically, who is clearly dedicated to her career.

It should be noted that the right of natural parents to custody of children, legitimate or illegitimate, is not absolute. The state has an indisputable authority to take custody out of the hands of both natural parents, if a third party is better equipped to care for the child. But this cannot be done without a hearing on the fitness of the natural parents. When a third party seeks custody, the biological parent must be found "unfit" before his or her custody can be terminated.

Conversely, of course, a court can also order joint custody, in which case again, the father obtains expanded rights to intervene in or control child-rearing.

Finally, according to the staff attorney for the Women's Legal Defense Fund in Washington, D.C., in most states both biological parents actually *have* equal rights to custody, unless there is a court order of custody.

This means, then, that the father "has" custody and can take the child at any time unless the mother obtains a custody order.

In practice, single mothers do not generally file custody papers; either they do not want to upset the precarious peace with the fathers or they do not want to have anything to do with them. But prospective single mothers should know that a father can exercise his rights over her wishes. And it is theoretically possible that after the baby's birth, a man might become more interested in actively fathering and so he might change his mind about accepting a minimal role. The fact that most of the men, in the cases reviewed here, took little or no interest in the baby, does not mean that some men might act differently.

VISITATION RIGHTS

The same logic applies to the determination of a biological father's right to visit his illegitimate child. The court dockets are filled with disputes over the visitation rights of unwed fathers.

Time after time the courts have held that the father has a right to visit his children when this is in their best interests.[21]

Some courts have added language to the effect that the father's right is conditioned on not only acknowledgment of paternity, but also on ongoing contributions of financial support or demonstrations of love, concern, and interest. Again, it is something to be determined by a hearing, case by case. For instance, a New York court ruled that allowing the putative father visitation rights was in the best interests of the child, given that the father demonstrated love, affection, and financial aid, and given psychiatric testimony that the child's growth would be enhanced by contact with the natural father.[22] Likewise, a Pennsylvania court said, "The putative father may, in many instances, instill in the child a sense of stability. He may develop qualities in the child which the mother is uninterested in, unwilling or incapable of developing. To the extent that he can perform such a valuable service, his presence becomes exceedingly important. Certainly, to the illegitimate child, the father is never putative."[23]

Specifically, then, the preferences or prejudices of the parents are not the issue; indeed, the burden of proof to show that the father's visits would be detrimental is on the mother.

On the other hand, the courts sometimes refuse to allow visitation by the father. An Ohio judge said that where the biological father had married and had a family of his own, and the mother had married a man who assumed the duties of a full-time father, granting visitation rights to the biological father was unwarranted.[24] When the biological father demonstrates no interest in the child the state may move quickly to terminate his rights.

It is amusing, but not surprising, to note that in 1981, California courts dismissed the suit of a girl trying to compel her natural father to visit her. Paternity had been established and the

[21] *Griffith vs. Gibson*, 73 Cal. App. 3d 465,142 Cal. Rptr. 176 (1977).

[22] *Pierce vs. Yerkovich*, 80 Misc. 2d 613, 363 N.Y.S. 2d 493, See also, *Pearson vs. Clark*, 382 So. 2d 482 (1980 Miss.).

[23] *Commonwealth vs. Rozanski*, 206 Pa. Super. 397, 213 A. 2d 155, 157, 15 A.L.R. 3d (1965).

[24] *In re: Connolly*, 43 Ohio App. 2d 38, 332 N.E. 2d 376.

natural father was paying support. The trial court held, and its decision was affirmed at the appellate level, that it can compel a child to visit the parent, but it cannot compel a parent to visit the child. Put another way, the court said it could compel a parent to provide monetary support, but it could not compel the family to stay together.[25] (A mother, however, could be ordered to promote and encourage a child's relationship with its father.)

CUSTODY BY LESBIAN MOTHERS

As we noted above, in custody disputes between a natural mother and natural father the standard or test on which the judge bases a decision is the "best interest of the child," a standard which, again, is purposefully vague and which allows the judge considerable discretion. In contrast, when the state attempts to take a child away from its natural parent, the state must show that the child has been neglected, or that the parent is somehow "depraved." Sixteen states permit immorality of parents to trigger neglect findings; thirty-one permit "unfit environment."[26]

It should be noted that custody decisions are never absolutely final. Courts do not like to switch, but if there is a "material change in circumstances," the losing parent can petition the court to reconsider its decision. In some cases, the natural father has asked for a reconsideration upon learning that the mother is involved in a lesbian relationship.

One judge, some twenty years ago, said that "(A) judge should not base his decision upon the disapproval of the morals or other personal characteristics of a parent that do not harm the child. It is not his function to punish a parent by taking away a child."[27] But according to the authors of a law review article on this question, even judges who in theory accept this view and who agree that homosexuality per se does not render a parent unfit, will tend to accept fairly weak demonstrations of harm.[28]

---

[25] *Loudin vs. Olpin,* 118 Cal. App. 3d 565, 173 Cal. Rptr. 447 (1981).

[26] Nan D. Hunter and Nancy D. Polikoff, "Custody Rights of Lesbian Mothers: Legal Theory and Litigation Strategy," 25 *Buffalo Law Rev.* at 714.

[27] *Stack vs. Stack,* 189 Ca. App. 2d 357, 371, 11 Cal. Rptr. 177, 187 (1961).

For example, the authors point to an Ohio court which granted custody to a sixty-five-year-old grandmother: the only specific point of injury to the children was the potential for being teased by peers on account of their mother's homosexuality.[29]

In the case cited above, the trial judge said, ''I don't say that a mother cannot be fit to rear her children even if she is a lesbian, but I wonder if she is fit when she boldly and brazenly sets up in the home where the children are to be reared, the lesbian practices which have been current there, clearly to the neglect of supervision of the children.''[30]

This court implied that the lesbian mother, who in fact suppressed her sexuality, who did not ''practice'' her sexual preference might not cause harm, but the mother who actually lived in a lesbian relationship would. Other courts have agreed, awarding custody to the lesbian mother only on the condition that she not live with another woman, or only associate with lesbians when the children were not home.[31]

CHILD SUPPORT

Put most simply, the biological father is regarded as having an obligation to support his children, although this was not the case with the old common law. This may be important for the mother who decides the father should pay; but it may be distressing for the mother who wishes nothing from the father and wants to reassure him that all she wants is his sperm.

It certainly has been significant for mothers who have applied for AFDC benefits, for the states have decided that they can reduce welfare expenditures by going after and collecting support payments from the absent father. In 1967 Congress enacted legislation requiring states to establish paternity and to seek support payments for children on AFDC who had been deserted by a parent (invariably the father). In 1975 a federal statute (Ti-

[28] Hunter, *op cit*.

[29] Hunter, p. 696–7, quoting *Townend vs. Townend*. 1 Fam. L. Rptr. 2830 (1975).

[30] Hunter, p. 697, quoting *Townend* at 2831.

[31] *Mitchell vs. Mitchell*, No. 240665 (Cal. Super. Ct., Santa Clara County, June 8, 1982).

tle IV-D), an amendment to the Social Security Act, put more teeth into this requirement. This Child Support Enforcement Program is designed to locate the parents who desert, to establish paternity of out-of-wedlock children, establish the legal obligation of the absent parent, and enforce that obligation. In 1978, over one million dollars was collected this way.[32] Families not on welfare can use this mechanism to obtain support payments.

At least one lawyer argues that, although so far paternity actions have only been initiated by the state because of the state's economic interest, that the state can bring an action without any economic interest.[33]

Originally a woman could decline to cooperate in naming the father but still receive AFDC only in cases of rape, incest, or adoption. As a result of both litigation and criticism, the duty of the AFDC mother to cooperate has been clarified and the circumstances under which she can legitimately refuse to identify the father have been expanded.[34] Now by federal statute, the "good cause exception" also provides for cases where identifying the father would cause serious physical or emotional harm to the child, or would emotionally or physically harm the mother to such a serious extent that she would not be able to care for her child adequately. In both conditions, the burden of proof is on the recipient mother; she must provide documentary corroborative evidence. But the validity of the rule requiring disclosure has been constitutionally tested.[35] (Presumably, this cannot apply to women artificially inseminated with the sperm of an anonymous donor.)

And if the mother refuses, she may withdraw her application, or her children may receive welfare aid (excluding any-

[32] Louis B. Hayes, "A National Overview from the Federal Perspective," in *A Legislator's Guide to Child Support Enforcement,* Carolyn K. Royce, ed. (Denver: National Conference of State Legislatures, 1980), 4–9.

[33] Donovan, *op cit.,* 213–14.

[34] Stephen Fleece, "A Review of Child Support Enforcement Program," *Journal of Family Law* 70:3 (1982): 489–522 at 506.

[35] *Maher vs. Doe,* 432 U.S. 526 (1977). A thorough explanation of the history and logic of the program, the rules and the good cause exemption is found in Krause, *Child Support in America,* 281–412, especially pp. 372–387.

thing for her needs) issued through a "Protective payee" (for example, a grandparent).

SUPPORT PAYMENTS

Usually a court will order that support be paid periodically. However, in some states, if it is in the child's best interests, the courts may instead order a lump sum payment or the purchase of an annuity. Courts vary in how they determine the amount of support to be paid and for how long (usually until the "age of majority"). According to the Uniform Parentage Act, the court may consider such things as the needs of the child, the standard of living and circumstances of the parents, the relative financial means and earning ability of the parents, the child's age and need for education, the financial resources and earning ability of the child, the responsibility of the parents for the support of others, and the value of services contributed by the custodial parent. Some state legislatures have designed tables—much like income tax tables—to calculate the support payment. For example, a 1978 Florida law established monthly payments of between $40 and $110 depending on the child's age.[36] But in most jurisdictions, determination of the amount is left to the court's discretion.

Once paternity is adjudicated or acknowledged, the father's obligation to provide child support can be enforced. Typically, the father's failure to obey a court order is considered contempt of court and can be punished as such.[37] But a father can also be prosecuted for criminal nonsupport—although a jail term hardly solves the problem and indeed may be counter-productive. On the other hand, in reality, support orders may not really cover (half) the costs; and many fathers pay neither the full amount nor on a regular basis.

Incidentally, according to the author of a major text on child support law, inability to pay is no excuse if the father has voluntarily brought the disability upon himself, nor is the mother's denial of or interference with visitation rights.[38] And in some

[36] Krause, *Child Support in America,* 10.

[37] Douthwaite, *Unmarried Couples,* 134–35.

states, the court must order a wage assignment (direct payment from the father's employer, taken out of salary) when he defaults on support payments.

Clearly a mother may actively seek to obtain child support against the wishes of the unwed father; we have several recent cases where the father resisted, unsuccessfully, for various reasons. A couple of courts have rejected men's claims that, because they had counselled abortion (had even offered to pay for abortion), they had no liability for child support.[39]

In a very famous case, paternity was readily established by testimony and by the H.L.A. blood tests. But the father said the mother told him she had been using contraceptives. Another witness testified that he had broken off a relationship with Pam P. after she told him she wanted to get pregnant and was therefore no longer taking birth control pills. When this witness refused to impregnate her, Pam P. told him she would get pregnant by Frank S., whether or not he wanted that. She wouldn't tell him of her plans. Frank S. said her deception violated his constitutional right to decide whether to beget a child. Therefore, he argued, he was not liable for child support.[40]

A lower court agreed with Frank S. that Pam P. had intentionally and deceitfully deprived him of choice in avoiding contraception; it said it would issue a support order against Frank S. only if Pam P. could not provide for the child. But the appeals court disagreed, reasoning that the amount parents should pay in child support must be determined only on the basis of the child's needs and the parents' abilities to pay. The notion of "fault" in conception is irrelevant. It went on to say a father does have a constitutionally protected right to decide whether to father a child—but that right does not encompass the right to avoid child support payments, once a child is born, just because the mother deceived him about her use of contraceptives.[41]

---

[38] Krause, *Child Support in America*, 66–67.

[39] *Harris v. State*, 356, So. 2d 623 (Ala. 1978); Dorsey v. English, 283 Md. 522, 528–29, 390 A. 2d 1133, 1138 (1978).

[40] Pamela P. vs. Frank S., 462 N.Y.S. 2d 819 (Ct. App. 1983).

[41] *Ibid.*

In another case, the unwed mother sought enforcement of a contract, signed and witnessed the day before the birth of the child, whereby the father would pay $25 a week.[42] According to the contract, the father agreed to pay, in exchange for which the mother relinquished her right to sue under applicable laws. She also gave the father liberal visitation rights and full guardianship, if the mother died while the child was still a minor.

The court said that a mother may elect either to upset or enforce an agreement that is not court-approved. Indeed, the court said that "it is in the best interests of an illegitimate child to encourage amiable agreement between the mother and putative father with respect to the child's custody and support; thus, an agreement privately negotiated without judicial proceedings is desirable and should be enforced by the courts . . ."[43]

And in a third case, when an unwed mother tried to enforce a child support order, the father contended he should not have to support a child who did not bear his name.[44] Actually, the mother twice (once at birth, once when the child was five) tried to get his permission to put his name on the birth certificate but the father had refused. Then, eighteen months after being ordered to pay support, the father said he would only pay if the child's surname was changed to his. This time the mother refused. And the court said it lacked the authority to change the child's name. It noted, however, that the father was not without remedy, adding that any determination on the name change would ultimately be based on the child's "best interest."[45]

The Uniform Parentage Act provides that the court apportion among the parties the costs of reasonable attorney's fees, experts, blood tests, and of the court actions; the state picks up the tab for those who can't afford this. The Act adds that any party may be represented by counsel; the court appoints counsel for someone who can't afford that, too.

[42] *Auleta vs. Bernadin*, 113 Misc. 2d 526 449 N.Y.S. 2d 395 (Sup. Ct. 1982).

[43] *Ibid.*

[44] *Dana A. Vs. Harry M.N.*, 113 Misc. 2d 635 449 N.Y.S. 2d 851 (Fam. Ct. 1982).

[45] *Ibid.*

ADOPTION BY A STEPFATHER

Most statutory and case law dealing with the adoption of illegitimate children refer to situations where the birth mother wants to give up the baby for adoption, or the state wants to take custody away from the biological parent. But what concerns us here is when the unwed mother, at some point after the birth of her child, marries, and her husband wishes officially to adopt the child. Can the biological father protest, and is his permission necessary? In many jurisdictions, the answer seems to be yes.

In the landmark case of *Stanley* vs. *Illinois,*[46] the Supreme Court held that a state could not take custody of the children of an unmarried father unless a hearing demonstrated his "unfitness." It's a matter of both equal protection and due process. This case, however, involved a man who lived with a woman and their three children for many years before her death. But in light of this case, many states said that consent of the putative father is necessary for an adoption, or at least he must be given notice of the adoption hearing.

Some states demand, when the whereabouts of the natural father are unknown, the publishing in an appropriate newspaper of a notice of the proposed adoption. New York, for example, maintains a "putative father registry"; a man who files a claim of paternity is therefore entitled to receive notice of any proceeding to adopt that child. New York also requires that notice be given to men who are adjudicated to be the father, who are identified on the birth certificate as the father or are identified as such in writing by the mother, or who live with the child and mother.[47] For example, in *In Re: Adoption of Zimmer,*[48] the trial court granted a stepfather's petition for adoption, based on the required report from the Department of Social Services. But the appellate court reversed this and sent the case back, saying that the court first should determine if the natural father had aban-

[46] *Stanley vs. Illinois,* 405 U.S. 645m 31 L. Ed. 2d 551, 92 Sup. Ct. 1208 (1972).

[47] New York Domestic Relations Law Sec. 111-a (2–4).

[48] *In Re: Adoption of Zimmer, 229 N.W. 2d 574 (S.D. 1980).*

doned the child. The best interests of the child and the determination of abandonment required separate evidentiary proceedings.

In *Cabin vs. Mohammed,* both natural parents had been "active" parents and the Supreme Court agreed with the father that he was owed equal protection, given his commitment to fulfilling parental responsibilities and his participation in the rearing of his two children. In this case, then, the father was successful in challenging the constitutionality of a New York law which had provided that children could be adopted without the father's consent, even though the mother's consent was required.[49]

But in many cases, the courts have said that the father's permission is not necessary, nor does the adoption court have to seek out the biological father and involve him in the decision. Where the father expresses no interest in the child, has no contact with him (because of sheer indifference or because he was confined in jail), the father has no say. For example, in a 1983 split decision, the Supreme Court refused to undo the adoption by the mother's new husband when the biological father never established any custodial, personal or financial relationship. The court emphasized that parental rights do not simply derive from blood, but from the emotional attachments that derive from the intimacy of association.[50]

A former New York family court judge commented that the *Lehr* decision "should end the exaggerated concern for the out-of-wedlock father and the pointless searches for him."[51] The Court rejected the claim of the natural father, Lehr, to equal rights with the mother and also the due process claim, for Lehr had not registered himself as the putative father with New York's postcard system.

---

[49] *Caban vs. Mohammed,* 441 U.S. 380 (1979).

[50] *Lehr v. Robertson,* 456 U.S. 970 (1983). *See also Quilloin V. Walcott,* 434 U.S. 246 (1978).

[51] Nanette Dembitz, "Supreme Court Report: Lehr Decision Helps Out-of-Wedlock Newborns Find Homes," *American Bar Association Journal,* 70 (January 1984): 126.

An interesting twist on the adoption issue involves a natural father who wished to adopt his child, with the mother's consent, but meanwhile preserving the mother's rights. The child had been deliberately conceived and born out-of-wedlock, but the unwed parents wanted the father to adopt, both to remove the stigma of illegitimacy and so that the child could inherit from the father. But the applicable New York law says a natural father could retain parental rights despite consenting to adoption only when the adoption was to be by the spouse of the natural parent. The court held here that the child should not be denied the privileges of legitimacy and care of the natural father simply because the parents refused to marry. The child's best interests were served by permitting the natural father to adopt as if he were the step-father by marriage to the natural mother.[52]

NAME CHANGES

Although statutes on name changes usually stipulate that both parents must consent to the name change, such statutes often do not apply to illegitimate children. For example, a North Carolina statute requiring both parents' consent was held inapplicable where the child was born out-of-wedlock, in view of another statute providing that the last name of a child born out-of-wedlock shall be the mother's.[53] And some statutes specifically provide that a single parent can unilaterally petition to change the child's name. The California Supreme Court has said quite clearly that the sole consideration for determining a child's surname, when it is contested, should be the child's best interests.[54]

In many cases, the natural father's failure to have contact with the child or care for it weakened the strength of his objection to changing the name to that of the stepfather. On the other hand, where the father had a continuing relationship, when the

---

[52] *In Re: A.J.J.*, 108 Misc. 2d 657, 438 N.Y.S. 2d 444 (Sup. Ct. 1981).

[53] *In Re: Dunston*, 18 NC App. 647, 197 SE 2d 560 (1973).

[54] *In Re: Marriage of Schiffman*, 28 Ca. 3d 640, 620 P. 2d 579. *See also Donald J. vs. Evna M.*, 81 Cal. App. 3d 929, 936, 147 Cal. Rptr. 15 (1978).

mother had promised in a contract not to change the name, when the mother couldn't demonstrate that bearing the natural father's name was injurious, when the court did not want to alienate the father from the child, did not want to injure the relationship of the child to the father, the name change was not allowed.

Ironically, a reverse situation is seen in a 1941 case involving the application, ostensibly by a six year old, to change the child's name from that of the mother to that of the putative father. The court noted that the father had denied paternity and objected to the use of his name, although he had been ordered to pay support. The court said there was no pressing need to adopt the new name and later on the child might not even want the father's name.[55]

CONTRACTS

According to Douthwaite, "a contract of a putative father to support his child is generally sustained if supported by adequate consideration. Most courts, far from regarding the agreement as violative of public policy, consider it as furthering the policy of the law, especially where a biological father owes a statutory duty to support."[56]

The Uniform Parentage Act, however, says that a natural father's promise in writing to furnish support for a child does not require consideration (that is, the father need not necessarily "get" something in return for his promise to provide support).

Either way, as long as an agreement of the parents provides for the best interests and welfare of the child, say the authors of a textbook in legal living-together agreements, "most courts, in most situations, will enforce it."[57] That is, the unwed mother and father can contractually agree on their relative shares of the total childrearing duty.

[55]*Application of Biegay*, 25 N.Y.S. 2d 85, (City Ct. 1941).

[56]Douthwaite, p. 136.

[57]Bernard E. Clair & Anthony Danielle, *Love Pact: A Layman's Complete Guide to Legal Living Together Agreements* (N.Y.: Grove Press/Evergreen, 1980).

Indeed, although these contracts are not legally binding, the biological parents can establish their intent and document their understanding of how the child should and will be reared. For example, if the biological parents agree, in a written contract, that the child will live with the mother in a communal household, then it will be more difficult for the father later to claim that no child should live in a communal household. The Lesbian Rights Project (1370 Mission Street, San Francisco, CA 94103) has prepared some sample contracts with appropriate provisions. Parents are thus able to choose how simple or complex they wish to make these.

What a mother cannot do, as we have suggested, is contract away her child's right to support from its father, or to sue for other forms of payments, such as social security benefits.

Indeed, it is because the UPA always allows for state, mother, and child to initiate action to declare paternity or obtain support, that Carol Donovan claims the UPA will "deter men from agreeing to intercourse with unmarried women who want to have a child," and thus "has a chilling effect on other unorthodox lifestyle choices."[58] Donovan proposes an amendment to the UPA which would allow preconception contracts. Donovan suggests that such a preconception contract take the following form:

> We, (man's name), as the potential impregnator of (woman's name), and (woman's name), do hereby voluntarily and unconditionally agree that (man's name) will have no legal rights or duties of any nature with respect to any child born to (woman's name), even though (man's name) may be the biological father of said child, that he will have no right to custody or of visitation with said child, or any other paternal rights, and that he will have no duty to support said child or any other paternal obligation. We understand this agreement is binding and final and cannot be revoked.[59]

[58] Donovan, p. 215.

[59] *Ibid.*

WRONGFUL DEATH STATUTES

According to traditional doctrine of early Anglo-American law, an illegitimate child was a *filius nullius,* a child of no one. As such, an illegitimate child could not inherit from either parent and indeed, under the old common law, only lineal descendants (i.e., not the natural parents) and the lawful spouse of an illegitimate could inherit from him. Until fairly recently, although a few states allowed an illegitimate child to sue for the wrongful death of its mother, most states did not allow recovery for the death of the father.

This has changed, with both state courts and, more importantly, the United States Supreme Court, saying that the law cannot discriminate against illegitimate children. To allow only legitimate children to sue for recovery from the wrongful death of a parent denies the illegitimate child equal protection guaranteed under the Fourteenth Amendment.

The Court began the move in 1968 with *Levy vs. Louisiana,* involving an attempt to recover for the wrongful death of the unwed mother.[60] The converse was also applied when that same year, the Supreme Court permitted an action by a mother under the wrongful death statute for the death of her (illegitimate) child, the Court adding that recognizing such a right would not necessarily encourage illegitimacy.[61]

It's worth quoting from two other decisions. The first involves workman's compensation benefits related to the death of the unwed father who did not acknowledge his child, and gives a good idea of just how emphatic the Court was:

"The status of illegitimacy has expressed through the ages society's condemnation of irresponsible liaisons beyond the bonds of marriage. But visiting this condemnation on the head of an infant is illogical and unjust. More-

[60] *Levy vs. Louisiana,* 391 U.S. 68, 20 L.Ed. 2d 436, 88 Sup. Ct. 1509 (1968).

[61] *Glona vs. American Guarantee & Liability Insurance Co.,* 391 U.S. 73 (1968).

over, imposing disabilities on the illegitimate child is contrary to the basic concept of our system that legal burdens should bear some relationship to individual responsibility or wrongdoing. Obviously, no child is responsible for his birth and penalizing the illegitimate child is an ineffectual—as well as unjust—way of deterring the parent."[62]

In *Gomez vs. Perez*, the Court looked at a state law involving support payments:

"We have held that under the Equal Protection Clause of the Fourteenth Amendment, a State may not create a right of action in favor of children for the wrongful death of a parent and exclude illegitimate children from the benefit of such a right. Similarly, we have held that illegitimate children may not be excluded from sharing equally with other children in the recovery of workmen's compensation benefits for the death of their parent. Under these decisions, a State may not invidiously discriminate against illegitimate children by denying them substantial benefits accorded children generally. We therefore hold that once a State posits a judicially enforceable right on behalf of children to needed support from their natural fathers there is no constitutionally sufficient justification for denying such an essential right to a child simply because her natural father has not married her mother. For a State to do so is 'illogical and unjust.' We recognize the lurking problems with respect to proof of paternity. These problems are not to be lightly brushed aside but neither can they be made into an impenetrable barrier that works to shield otherwise invidious discrimination."[63]

[62] *Weber vs. Aetna Casualty & Surety Company*, 92 S. Ct. 1400 at 1406–7 (1972).

[63] *Gomez vs. Perez*, 93 S. Ct. 872, 874–75 (1973) citations omitted.

On the other hand, such Supreme Court judgments themselves do not offer absolute protection in a practical sense to the illegitimate child. As Professor Harry Krause, one of the foremost experts on family law, notes, the mandates of the Court have not yet been fully understood or embraced by some state legislatures. While many discriminatory statutes have been repealed, "Some lead a twilight existence in the shadow of doubtful constitutionality."[64]

Since the *Levy* case involved the death of the mother, paternity (or rather maternity) was clear. But whether paternity actually must be acknowledged by the father before the child can bring a wrongful death action varies from jurisdiction to jurisdiction. Some courts say yes. Some, perhaps more, say no— that if dependency and paternity are all that legitimate children must prove, then illegitimate children must prove no more. Besides, if dependency and paternity are proven, fraud is unlikely.[65]

One legal expert explains that the federal statute on social security benefits recognizes a child as a dependent of a deceased natural father, "(i) if the decedent (I) had acknowledged in writing that the applicant is his child; (II) had been decreed by a court to be the father of the applicant; or (III) had been ordered by a court to contribute to the support of the applicant because the applicant was his son or daughter, and such acknowledgment, court decree, or court order was made before the death of the individual involved, or (ii) if the decedent is shown by satisfactory evidence to have been the father of the applicant, and such insured individual was living with or contributing to the support of the applicant at the time of death."[66] Thus, the federal social security statute does not treat illegitimate and legitimate children exactly equal, but Douthwaite adds that presum-

---

[64] Krause, p. 134.

[65] *See,* for yes, *Sanders vs. Tillman,* 245 So. 2d 198 Miss. (1971). For no, *see Evans vs. Atlantic Cement Co.,* 272 So. 2d 538 Fla. App. D4 (1973); *In Re: Claim of Burns,* 55 N.Y. 2d 501, 435 N.E. 2d 390, 450 N.Y.S. 2d 173 (1982).

[66] Douthwaite, p. 52.

ably the government has a justifiable interest in ensuring that the applicant is indeed the child of the wage earner and that the wage earner had a legal duty to support that child[67] (i.e., that the child was a dependent).

INHERITANCE

A statute which prohibited natural parents from bequeathing property to an "adulterously conceived illegitimate child" has been held unconstitutional.[68] Not only can a parent bequeath property to an illegitimate child (although this is sometimes limited or restricted when there are also legitimate heirs or a lawful spouse), but American courts tend to define the word "children," when the will simply bequeaths to "children," as including illegitimate children.[69]

But the issue of inheritance is quite complex, especially regarding the estates of fathers who die intestate, or without a will. First, the Supreme Court, for all the strong language quoted above, did not absolutely preclude any and all distinctions in the treatment of illegitimate children. Further, the court has said that special conditions or limitations placed on illegitimate children must bear some rational relationship to a legitimate state objective (such as preventing spurious and false claims). States which do allow illegitimate children to inherit from an intestate father usually condition this on legitimation, written acknowledgment, etc.; and various courts have found various reasons for accepting such conditions as not unconstitutional. The Supreme Court is not wholly precise, consistent, or unanimous on this point, as demonstrated in a succession of famous cases (such as *Labine vs. Vincent, Mathews vs. Lucas, Trimble vs. Gordon*). In the most recent case, *Lalli vs. Lalli*, the Supreme Court, in a 5–4 decision, upheld as constitutional a New York statute which said, essentially, that an illegitimate child could not inherit from a fa-

---

[67] Douthwaite, p. 52–53.

[68] Douthwaite, p. 122 ft. summarizing Succession of Robins, 349 So. 2d 276 (La. 1977).

[69] Douthwaite, *op cit.*

ther who died intestate unless the father had been adjudicated as such.[70] But as Douthwaite notes, there obviously are situations where the father will have acknowledged paternity and discharged his obligations as such without litigation.[71]

ADOPTION BY A SINGLE WOMAN

As of this writing no state expressly (by statute) forbids a single person from adopting a child; in fact some states specifically authorize it.[72] As we have said, it may be difficult or practically impossible for a single woman to get a healthy American infant from a recognized child placement agency, but it's not illegal. (In some states, however, the religious or ethnic background of the child and proposed parent are given "due regard.")

For women who want a healthy infant, then adopting a foreign child or adopting through the black market (essentially buying a baby from someone who locates and sells babies for a profit) or the gray market (private placement of a child through an unpaid intermediary) are the options. However, with black market babies, one noted legal authority says simply, "chances of securing a judicial degree of adoption in respect of a child so procured are slim indeed."[73]

Most states do not prohibit gray market adoption, but they somehow regulate it. For example, the state may require a state agency to investigate and report on the domestic situation before issuing a decree, or the state may require disclosure of expenses and agreements involved. Some agencies, of course, are more tolerant and supportive of single parenting than others.

Women who want to adopt a foreign child should work with an authorized international agency, for getting the child out of the country can be a complicated matter. Adoption procedures

---

[70]*Lalli vs. Lalli,* 439 U.S. 259, 99 Sup. Ct. 518 (1978).

[71]Douthwaite, p. 128.

[72]Douthwaite, p. 45; Robert Farmer, *How to Adopt a Child,* (Arco Publishing Co., Inc. N.Y. 1968), p. 15.

[73]Douthwaite, p. 45.

themselves do not differ in terms of legalities for foreign children. But adoption by an American citizen does not automatically confer citizenship: therefore a separate naturalization procedure is necessary. On the other hand, a special streamlined procedure is available for naturalizing a child.[74] A local lawyer or the U.S. Immigration and Naturalization Service can provide advice on this. Some states also have restrictions on bringing children into the state for adoption purposes.[75]

The Uniform Adoption Act was approved by the National Conference of Commissioners on Uniform state laws in 1953, and many states follow this. The procedure for adoption is fairly straightforward. But some state statutes may be different, and so a lawyer should be consulted.[76]

Typically the person wanting to adopt brings a petition for adoption before a state court. The petition contains the consent of the necessary parties; in nearly all states, if the child is old enough (probably over ten years old) that his consent would be meaningful, it must be obtained. A hearing is held—usually in the judge's private chambers—and if the judge decides adoption is "in the best interests of the child," a provisional decree is issued. (This is usually waived if the "natural" parent is adopting and thereby legitimizing the child.)

In most states, a final formal decree is not issued until after the test period (usually six to twelve months). During that time a state agency may periodically investigate.

No laws prohibit lesbians from adopting children (and most adoption agencies do not investigate the sexual preferences of their clients). On the other hand, unmarried couples—lesbian or heterosexual—cannot adopt a child together. A single mother (by conception or adoption) who becomes involved in a long-term relationship cannot have her lover (man or woman) officially adopt the child. So a lesbian "co-parent" legally has no rights or obligations with respect to a child.

[74] Farmer, p. 51.

[75] Farmer, p. 9.

[76] Farmer explains the various restrictions on a state-by-state basis, p. 7–9.

On the other hand, the lesbian mother (who conceives her child by a man or through artificial insemination with a known donor) can still work out an informal agreement with the biological father and her lover who wishes to co-parent. It's not absolutely binding, but at least such an agreement could establish the original intent of the parents. For example, the biological mother can sometimes, if the biological father agrees, name her lover as guardian; the procedure varies in the states where this is allowed.

ARTIFICIAL INSEMINATION

The Uniform Parentage Act deals briefly with artificial insemination. It says that when a married woman is inseminated with a donor's sperm, her husband (not the donor) is the legal father, provided that he agreed to the procedure. But the UPA says nothing about artificial insemination of unmarried women, leaving the status of the resulting children uncertain.

Of the non-UPA states, eleven have provisions for artificial insemination but say nothing about this for unmarried women; and in two states, the statutes specify that the semen donor has no duties with respect to the unmarried mother and child. California, Colorado, and Wyoming modified the UPA so that the section on artificial insemination with a donor (AID) applies to married and unmarried women; they provide specifically that the donor is not the legal father when the insemination is performed by a licensed physician. Washington law provides that the semen donor is not the legal father unless he and the mother agree in writing in advance that he will be. Ten other UPA states say nothing about the artificial insemination of a single woman.[77] Thus in only six states is it fairly clear that the single mother is the sole legal parent; the child has no interest in the donor's estate, and so forth.

Connecticut, Kansas and Oklahoma have language to the effect that a doctor can only perform AID with the consent of both

[77] Donovan, p. 218.

husband and wife. Some lawyers do not see this as actually prohibiting AID for single women, although one lawyer says this
means that it is prohibited.[78]

But even if these states are prohibiting AID for single women,
one legal scholar notes that "the doctors, when acting on their
own, are not engaged in state action and hence are not subject
to the relevant constitutional strictures.[79] Moreover, this writer
suggests that the laws prohibiting women from obtaining AID
may be unconstitutional. The Supreme Court has said that the
decision to procreate is part of one's right to privacy; Supreme
Court decisions on abortion and contraception, then, protect the
right of unmarried and married persons to decide whether or not
to procreate. Shaman suggests, quite reasonably, that the right
to decide is infringed as much by prohibitions upon initiating
procreation as by prohibitions on preventing it.[80]

On the other hand, "fundamental interests" can be restricted by state law if the state has compelling reason to do so.
And states may argue that they have such reasons. In any case,
says Shaman, "it is difficult, if not impossible to predict how
the courts will rule on this matter."[81]

The Uniform Parentage Act provides that AID records be
kept confidential and sealed, and shown only for good reasons
by order of the court (presumably for medical reasons). This also
has not yet been tested, although the many cases where adopted
children have gotten access to information about their biological
parents (but not the identity itself) may serve as a precedent for
AID.

The artificial insemination of a single women with the sperm
of a known donor resulted in an interesting case in 1977.[82] C.C.
was a single woman who wanted to have a child but did not

[78] Donovan, p. 219.

[79] Jeffrey M. Shaman, "Legal Aspects of Artificial Insemination," *Journal of Family Law*
18 (1979–80): 331–351 at 338.

[80] Shaman, p. 345.

[81] Shaman, p. 346.

[82] *C.M. vs. C.C.*, 152 N.J. Super. 160, 377 a. 2d 821 (Cumberland County Ct. 1977).

want to marry, or have premarital sex. The doctor at the local sperm bank refused to accept her, but she learned from him how to inseminate herself. She discussed having a child by AID with her boyfriend C.M. and she asked if a friend of his would supply the sperm. C.M. said he himself would, and she accepted the offer. Over a period of months, she went to his apartment and tried to inseminate herself (C.M. stayed in a separate room). Eventually it worked. C.M. testified that until the third month of C.C.'s pregnancy, he assumed he would treat the child as a father would. C.C. denied that this was the agreement. By the time the child was born, the relationship ended and she refused to let him visit. So he sued for visitation rights.

The court granted his request for visitation and ordered him to pay child support on the grounds that, as the natural father, he should be allowed to exercise the responsibility of parenthood as he intended when he donated the sperm. The Court noted that no other person was available to act as father, and that "It is in the child's best interests to have two parents whenever possible."[83] Later the father won[84] the right to have his name entered on the birth certificate as the father.

The facts of this case are unique, so this case may be unimportant as precedent. But the opinion illustrates the potential problems for single women opting for artificial insemination with sperm from a known donor.

CONCLUSION

In this appendix we have attempted to highlight some of the legal issues involved in single parenting. We hope we've given you a general sense of some of the relevant legal principles and the way that they are applied. But there are variations over time and from state to state and case to case. As Professor Harry Krause wrote in 1981: "So far state legislatures have made inadequate efforts to enact new laws to conform to the constitu-

[83] Ibid. 152 J. J. Super. at 167, 377 A. 2d at 825.

[84] *C.M. v. C.C.*, 170 N.J. Super. 586, 407 A. 2d 849 (Juv. and Dom. Rel. Ct. 1979).

tional mandate of equality. This failing is unfortunate though perhaps forgivable—in view of the confusing judicial signals. Consequently, the gulf between the abstract constitutional principle and the practical realization of legal equality (between marital and nonmarital children) continues to loom wide.''[85] Then, too, is the question of the rights of a single woman who wishes nothing for or from the biological father. Again, we urge you to consult with an attorney.

[85] Krause, *Child Support in America*, p. 161.

INDEX